LIBRARY IN A BOOK

EDUCATION REFORM

Ian C. Friedman

Facts On File, Inc.

EDUCATION REFORM

Facts On File, Inc.
132 West 31st Street
New York NY 10001

Library of Congress Cataloging-in-Publication Data
Friedman, Ian C.
    Education reform / Ian C. Friedman.
        p. cm.—(Library in a book)
Includes bibliographical references and index.
    ISBN 0-8160-4962-9
        1. Educational change—United States—History. 2. Educational change—Research—United States. 3. Education—Aims and objectives—United States. I. Title. II. Series.
    LA212. F75 2004
    370′ .973—dc21   2003003502

Facts On File books are available at special discounts when purchased in bulk quantities for businesses, associations, institutions, or sales promotions. Please call our Special Sales Department in New York at (212) 967-8800 or (800) 322-8755.

You can find Facts On File on the World Wide Web at http://www.factsonfile.com

Text design by Ron Monteleone
Cover design by Cathy Rincon

Printed in the United States of America

MP Hermitage 10   9   8   7   6   5   4   3   2   1

This book is printed on acid-free paper.

For Lene

CONTENTS

PART III
APPENDICES

ACKNOWLEDGMENTS

I would like to thank my editor at Facts On File, Nicole Bowen, for taking a chance on a first-time author and for her valuable guidance and support.

I am also grateful to my entire family, particularly my parents, Marcia and Leon Friedman, for always encouraging me to pursue my interests and for providing an environment in which education is respected, valued, and enjoyed. Thanks also to my brother Keith for consistently coming through with much needed technical assistance and fun conversation during the time I was writing this book.

To my wife, Darlene, my thanks for her always strong faith, encouragement, and love.

Finally, to my sons Evan and Mason, my deep gratitude and love for their gifts of perspective, inspiration, and happiness that they bring to me every day.

PART I

OVERVIEW OF THE TOPIC

CHAPTER 1

INTRODUCTION TO
EDUCATION REFORM

It seems appropriate that a book about education reform in the United States begin with a standby of American schooling—a multiple-choice question. *Analyze the quotations below and answer the question that follows.*

> "The educational foundations of our society are presently being eroded by a rising tide of mediocrity that threatens our very future as a nation and a people."
>
> "Our standard for high school graduation has slipped badly. Fifty years ago a high-school diploma meant something."
>
> "Whether we like it or not, we're beginning to see that we're pitted against the world in a gigantic battle of brains and skills."

The quotations above reflect beliefs about the condition of U.S. public education commonly held in the

A 1980s
B 1950s
C early 1900s
D all of the above

The correct answer is D.

The first quotation is from the landmark 1983 publication *A Nation at Risk*, which served as a key catalyst for the growth of education reform ac-

3

tivity over the past 20 years. The second quotation is from a 1958 *U.S. News and World Report* interview of education historian and author Arthur Bestor. The "fifty years ago" referred to by Bestor is almost exactly the date of the third quotation, taken from Stanford education dean Ellwood Cubberley's 1909 book *Changing Conceptions of Education.*

Although more than 20 years have passed since the most recent of these quotations, each would be entirely plausible in the context of today's debate on education reform. The issue of education reform—the effort to improve the quality, methods, and purpose of elementary and secondary schooling in the United States—traces its origins to the inception of public schools, which preceded the founding of the nation by almost 150 years.

Since that time, education reform has both reflected and led social change in United States. The widely held belief that schools play a critically important role in shaping the nation's future has led to intense discussion on a variety of issues, including assimilation of immigrants, integration of African Americans, economic strength, the role of the federal government, constitutional rights of parents and children, and opportunity for individuals from lower economic backgrounds.

At present, as in the past, issues of effectiveness, fairness, and competitiveness shape the arguments over education reform. Advocates often have sharply contrasting views on such leading questions as

- Can school choice, including vouchers, charter schools, and privatization, successfully combat the cycle of poor children trapped in failing schools?
- What are the causes, outcomes, and implications of homeschooling?
- What are effective accountability measures for students and schools? Do curriculum standards and reliance on standardized assessments promote academic achievement? Are policies ending social promotion and bilingual instruction helpful and fair to students?
- Who will teach, particularly in chronically underserved areas? How can teaching become a profession that attracts, trains, and retains top candidates, especially in light of an expected teaching shortage?
- How can the culture within schools be strengthened to promote learning and safety? Are class-size reduction initiatives, zero-tolerance policies, and dress codes effective?

The background, themes, events, people, and movements that have shaped the history of education reform in the United States reveal a consistent though paradoxical tradition in which Americans maintain enormous faith in public schools while combating the nagging fear of their failure. This tradition is now at a critical juncture as the key issues of education reform evolve and assume an increasingly prominent place in U.S. politics, culture, and society.

PHILOSOPHICAL FOUNDATIONS OF U.S. EDUCATION

The roots of American notions of education reach back to ancient Greece and ancient Rome. The link between the state and support of the educational system was first described in Plato's *Republic* written around 360 B.C. The Greek philosopher's beliefs that the most intelligent were best able to lead the state and that education promotes the happiness and fulfillment of the individual by fitting him or her into his or her role in society have been espoused by education reformers of various ideological and pedagogical persuasions. Plato also expressed the belief that education could prepare individuals to function positively within society. Roman educator Quintilian extended these thoughts in the first century A.D. by emphasizing the advantages public forms of education could have, particularly on the socialization of a person. Quintilian, the tutor of the emperor's grandsons, believed that education should be concerned with a person's whole intellectual and moral nature, with the goal of producing an effective person in society. He recommended a broad literary education that included music, astronomy, geometry, and philosophy, preferably in public schools where a student could develop relationships and learn from his peers. Quintilian's views and methods helped establish a foundation for the education reformers in the United States, particularly leaders of the Progressive movement, who would follow almost 2,000 years later.

The Renaissance in Europe, which began in the 13th century and lasted more than 300 years, also had a significant impact on the development of U.S. educational thought and practice. Early in this period, Dominican monk and scholar Thomas Aquinas (1224–74) advanced reason, as well as faith, as sources of truth, helping to provide the basis for formal Roman Catholic education through curriculum that contained both theology and the liberal arts. Toward the end of the Renaissance, Dutch humanist and writer Desiderius Erasmus (ca. 1466–1536) criticized the ignorance of the clergy and the injustice of society, advancing public education as a means of equity. His calls for the systematic training of teachers, abolition of corporal punishment of students, and recognition of the value of play and the importance of understanding the student's individual needs and abilities helped provide a philosophical base for subsequent education reform in the United States, including the current debates.

Other important contributors to Western educational thought included Martin Luther (1483–1546), John Calvin (1509–64), John Locke (1632–1704), and Jean-Jacques Rousseau (1712–78). Luther advanced the resounding notion that education is necessary for the economic well-being of the state and that it should include vocational training. Luther's views influenced development of the concept of free and compulsory education as well as the concept of universal literacy, which became essential components of U.S. education. Calvin extended Luther's thought by stressing the need for elementary schools for the masses where they could learn to read the Bible and secondary schools to prepare the leaders of church and state. This helped establish a European tradition of a two-track system that was imported to the colonies and eventually spread throughout the United States.

British philosopher Locke and French philosopher Rousseau were leading advocates of education that promoted the development of reason, morality, and individual freedom. Locke's views helped establish a strong link between learning and participatory democracy, and Rousseau's beliefs—which led him to be considered by many the "father of modern child psychology"[1]—were instrumental in establishing the adaptation of instruction for children at different stages of development. Although their impact on U.S. schools has been enduring, the extent to which Locke's views of civic education and Rousseau's belief in adapted instruction should be implemented have been argued throughout U.S. education reform history.

EDUCATION IN EARLY AMERICA

The English, the predominant settlers of the North American colonies, had the greatest influence on the educational system that emerged in early America, though the cultural diversity and the presence of many different religious denominations in the colonies had a considerable impact on schooling. Colonial governments allowed individuals and religious groups to establish schools of their own. In general, colonial governments did not engage in close supervision of such schools. This early form of church-state separation came about largely due to the variety of religious denominations in the colonies, each seeking freedom of worship and each uninterested or unable to reach consensus regarding religious principles to be taught in schools founded by civil authorities.

Social and economic differences among colonial regions of British North America were also reflected in the formation of schools. In the southern colonies, religion was reverently practiced but was not the dominating force of life, as it was in New England. Therefore, the desire to have each person educated so that he or she could read the Bible was not of high importance to the wealthy English gentleman governing the southern colonies. This commonly held attitude was expressed in 1671 by Virginia governor Sir William Berkeley, who believed that every man should instruct his own children according to his means, explaining: "I thank God that there are no free schools nor printing, . . . for learning has brought disobedience and heresy, and sects into the world."[2]

Some efforts at organized schooling did exist in the southern colonies, though the financial commitment to them was usually lacking. Educational opportunity was determined almost exclusively by social class, and many wealthy families sent their children to tutorial schools, essentially private institutions in which a tutor would instruct young people. Dame schools in which a woman would provide rudimentary instruction in her own home, often while carrying on household tasks, were also common throughout the colonies, including the South.

The Middle Colonies featured a striking diversity of faiths, languages, and cultures and tended to develop many different kinds of schools. This diversity prevented one particular group from imposing its will on the others and created a kind of tolerance of necessity. As a result of this, a coordinated system of public schools and state support or regulation of public schools failed to develop.

Among the Middle Colonies groups, the Quakers of Pennsylvania were the most active in education, particularly at the elementary level. Quaker schools were open to girls and the poor, and some provided education for free blacks.[3] Practical education, similar to what would later be termed vocational education, offering training in merchandising, navigation, trade, and mechanics, was emphasized at Benjamin Franklin's academy in Philadelphia, which opened in 1751.

New England was witness to the greatest and most influential educational endeavors of all the colonial regions. Education in New England during the colonial period was driven by the Puritan philosophy, a tenet of which was that man's sinful nature required activity to prevent idleness and instruction to avert evil.[4] New England had less fertile land than the rest of colonial America and consequently developed a greater emphasis on such occupations as shipbuilding, manufacturing, and trade. Because of this economic activity, it was essential to have people able to read, write, and think efficiently. The establishment of schools served the specific desires and needs of the people in this region.

In 1635, the Boston Latin School became the first public school in the British colonies. Seven years later, the first compulsory education law in the colonies was enacted with the passage of the Massachusetts Act of 1642. This law stated that parents and masters of those children apprenticed to them were responsible for their basic education and literacy. It also stated that should parents and masters not meet their educational responsibility, the government would have the right to remove the child from the home and place the child where he or she could receive adequate instruction. A half-decade later, Massachusetts again led the way in education legislation with the passage of the Massachusetts Law of 1647, also known as the Old Deluder Satan Act. Provisions of this law required the establishment of elementary schools in all towns of 50 or more families and the establishment of secondary schools in towns of more than 100 families.

The significance of colonial education in New England was enormous, particularly in forming the traditions of public support for district schools, local autonomy, compulsory education, and distinct educational levels. Although New England's schools had, by modern standards, a rudimentary form, narrow curriculum, and weak support, they were the forerunners for what would eventually become the public education system in the United States.

In the years leading up to the American Revolution, education for the young was growing among the thirteen colonies, which had a total population of 2 million people. The ideas of the Revolution, such as those of Locke, were particularly influential. Locke believed that ideas came from experience and that the measure of truth of an idea is its correspondence with concrete, objective, commonsense reality. These beliefs helped lead to the growth of the kind of practical education programs supported by leaders such as Franklin.

The Revolution temporarily interrupted the momentum of education but eventually served to advance a unique form of American schooling. Though the formal bonds to Great Britain were broken, and with that any financial support previously provided, the United States began to define its own vision of public education. Among the primary architects of this vision were Noah Webster and Thomas Jefferson.

Webster, known as the "Schoolmaster to America," wrote the *Compendious Dictionary* in 1806, the first in a series of dictionaries that validated and disseminated an American lexicon. Also, Webster's *Elementary Spelling Book*, often referred to as the "Blue-Back Speller," was the most successful textbook ever produced in America, with an estimated almost 20 million sold by the time of his death in 1843. The book reflected Webster's strong nationalism and emphasis on the virtues of liberty, hard work, and morality. Accordingly, Webster vigorously supported legislative action leading to free schools in which U.S. children could learn these virtues.

Jefferson's impact on U.S. education was prodigious and mainly the result of efforts unrelated to his presidency. His support for the expansion of educational opportunity to ensure a wise populace that could protect democracy was evidenced with his 1778 proposal in the Virginia legislature known as the Bill for the More General Diffusion of Knowledge. The plan called for a state system of free elementary schools with local control of secondary schools supported by tuition and scholarships to help pave the way for poor boys. Although these provisions of the bill were not passed, it provided an often-imitated framework for future school systems, particularly the pattern of decentralized control and localization of financial responsibility. Jefferson's advocacy of the bill also served to help reduce the stigma of poverty as a barrier to receiving an elementary education and helped establish an American perception of educational equity, which is often at the center of today's education reform discussions.

The U.S. Constitution, ratified in 1789, did not explicitly mention education. The First Amendment's prohibition of government establishment of religion or religious practice did set a critical and oft-debated precedent separating state support for religious schools, though schools of all types continued to use religious material in instruction. The federal government supported the promulgation of schooling in the early republic through such acts as the Northwest Ordinance of 1785, which reserved a section in each township for schools and stated that schools and education should always be encouraged in the newly added regions covered by the act.

States emulated such support for provisions in their constitutions establishing funding for the creation of schools. The Pennsylvania Constitution, adopted in 1776, became a model for many states with its requirement that the state pay the salaries of public-school teachers. By the beginning of the 19th century most states had set up a system of schools with their constitutions. Formal education was not yet widespread, but the character and foundation of U.S. public education was established and ready to expand.

THE NINETEENTH CENTURY AND BEYOND

The first half of the 19th century in the United States saw social, economic, and political developments that led to the advancement of what is often referred to as the "common man." This increased adherence to the notion of equality led many citizens to believe that all should be able to read in order to a participate in government and improve their standing in society.

One important factor in the growth of public education during this time was the rise of industrialization. During the early stages of America's Industrial Revolution, efforts to promote public education suffered because so many children were part of the working force. For example, in New England during the 1830s, approximately 40 percent of children under the age of 16 were employed in industrial occupations. However, industrialization also required training and often led to a need for affordable activities for the children of working-class parents. In addition, many reformers viewed education as a means of combating the negative effects of industrialization, such as urban poverty.

Industrialization also led to a population boom in the United States, particularly in northern and eastern cities. Much of this growth was the result of huge waves of immigration from Europe. Schools were seen by many as an excellent tool to Americanize these newcomers, whose language and customs were different and often viewed as a threat to those of the native-born. Simultaneously, western settlers on America's frontier established one-room schoolhouses, often the only public building in a community, to educate their children. They were generally more reluctant than those in urban areas were to allow government influence over their educational institutions, reflecting an attitude that would be echoed decades later by advocates of homeschooling across the United States.

The emerging publicly supported common schools of the mid-1800s varied in size, organization, and curriculum. In rural areas, the one- or two-room schoolhouse was dominant. Progress in these schools was not marked by movement from one grade to another but rather by completing one text and beginning another. On the frontier, where there remained some distrust of too much education, the curriculum was limited to reading, writing, and arithmetic, while in larger cities the curriculum tended to be broader.[5] A wider variety of textbooks began to appear in common schools by the late 19th century, and the popular practice of rote learning, drill, and practice was beginning to be chipped away by early and sporadic measures of reform aimed at developing the individual talents of a child.

During the first half of the 19th century, states had gradually moved toward establishing educational systems. State superintendents, as educational officers were often called, of free schools, or common schools, usually had weak powers. Legal requirements for the collection of school taxes and compulsory attendance were often ignored as the tradition of parental and church responsibility for the education of children remained resilient.[6]

Two important leaders of this time who helped to propel state systems of education were Horace Mann and Henry Barnard. Mann was a Massachusetts legislator who led the effort to create a state board of education. When this measure was approved, he resigned to become the board's first secretary. During his 12 years in the post (1837–49), Mann was the most active leader of the common school education movement in the country. He succeeded in attaining state tax support for teacher salaries and new buildings, creating three of the first normal, or teacher training, schools in the country and establishing 50 new high schools. Attendance increased dramatically during Mann's tenure. Mann's educational philosophy influenced many other states and has had a profound impact on current mainstream thought.

Barnard, another important state education leader of the mid-19th century, had been a Connecticut state legislator before becoming secretary of the state board of education there and later in Rhode Island. Also like Mann, he espoused a democratic philosophy of education and was effective in spreading his message through the publication of the *American Journal of Education*.

Introduction to Education Reform

The first half of the 19th century had also witnessed the emergence of the public high school. In 1821 the English Classical School was opened in Boston, becoming the first of its kind in the United States. High school growth remained weak over the course of the next few decades because of opposition to paying taxes for their support and the popularity of private academies, which had spread since the late 18th century and encompassed prestigious, exclusive institutions, as well as practical, religious, and military schools. By the 1860s there were only 300 high schools in the United States, one-third of which were in Massachusetts; however, the idea of free secondary education grew in popularity, particularly among the growing numbers of middle-class citizens who viewed a high school educational as necessary to fully realize one's social and economic goals. In addition normal schools, named for the standard or normal curriculum that was followed, sprang up in the 1840s establishing a model for state-supported training of teachers.

Despite these advancements in U.S. public education, African Americans and Native Americans were almost always systematically neglected. Education for blacks during this time was limited in the North and almost nonexistent in the South. Formal education for Native Americans, guaranteed in the many treaties signed between the U.S. government and various Native tribes, was usually provided in the form of substandard mission schools that emphasized basic literacy and vocational and agricultural instruction. This educational negligence would reap generations of dissatisfaction still found at the center of some of the most intensely argued education reform issues, such as bilingual education, standards and assessments, and school choice.

The common school period came to a halt with the Civil War. The disruption inflicted on education was pervasive, particularly in the South where the damage done to an already-less-developed system was severe. Reconstruction-era efforts to build the southern education system, particularly attempts to instruct the more than 4 million newly freed slaves, were insufficiently supported or actively resisted. Proposed legislation in the U.S. Congress to boost education systems in areas devastated by war were also unsuccessful. In 1870, Massachusetts congressman George Hoar introduced a bill designed to establish a federal school system in southern states. This measure was defeated and served as a symbol of U.S. hesitance to cede too much autonomy on education matters to the federal government. The 1882, Blair Bill, named for its sponsor, New Hampshire senator Henry Blair, passed the Senate three different times but never passed in the House of Representatives. It proposed the application of almost $80 million for states to use as they saw fit to fight illiteracy.

Despite the difficulties experienced in the South, high school growth accelerated significantly following Reconstruction elsewhere. In 1875, fewer than

25,000 students were enrolled in public high schools, but that number jumped to more than 500,000 by 1900. Part of this growth was due to the legal precedent set by the 1874 Kalamazoo Michigan School Case *(Stewart et al. v. School District No. 1 of the village of Kalamazoo)*, in which the state supreme court held that the state had the right to levy taxes to support high schools.

One problem confronting the rapid rise in high school enrollment was the standardization of curriculum. High schools offered traditional and practical programs, with emphasis usually on college preparatory curriculum, even though only about 10 percent of high school students in 1900 would attend college. The menu of courses from school to school varied extensively in scope and nature.

Two important events then took place to reform this lack of standardization: the creation of the National Education Association (NEA) in 1870 and that body's formation of the Committee of Ten in 1892. For decades, a variety of regional educational associations formed to deal with high school standardization issues such as curriculum, school day length, and quality of instruction. In 1870, the largest of these professional organizations—the National Teachers Association, the National Association of School Superintendents, and the American Normal School Association—merged to create the NEA, which quickly became recognized as the leading education group in the country.[7]

In 1892, the NEA convened the Committee of Ten to study and put forth recommendations relating to confusion over secondary schools' standards, curriculum, methods, and programs. The committee's name was a reflection of its composition: five college presidents, two headmasters, the U.S. education commissioner, a professor, and a high school administrator. Absent was any high school teacher.

The Committee of Ten's report reflected the group's college orientation, supporting an increased focus on general education subjects such as Latin, English, math, physical and biological sciences, history, and geography. Vocational and commercial subjects were largely ignored. The committee's recommendations further advanced the practice of studying each subject for one period each day, five days a week for a year. As a result of the report, the standard unit of credit for high school subjects, often referred to as a Carnegie unit, was established. The Committee of Ten also supported an eight-year elementary school followed by a four-year high school, though special subjects and methods were not suggested for students who did not expect a good college. Taken together, the Committee of Ten's efforts were critical in bringing a sense of unification to a national system of public education.

Vocational and manual training schools sought to fill the void that grew following the implementation of many of the Committee of Ten's recommendations, especially with the late 19th century's need for skilled workers, who often wanted a high school education but had no intentions of attending college. Some teacher training colleges designed programs for vocational educators and the Industrial Education Association was formed in 1884.

Along with the growth of schools came a marked increase in teacher training schools. The number of such public and private normal schools more than tripled between 1871 and 1900 (from 114 schools to 345).[8] Despite this growth, fewer than half of the trained teachers that were needed to staff public schools were provided by normal schools or other teacher training programs. Most classrooms continued to be taught by low-paid young women, often with little education beyond elementary school. These conditions in the teaching profession were cause for concern at the time, leading U.S. commissioner of education Henry Barnard to express what would become a frequently heard expression of frustration with teacher quality, preparation, and status. As reported in the July 13, 1867, *Boston Examiner,* Barnard explained:

> *Too many of those we have entrusted to guide and guard our nation's youth have little knowledge beyond that which they are attempting to impart. Indeed, we might well question whether their knowledge is superior to that of many of their fellow tradesmen. Not only is the depth and breadth of their knowledge of the curriculum matter a subject of concern, but where knowledge is possessed, there exists most often an absence of any training in pedagogy . . . teachers will not be elevated to that place in society and receive that compensation they so richly deserve until they are required to undertake a special course of study and training to qualify them for their new office.[9]*

Private schools also became more established in the late 1800s, even as their student body became more conspicuously composed of the wealthy, those gaining military training, and Catholics, who were often shunned in schools that were overwhelmingly Protestant and nativist. The 1875 proposal of the Blaine Amendment, named for its sponsor, Speaker of the House of Representatives James Blaine, sought to prohibit the use of state funds for "sectarian" schools. Though this legislation narrowly failed to pass in the U.S. Congress, supporters of the amendment turned their attention to the individual states, where they had much more success. Blaine amendments were critical in the development of an organized private, Catholic educational system in the United States, and they have contributed to the broad conception of the separation of church and state.

As the 19th century came to a close, education in the United States was far different from what it had been 100 years earlier. Well established was a de jure expression of belief in free opportunity for all citizens, and with that, came a dramatic increase in school enrollment and prominence in society. Also well established was the foundation for future arguments of education reform, including the role of government and religion in schools, teacher quality, and standards and curricula. This rapid and meaningful pace of change witnessed in the 19th century would only accelerate in the 20th century.

THE EMERGENCE OF EDUCATION'S
PROGRESSIVE MOVEMENT

In the early 1900s, most Americans felt pride in their public schools. Specifically, they believed that schools could enable children of humble origins to climb an educational ladder toward greater opportunity. Implicit in this widespread conception was the promise of a liberal education's role in providing access to knowledge previously only available to the elite. A movement was mobilizing, however, that would change the nature and purpose of American schools.

Central to the new education supported by the early 20th-century reformers was a focus on targeting instruction for practical subjects that would fit the future occupations of most students whose members were steadily climbing due to immigration, prosperity, and the implementation of laws preventing child labor. The primary proponents of such education were business leaders who wanted prepared and efficient workers and educators who would come to be known as progressive educators. Most of the progressives were teaching in the nation's burgeoning colleges of education and wanted the curriculum to serve the needs of society and the industrial age.

The leading colleges of education were Columbia University's Teachers College, Stanford, the University of Chicago, and Harvard. Teachers College professors were most prominent in combating many of what they considered conservative tendencies of a U.S. educational system that ignored the benefits of modern science. The establishment of these colleges of education played a significant role in wresting the authority of American education from school superintendents to professors in schools of education. From these schools came the ideas that powered the progressive education movement.

The progressive education movement had a variety of goals, including making school instruction more practical, introducing modern methods of teaching that recognize that students learn in different ways, and giving more attention to the health of students. It also sought to make education into a profession and in doing so, reduced the school-related influence of laypeople, especially in poor and immigrant neighborhoods. Toward these ends progressive reformers supported the creation of centralized school bureaucracies and civil service systems, particularly in urban districts. Progressive educators of the early 20th century often attacked the high school curriculum as rigid, elitist, and an obstacle to social progress, particularly for the masses of poor and immigrant students in urban schools.

The leading spokesman of progressive education was John Dewey during the 1890s and into the new century. At the age of 35, the former teacher and professor assumed the chairmanship of the University of Chicago's Department of Psychology, Philosophy, and Pedagogy. Two years later, Dewey opened the University of Chicago Laboratory School to test new approaches to education.

Dewey believed that education, "must represent present life—life as real and vital to the child as that which he carries on in the home, in the neighborhood, or on the playground." He generally opposed the common practice of teaching by recitation. He advanced the notion that schools were instrumental to social reform, and he sought to create schools with, "an active community life, instead of a place set apart in which to learn lessons."[10] For example, in Dewey's vision students should learn biology not by memorizing the technical names for different plants and their parts, but rather by observing the growth and considering the factors that affected their life. Dewey believed that the child should be viewed as a total organism and that education is most effective when it considers not only the intellectual but also the social, emotional, and physical needs of the child. He held that education was a lifelong process and that the school should be an integral part of community life, a concept that gave support to the development of the community school. Dewey wrote more than 500 articles and 40 books, and his imprint on education in the United States was unparalleled in the 20th century.[11]

Dewey's leadership brought cohesion and credibility to progressive education and helped the movement become the dominant doctrine in the new influential schools of pedagogy. The key ideas of the movement included the following:

- Education was a science, and the methods and results of education could be precisely measured.
- The methods and ends of education could be effectively derived from assessing the innate needs and nature of the child.
- The proper approaches and outcomes of education could be determined by assessing the needs of society and then fitting the student for his or her role in society.
- Education could effectively reform society.[12]

In order to determine the ways in which schools could advance society, progressive education theorists developed the concept of social efficiency. In this framework, the value of academic subjects was evaluated by the degree that they served the purpose outside the classroom. According to this standard, many academic subjects, or at least the traditional approaches to them, lacked relevance for the great majority of students, who would most likely become workers or homemakers after they left school.

A leading figure in the social efficiency movement was the Massachusetts commissioner of education David Snedden. He believed that students should be assigned to different curricular tracks based on sociological criteria and that these differentiated curricula could be implemented for students by the age of 14 by scientifically trained educational experts.

In line with notions of school efficiency was the development of industrial education. In 1907, this aspect of education reform was notably boosted by President Theodore Roosevelt who stated, "our school system is gravely defective in so far as it puts a premium upon mere literacy training and tends therefore to train the boy away from the farm and workshop. Nothing is more needed than the best type of industrial school, the school for mechanical industries in the city, the school for practically teaching agriculture in the country."[13] Support such as this, the additional affirmations from the NEA and other prominent professional educators, and the defections of previous advocates of traditional academic education such as former Committee of Ten member Charles Elliott led to a marked shift in the orientation of U.S. public schools, particularly at the secondary level. With remarkable speed, the meaning of public education had been redefined by progressive theorists, from the relatively standardized academic ladder to a variety of paths leading to different destinations, with future professionals preparing for college, future farmers studying agriculture, future homemakers studying household management, and future industrial workers studying metalworking and woodworking. The view that all students take college preparatory courses was now usually seen as elitist, inappropriate, and undemocratic.

Advancing these views was Ellwood Cubberley, a former teacher, school superintendent, and education professor at Stanford. His books on education history and school administration describing the school's role in assimilating immigrants and training workers were standard reading in schools of education and remained so for many years. Also influential was his support for vocational education and curricular differentiation.

High school enrollment continued to boom throughout the early 20th century. In 1900, only 10 percent of those ages 14 to 17 attended high school, but by 1920, the percentage had increased to 31 percent. The obvious heightened prominence of high schools combined with the momentum of progressive educational thought led to the emergence of the school survey movement, designed to assess the efficiency of public schools.

The efficiency experts were largely the leading progressive theorists, and their evaluations and recommendations given to school systems reflected their support of changes, including intelligence testing and standardized testing for the classification of students. The results of the school survey movement was a continued rejection of the kind of broad education advocated at the turn of the century in favor of a socially efficient curriculum strengthened by tax-supported improvements to facilities and programs addressing specific needs of students. The movement also helped open the door to major battles over curriculum standards and the purpose and scope of testing that continue to rage to this day.

The reforms ushered in by the efficiency experts and progressive educators were essentially shut out of schools for African Americans. Black schools, particularly in the South, were woefully underfunded and inadequate compared to those for whites. Arguments about how best to educate black students included renowned scholar W. E. B. DuBois's belief in access to academic curriculum and educator Booker T. Washington's more accepted advocacy of the benefits of vocational education.

Critics of the progressive education movement, though dwindling in number, often spoke out against the proposed and implemented reforms. Among the critics were New York City superintendent William Henry Maxwell and University of Illinois education professor William Bagley. Bagley and Massachusetts education commissioner Snedden debated the merits of many progressive education reforms at a 1914 NEA conference, but it became clear to Bagley that he was fighting a futile battle, as evidenced in 1917, when the U.S. Congress passed the Smith-Hughes Act, establishing federal aid for vocational education. This act was the first federal program of any kind for public education.

In 1918, progressive education took another step forward with the publication of the *Cardinal Principles of Secondary Education*. This report was prepared by the NEA's Commission on the Reorganization of Secondary Education (CRSE), and it appeared exactly a quarter century after the Committee of Ten's report.

The *Cardinal Principles*, however, were very different in content and sensibility from the Committee of Ten's report. The composition of the CRSE was primarily made up of education professors who espoused the belief that high schools should promote different curricula for different groups depending on their likely future occupations. The CRSE explained that such reforms were necessary because schools needed to respond to new social realities, particularly increased industrialization; to support a larger and more diverse student population; and to apply advances in educational understanding.

17

Based on these assertions, the CRSE identified the main objectives of secondary education as:

1. Health
2. Command of fundamental processes
3. Worthy home membership
4. Vocation
5. Citizenship
6. Worthy use of leisure
7. Ethical character

Further, the CRSE noted that, "the purpose of democracy is so to organize society that each member may develop his personality through activities designed for the well-being of his fellow members and of society as a whole."[14]

The CRSE report was a critical milestone in the history of U.S. education. It crystallized and represented a new consensus about the direction of secondary education, one that emphasized social efficiency, socialization, and the authority of professional educators and education reformers.

Following the completion of World War I, education reform delved into an area that would prove to be a constant battleground: intelligence and standardized testing. This field of testing expanded during the war, and many educational theorists and practitioners believed that these kinds of testing procedures could be beneficial in constructing appropriate and effective public school curricula.

The group intelligence tests that had been administered in the U.S. Army during World War I were well suited for adaptation for schools, largely because they were relatively inexpensive, easy to administer, and resulted in the listing of group norms, which led to the assignment of students to the differentiated curriculum programs growing in popularity. The test quickly became a regular component of the public school experience, as evidenced by a 1925 U.S. Bureau of Education survey of 215 cities that reported that intelligence tests were used to classify students into homogenous groups by 64 percent of elementary schools, 56 percent of junior high schools, and 40 percent of high schools. These tests, a key component of what is sometimes called the measurement movement, allowed schools to classify, assign, and compare students, as well as diagnose learning difficulties and aptitudes. Opponents of widespread testing, then as now, decried the abuse of such assessment, arguing that the tests often led to faulty judgments about the quality of teaching and subjective judgments about students' potential.

Critics included William Bagley who warned of the "fatalistic inferences" of the tests and argued against the intentions of the testers, labeling them "educational determinists."[15] Popular newspaper columnist Walter Lippmann echoed such opinion during the 1920s, criticizing how these tests provided fodder to anti-immigrant sentiment and noted that the purpose of the school was to increase, not measure, a student's capacities. Despite such arguments, intelligence and standardized achievement testing took hold in public schools.

The 1920s also were a period in which a great deal of attention was given to creating curricula that would support progressive educational theory. The rising prominence of curriculum experts, steeped in scientific research, signaled growth in the transfer of educational influence away from parents and teachers and toward these specialists who had control over many districts' curriculum.

Among the primary curriculum experts was John Franklin Bobbitt, author of *The Curriculum*, the first textbook of the theory of curriculum construction, which became a standard in teaching training institutions. Bobbitt likened his role to that of an educational engineer who could establish precisely what students needed to learn in order to function effectively in life and contribute to society. He sought to design curricula that could address deficiencies in the social order, believing, for instance, that if agricultural production dropped, it was the job of the school to provide better agricultural education.

Dewey's advocacy of the child-centered movement was another example of leading 1920s curricular thought. Inspired by Jean-Jacques Rousseau's book *Emile*, Dewey emphasized the value of what a student learns in the ordinary course of living. At his Laboratory School, Dewey sought to demonstrate how traditional subjects, often taught through unimaginative drudgery, could be exciting and meaningful through projects and activities that appealed to a child's interests and therefore unleashed his or her intellectual energies.

Other key curriculum experts included William Heard Kilpatrick, who helped popularize and extend progressive practice of project-based learning, curriculum integration, and whole child education, which sought to balance intellectual, physical, and emotional development, and Harold Rugg, who developed a new social studies curriculum intended to replace traditional instruction of history, geography, and civics. They, of course, had their critics, including steadfast supporters of traditional liberal and classical education, as well as Dewey, who feared that some proponents of child-centered education went too far by not providing sufficient adult guidance to instructional activities.

The Great Depression that struck the United States in October 1929 both interrupted the progressive education reform momentum and galvanized its proponents who viewed the crisis as an example of how schools needed to reform society. During this time, progressive education's left wing was articulated by leaders such as George Counts, a Teachers College educational sociologist, who, following a trip to the Soviet Union, promoted the abandonment of traditional American individualism and capitalism in the journal *The Social Frontier*. At the other end of the progressive education's ideological spectrum was Counts's colleague at Teachers College, Isaac Kandel, who ridiculed the notion that schools should be expected to build a new social order, nothing the irony that the same progressive educators who had consistently opposed efforts at a planned curriculum now advocated a centrally planned society.

From 1920 to 1940 U. S. schools experienced another surge in enrollment, particularly in high schools where the number of students attending rose from 2.2 million in 1920 to 4.4 million in 1930 and 6.6 million in 1940.[16] Many schools were built and additional teachers hired to deal with this new reality. Inside schools, the results of progressive education reforms were visible, often in the form of implementation of revised curricula. The vast majority of such changes reflected the progressive preference of experience-based over academic instruction.

One strand of curriculum revision, the activity movement, emphasized project-based learning evolving from student's interests. Many cities, including Ann Arbor, Michigan; Los Angeles; and New York City, launched ambitious activity programs in elementary schools. Even in these settings, however, the instructional result was often a modified version of traditional education, with the fundamental aspects of the classroom experience—the physical layout of the room, class size, rules, evaluation, and supervision—only marginally affected, despite the prolific use of progressive jargon.

The conflict between the needs of youth and academic curricula remained a volatile one during the late 1930s. The Progressive Education Association (PEA), an advocacy group for child-centered education, actively promoted the campaign contending that U. S. high schools needed to increase their emphasis of students' personal, emotional, and social problems and decrease their emphasis on academic studies and traditional forms of school structure. Formed in 1919, the PEA's guiding principles reflected the widespread beliefs of the increasingly influential movement. They included the following:

1. The child should be given the freedom to develop naturally.
2. Interest provides the motivation for all work.
3. The teacher should be a guide in the learning process, not the taskmaster.
4. The scientific study of pupil development should be promoted by the refocusing of information to be included on school records.
5. Greater attention should be given to everything that affects the child's physical development.

6. The school and home should cooperate to meet the natural interests and activities of the child.
7. The progressive school of thought should be a leader in educational movements.[17]

The PEA was joined in its efforts against the traditional academic curriculum by individuals and groups considered more mainstream, such as the NEA.

The academic curriculum remained a potent and steady force in U.S. schools, nonetheless, largely because achievement and academic coursework was still an essential measure determining college admission. In 1930, the PEA undertook what became known as the Eight-Year Study to demonstrate that such academic requirements for college admission were unnecessary. Results of the study, in which evaluations were made of college students admitted on the basis of following successful completion of required courses and exams and those admitted largely on the basis of recommendations, interests, and aptitude tests, supported their contention. Yet many observers questioned the reliability of the study and claimed that it lacked credibility because Ivy League schools did not participate. The academic curriculum survived but more than ever was associated primarily with the college bound and not with future farmers, housewives, and factory workers.

EVOLUTION, CRITICISM, AND CHANGE

The pervasive effects of progressive education were highlighted by a 1938 *Time* magazine cover article, entitled "Progressives' Progress," that noted, "No U. S. school has completely escaped its influence."[18] Yet efforts by critics of progressive education, led by Bagley and other essentialists who stressed rigorous standards and a common academically oriented curriculum, continued, even as public attention remained focused on the economic crises at home and growing conflicts overseas.

Other prominent critics of this period included Robert Maynard Hutchins and Mortimer Adler. Hutchins was a high-profile educator who in 1929, at age 30, became president of the University of Chicago. Adler was then brought to the university by Hutchins to advance his Great Books curriculum, which focused on an academically oriented examination of classic works, which they believed could help counter what they viewed as the anti-intellectual aimlessness of many progressive education reforms, such as child-centered education.

Largely in response to such criticism, progressive education's towering figure, John Dewey, published *Experience and Education* in 1938. In this book, his last major work on education, Dewey sought to temper the accusations of laissez-faire individualism and radicalism that sometimes were lobbed at progressive education by opponents. However, the tension among factions in education reform remained severe.

As the 1930s came to a close, the issue of teacher training and certification began to assume more prominence in the education reform debate. A leading advocate for national teacher testing was Teachers College professor Isaac Kandel. He defended the administration of the National Teachers Examinations, which were developed during the Great Depression when there were more teaching applicants than available teaching positions. The exams were first offered in 1940 in 20 areas, including such cities as Philadelphia, Atlanta, and Boston. The 10- to 12-hour exams, developed by the American Council on Education, assessed the teacher candidate's command of such fields as English expression, reasoning, quantitative skills, literature, science, history, fine arts, and current issues, as well as teaching methods and educational history, psychology, and philosophy.

Those opposed to these exams feared that they would lead to greater uniformity and would place too much emphasis on teachers' factual knowledge rather than their ability to teach. The conflict over teacher testing subsided when World War II created a teacher shortage, puncturing reliance on the test. However, the questions of who should teach, how the individual is prepared, and how visions of curricular standards relate to strengthening public schools had established a prominent place on the education reform menu.

By the end of World War II, a half century after the movement had begun, progressive education was the reigning ideology of U.S. public education. In the mid 1940s, the NEA published *Education for All American Youth*. The report, endorsed by the leading school administrators' and principals' organizations, defined the role of public schools as oriented toward effective career guidance. As a result of the report, increased emphasis was placed on aptitude and intelligence tests for college admissions and the classification of subjects such as physics, chemistry, history, and algebra as elective courses. Hollis Caswell, dean of Teachers College, helped advocate these and other curriculum reforms that sought to have a direct impact not only on theory but also on classroom practice.

The 1950s, though often characterized by its sense of societal conformity and political conservatism, was also an era of significant ferment in education reform, signaling many of the key battles of the coming decades. Critics of public schooling spanned the ideological and cultural range. Included among them were those who believed that a jargon-intensive education establishment, disconnected from parents and community, had lost sight of education's central purpose of developing the knowledge and intellect of students in favor of efforts to place young people within society according to their perceived personal needs. More religious and cultural conservative types worried that public schools would become too secular, undermining the nation's moral and spiritual foundation. Others, fueled by McCarthy-era fears of communist influence, blamed lax public school standards for such ills as diminished respect for authority and decreased school discipline, as featured in the popular 1955 film *Blackboard Jungle*. Largely as a result of such concerns, a push for increased recitation of the Pledge of Allegiance (with the words *under God* added in 1954) gained momentum, as did calls for more school prayer. However, proponents of prayer in public schools suffered a major setback when the U.S Supreme Court ruled in 1962's *Engel v. Vitale* that public schools may not require the recitation of prayers.

A common complaint of 1950s public schools was that while schools of education required the study of teaching methods, they did not require teachers or administrators to be well educated. This, they asserted, was reflected in the de-emphasis of academic studies in high schools, and these critics pointed to statistics for support. High school enrollment in academic subjects such as physics, foreign languages, and geometry had significantly declined since the beginning of the 20th century.

Critics of public school standards enjoyed a breakthrough with the enormous popularity of Arthur Bestor's 1953 book, *Educational Wastelands*, and Rudolf Flesch's 1955 book, *Why Johnny Can't Read*. Flesch argued that modern reading approaches such as the look-see method found in the Dick and Jane readers often used in elementary schools were not as effective as traditional phonics instruction. Flesch noted that, "reading isn't taught at all. Books are put in front of the children and they're told to guess at the word or wait until the teacher tells them. But they're not *taught* to read."

Why Johnny Can't Read set off a national debate about literacy instruction and more broadly the common teaching practices of public schools. Most reviewers and the general public embraced its viewpoints, and it remained on the national best-seller lists for 30 weeks. But most prominent educators rejected its premise. The book spurred a Carnegie Corporation study led by Jean Chall of the Harvard Graduate School of Education and designed to determine the most effective method of reading instruction. Chall's three-year study concluded that both approaches were effective, with phonics instruction better suited for young readers and those from low socioeconomic backgrounds.

In response to Chall's report, most early to mid-1960s reading textbooks for early readers emphasized instruction in phonics. But, like the vast majority of other education reform issues, this trend was temporary, and the reading curriculum war would rage again later.

Progressive education encountered other challenges to its wisdom and authority during the late 1950s. In 1955, the PEA, unable to raise sufficient money or recruit members, closed its doors. Increasingly, the perceived excessiveness of the movement's methods and practices were mocked, as evidenced by satirist Tom Lehrer's song "New Math":

Hooray for new math,
New-hoo-hoo-math,
It won't do you a bit of good to review math.
It's so simple,
So very simple,
That only a child can do it![19]

But the biggest blow to progressive education practice in the 1950s occurred outside the realm public schools. The Soviet Union's 1957 successful launch of the space satellite *Sputnik* struck fear in Americans and served as a symbol of the lagging quality of U.S. schools. In 1958, President Dwight Eisenhower and Congress passed the National Defense Education Act, which among other provisions, included unprecedented federal aid for school construction and for math, science, and foreign language curriculum support. Admiral Hyman Rickover reflected this shifting in the popular view of education's purpose and signaled future debate over standards in his 1959 book *Education and Freedom*, noting,

life in a modern industrial state demands a great deal more "book learning"
of everyone who wants to make a good living for himself and his family . . .
the schools must now . . . concentrate on bringing the intellectual powers of
the child to the highest possible level. Even the average child now needs al-
most as good an education as the average middle and upper class child used to
get in the college preparatory schools.[20]

Defending public schools was former Harvard president James Conant, whose 1959 Carnegie Corporation–sponsored book, *The American High School Today*, became a national best-seller. Among Conant's key points was that large comprehensive high schools that offered multiple curricula were most effective. He also asserted that every high school needed to have a high-quality counseling staff to help its students into the right program. He described the often-followed practice of requiring four years of English, three or four years of social studies, one year of science and math, with all other courses selected as electives, largely based on aptitude tests. Conant also endorsed social promotion in the required courses, which resulted in students moving on to the next grade based more on factors such as their age rather than academic achievement. *The American High School Today*, which did not refer to its recommendations as progressive education, was very influential in reducing the number of small high schools that could not provide a full array of academic, vocational, and general courses and in blunting the attacks of 1950s public school critics.

Among the most dissatisfied participants in public education during this time were African Americans and others who supported their access to education. The frustration over the substandard conditions of the largely segregated public school system could no longer be overlooked following the U.S. Supreme Court's unanimous, landmark 1954 decision in *Brown v. Board of Education*, which prohibited state-imposed racial segregation in public schools. However, despite the civil rights significance of this decision, education of black students still suffered. Resistance to the ruling in the South was widespread. In the North continued white flight to the suburbs contributed to the deterioration of public schools.

Educational researcher Kenneth Clark, whose work was a key factor in demonstrating the harmful effects of segregation in the *Brown* case, advocated an emphasis on raising standards in the now notoriously underachieving larger urban schools, most of which had a high concentration of blacks. Such calls were largely drowned out by the din of political struggles and crises that engulfed the nation and its public schools throughout the 1960s, although the standards debate would emerge a generation later.

The role of the federal government in education reform took a giant step forward in 1965 with the passage of the Elementary and Secondary Education Act. This legislation, providing the largest infusion of federal funding for public schools ever, was a key component of President Lyndon Johnson's Great Society program. The law's Title I provision of approximately $1 billion to help improve education in the nation's poorest areas represented an unprecedented and to many unwelcome commitment of federal government in local schools. While among many there was enormous optimism that poverty and its related ills, such as inadequate education, could actually be overcome, the late 1960s were a time of great discord and criticism for public education, creating fertile ground for the proposition of sometimes radical reforms.

In 1964, private school teacher John Holt published *Why Children Fail*, ripping tests, grades, curricula, and other aspects of the schooling experience. His work is often credited with providing an articulation of the philosophical foundation for the homeschooling movement. Another important pen of reform was provided by teacher Jonathan Kozol, whose 1967 book, *Death at an Early Age*, won the National Book Award for its portrayal of the appalling conditions, including insensitive and unresponsive bureaucracy and incompetent and indifferent teachers, in the Boston public schools.

One proposed solution to the problems of urban schools and to the malaise of other public schools was the open education movement. The movement grew in popularity following the 1967 publication in *The New*

Republic of a series of articles by American social critic Joseph Featherstone that described open education in Britain, in which the routine of the day "is left completely up to the teacher and the teacher, in turn leaves options open to the students." Partly as a result of this movement, multiage groups, activity centers, and other aspects similar to the child-centered movement of the 1930s became more common. Journalist Charles Silberman's popular book *Crisis in the Classroom* helped propel the movement and by the early 1970s many schools had been modified to fit the tenets of open education. However, this movement fizzled almost as quickly as it grew. Many ambitious but poorly planned open education experiments failed miserably, as depicted in Massachusetts principal Roland Barth's book *Open Education and the American School.*

In 1969, a Gallup poll of Americans listed "lack of discipline" as the school's leading problem.[21] The real and perceived problems that resulted from the late 1960s and early 1970s, namely the easing of graduation requirements, bilingual education programs, dress codes, and disciplinary rules, led to a groundswell of support for a back-to-basics movement in education. This growing contingent of citizens who believed that schools had lost their focus of teaching young people in a morass of ill-conceived programs, services, and curricular trends would find hospitable terrain in the more conservative political environment of the early 1980s.

SEEKING SECURITY IN A NATION AT RISK

In 1983, the debate over education reform was redefined with the publication of *A Nation at Risk.* The controversial report issued by the National Commission on Excellence in Education, whose members had been appointed by President Ronald Reagan's secretary of education, Terrell Bell, warned of the dire consequences of U.S. educational decline. It charged that lax academic standards in American schools were clearly related to the drop in behavioral standards and that the failure to address these conditions could result in educational catastrophe. The report stated, "if an unfriendly foreign power had attempted to impose on America the mediocre educational performance that exists today, we might well have viewed it as an act of war."[22]

A Nation at Risk asserted that four aspects of schooling needed to change: content, expectations, time, and teaching. The report claimed that high school content had been, "homogenized, diluted, and diffused" to the point that it was a "cafeteria-style curriculum in which the appetizers and desserts can easily be mistaken for the main courses." *A Nation at Risk* continued to claim that expectations had been unacceptably watered down by grade inflation and weak promotion policies such as those found in the majority of states requiring only one year of math and science for high school graduation.

The report also compared the length of the school day and the school year in the United States and other industrialized nations and found that American students spent an insufficient amount of time pursuing academic study. In addition, the report argued that standards for teachers were in need of significant improvement by criticizing the relatively low academic achievement of teacher candidates and the heavy methods orientation of teacher education programs. Among the report's recommendations were the standardization of high school graduation criteria, including the requirement of successful completion of the "new basics": four years of English, three years of math, science, and social studies, and a half year of computer science.

Intense and ideologically diverse debate over the best ways to address the deficiencies of U.S. public schools followed the highly publicized release of *A Nation at Risk*. A first wave of reform resulted in top-down types of measures, including state legislation enacting higher graduation requirements, standardized curriculum mandates, increased testing of students and teachers, raised certification requirements for teachers, minimum standards for participation in athletics, and in some cases the lengthening of the school day and school year. A second wave of reform focused on bottom-up changes, such as increased local control of schools and site-based management, teacher empowerment, parental involvement, and various forms of school choice.

Two significant curricular schools of thought during this period were the modern tradition of progressive education of Ted Sizer and the academic curriculum emphasis of E. D. Hirsch. Sizer, former dean of the Harvard Graduate School of Education, published *Horace's Compromise* in 1983. In it, he melded traditional progressive education principles while shedding some of the more discredited notions of the movement. The book decried the low expectations and dull routine of most U.S. high schools. To counter this, Sizer advocated for increased authority for the teachers, administrators, and parents at local schools. For students, he recommended a greater emphasis on demonstrations of mastery rather than reliance on standardized tests. He created the Coalition of Essential Schools to advance reform ideas.[23] Among these schools was Central Park East School in Harlem, led by prominent education reformer Deborah Meier. By 2000, more than 1,200 schools were part of this coalition.

In the early 1980s, E. D. Hirsch was an English professor at the University of Virginia, and was not particularly well known outside Charlottesville. However, in 1987 his book *Cultural Literacy* was published and quickly became an education reform lightning rod. Supporters of the book lauded its purpose of transmitting "the basic information needed to thrive in the modern world" and backed Hirsch's claim that the understanding of a common, explicit curriculum was "the only way of combating the social determinism that condemns [students] to remain in the same social and educational condition as their parents."[24] Critics disparaged Hirsch's dictionary-like collection of information as trivia, but well over 1 million purchasers of the book found it to be relevant.

One common thread running through the major education reforms of the 1980s was a focus on academic standards. Increased economic globalization and rapidly advancing technology led many, particularly in the business community, to worry that American students would not be sufficiently prepared to lead the U.S. economy in a more competitive environment. Critical input from within the education community on the standards debate was provided by American Federation of Teachers president Albert Shanker. As the leader of the nation's largest teachers' union, Shanker exerted his considerable influence through regular newspaper op-ed pieces advocating clear standards and assessments that would strengthen the meaning and consequences of schooling for students. Soon elected officials were promoting standards as well, leading to President George H.W. Bush's 1989 Education Summit with the nation's governors to promote national education goals. This culminated in 1994 with President Bill Clinton signing the GOALS 2000: Educate America Act.

Despite the apparent middle ground consensus on curriculum standards, battles, particularly relating to U.S. history, raged. In 1994, University of California Los Angeles's Center for History in the Schools prepared a federally funded project of National History Standards. Even before the release, they were the focus of severe criticism. Lynne Cheney, former chairwoman of the National Endowment for the Humanities, attacked them for political bias, noting how the standards mentioned such shameful figures as Joseph McCarthy 19 times and the Ku Klux Klan 17 times yet omitted figures generally regarded as heroic, such as Paul Revere and Thomas Edison.[25] Although many, including the editorial boards of the *New York Times* and Los Angeles Times, endorsed the standards and their reflection of a multicultural curriculum emphasis, public sentiment was largely opposed to them. The U.S. Senate passed a resolution condemning them 99–1 (the one opponent wanted a harsher condemnation). President Clinton's secretary of education, Richard Riley, distanced the administration from them saying, "this is not my view of how history should be taught in America's classrooms . . . our schools should teach our students to be proud of the Americans."[26] The National History Standards were eventually revised but also largely ignored by states and districts, highlighting the historic difficulty of reaching a meaningful consensus in education reform in light of consistently deep ideological divisions.

CURRENT ISSUES IN EDUCATION REFORM

The impact and implications of education reform's history have merged with key current issues since the 1990s and into the 21st century. Following is an examination of the most prominent present-day issues in education reform, including choice, vouchers, and charter schools; privatization; homeschooling; accountability, standards, and assessments; teacher quality, school environment, and school financing.

CHOICE

School choice initiatives are based on the premise that allowing parents to choose which schools their children attend is not only the fair thing to do but also an important strategy for improving public education. Instead of a one-size-fits-all model, choice programs are designed to offer parents various alternatives from which to pick the educational settings that they believe work best for their children.

The earliest expression of this critical and increasingly prominent aspect of education reform is often credited to the free-market champion author of the 1776 book *Wealth of Nations*, Adam Smith. In that book, Smith argued that parents are in the best position to decide how their children should be educated and that the state should give parents the money to hire suitable teachers. The view that the state should provide funding for poor families to secure a basic education for their children was also endorsed by famous patriot and writer Thomas Paine toward the end of the 18th century.

However, circumstances in 19th-century America would lead to a general consensus against the embryonic notions of school or education vouchers. Especially damaging was the prevalent anti-Catholic bias that existed in the United States following the large influx of largely Catholic immigrant groups. Because of what he viewed as the intolerable resistance of non-Catholics, New York City bishop John Hughes asked the Public School Society of New York for state aid for Catholic schools in 1840. After his request was denied, Hughes built his own system with private funds. Three decades later, President Ulysses Grant helped certify the United States's educational separation of church and state by explaining, "Not one dollar . . . shall be appropriated to the support of any sectarian schools."[27]

Vouchers

The push for vouchers remained essentially dormant for almost a century. Despite support for voucher programs from advocates such as economist Milton

Friedman, who first proposed vouchers in 1955, popular and legal opposition to the practice of using public funds for private religious education was formidable. The period of the 1960s and 1970s were witness to a series of Supreme Court cases, including 1971's *Lemon v. Kurtzman*, that struck down attempts to provide state aid to religious schools in the form of teachers' salaries and instructional materials. During this time different forms of school choice began to emerge, including public school choice, in which students were able to attend schools outside their neighborhood but within their public school district.

Like many other education reforms, the choice movement owes a debt of gratitude to the 1983 report *A Nation at Risk*. This highly critical evaluation of U.S. public schools both reflected and initiated concern about the failure of schools and helped create an environment in which more radical approaches could be encouraged. A new openness to vouchers for private schools was evident in the 1983 Supreme Court case *Mueller v. Allen*. In a 5-4 decision, the Court supported the concept of tuition tax credits, holding that a state government (in this case Minnesota) could allow taxpayers to deduct expenses incurred due to "tuition, textbooks, and transportation" at religious, elementary, and secondary schools.[28]

Momentum for vouchers also grew in 1990 following the release of John Chubb and Terry Moe's book *Politics, Markets, and American Schools*, in which they claimed that "choice, all by itself, has the capacity to bring about a transformation in public education." A dramatic expansion then took place throughout the 1990s in the use of public school choice and in the more controversial private and religious school choice programs based on vouchers. The most renowned and contested of these programs were the Milwaukee Parental Choice Program, the Cleveland Scholarship Program, and the Florida A+ Plan.

There are three different types of options that fit the umbrella term of *school choice*. The least disputed and most common of these is intradistrict choice. This is the kind of public choice that allows parents to select among schools within their home district. Magnet schools, which typically focus on a specialization, such as technology or fine arts, are examples of intradistrict choice, as much or all of their enrollment is made up of students from all parts of the district and admission is based on lottery and/or the demonstration of academic achievement.

A less frequent but similarly oriented choice plan is statewide or interdistrict choice. Under these programs, students are allowed to attend public schools outside their home district. Minnesota has led the way for such initiatives with 13 other states creating similar legislation. The majority of states without interdistrict laws are currently considering them.

The issue of vouchers is most associated with private school choice. These programs, which usually are at the center of arguments about choice, permit parents to use public funds to send their children to private schools and, in many cases, religious schools.

Few issues in education, if any, are as intensely debated as private school vouchers. Supporters of the practice often argue that private school vouchers encourage equity by enabling students from families of low socioeconomic status, like their wealthier peers, to escape the troubled and inadequate public schools. In addition, these proponents also claim that private school vouchers will create competition that will spur innovation, accountability, and improvement in a public school system that serves as a monopoly providing poor services to its most vulnerable clients.

Opponents of private school vouchers generally contend these programs endanger the ideal of offering every student access to high-quality education by treating learning as a commodity rather than a public good. They point out how this competitive conception does not always work in the interest of the consumer. At best, they claim, private school vouchers are a kind of lifeboat that may help the fortunate few while leaving the majority of others stranded in a public system with depleted resources. In addition, voucher foes assert that allowing private schools to take public money with little oversight may lead to mismanagement or corruption.

Although the ideological divisions in the voucher debate are clear, they often do not fall along the common political or demographic lines. Vouchers are generally presented as something that conservatives and business types support and liberals and teachers' unions oppose. While that is often true, some of the strongest support for vouchers has come from individuals and groups that rarely endorse policies considered conservative. For instance, many recent studies have indicated that African Americans have posted higher levels of support for some form of private school vouchers than the general public.[29]

So how does the American public view private school vouchers, an issue almost completely off the radar less than 25 years ago? According to the 2002 Phi Beta Kappa/Gallup Poll on the Public's Attitudes Towards the Public Schools, the general public is split but increasingly supportive of the notion. In the poll, 52 percent of those surveyed said that they oppose allowing students to attend private school at "public expense." However, support for private school vouchers jumped 12 percentage points in just one year—from 34 to 46 percent. When this same question dropped the phrase "public expense," instead stating "the government would pay all or part of the tuition," 52 percent of respondents supported private school vouchers, an increase from 44 percent in 2001.[30]

Reasons for this increase of support may include the Supreme Court's provoucher decision in the 2002 case *Zelman v. Simmons-Harris* and a high approval rating at the time of the survey for President George W. Bush, who has publicly endorsed private school vouchers. However, when school voucher programs have been decided at the ballot box, the voters have usually defeated them by significant margins, as they did in Michigan and California initiatives during the 1990s.

The key questions of the voucher debate involve a wide range of legal, fiscal, social, and practical issues with potentially far-reaching implications: Are vouchers constitutional? Do they work? Do vouchers drain money from public schools? And, is there capacity to handle potentially expanded voucher programs?

The most vigorous arguments about vouchers often revolve around their constitutionality, specifically whether they infringe on church-state separation. Supporters of vouchers, who often draw comparisons between these programs and the enormously popular 1944 GI Bill, which provided educational support for veterans, claim the government has allowed public money in the past to go to private religious education and continues to do so, when, for instance, a student attending Notre Dame receives financial aid.[31] Proponents also point to recent state and Supreme Court rulings that have allowed more lenience in the application of public funds toward religious institutions.

Opponents of vouchers consistently assert that such mingling of public money and sectarian groups is a clear violation of the First Amendment's establishment clause, prohibiting government establishment or endorsement of religion. They often counter arguments that parents, not the government, actually would pay religious schools under voucher plans as legally irrelevant because public funds could still be used for religious instruction. As for claims that voucher funding would only pay for secular subjects, opponents argue that this would be impossible to enforce and further, that the public funds could actually violate discrimination laws in schools that make personnel decisions based on such factors as religious faith and sexual orientation.

The academic effectiveness of voucher programs is a particularly muddled aspect of the voucher debate. Despite the growing national dialogue about vouchers, many education reform experts explain that there are few studies about them that have been conducted by objective researchers with sound methodology. In addition, because there have been so few voucher programs, and those that exist have been in place for a relatively brief amount of time, reliable statistics demonstrating whether students and schools actually benefit from these programs are in short supply. Not surprisingly, many of the studies that are referenced point out that voucher programs are either great saviors or horrific failures.

Advocates on both sides of the voucher issue also argue about whether these programs are fiscally fair. Supporters believe that they are because they enable students from poor families to gain resources that can help them attend better and safer schools. They claim that voucher programs are designed to provide additional money for educational support so that they do not poach already determined spending allocations. Regarding charges that broader voucher plans would unfairly deplete funding available to public schools, supporters explain that if public schools receive the same amount of money per pupil they will not suffer.

Opponents argue that even the most ambitious and supportive voucher plans usually are not able to cover a student's entire tuition, making such plans useful for the wealthy and perhaps the middle class but not for the poor, whom the programs are ostensibly designed to help. They usually believe that money that could go toward the establishment and maintenance of a voucher program would be more wisely spent on measures designed to improve instruction in struggling public schools, such as initiatives to reduce class size and to improve reading instruction.

Voucher combatants also disagree on the fundamental question of whether voucher programs are socially practical. Supporters assert that they are, pointing out that vouchers will lead to public school improvement, and over time, fewer transfers to private schools. This will help allow private schools to absorb more easily incoming students, and if there are too many students leaving public schools, more private schools will be created.

Those opposed to voucher programs argue that such plans undermine society's commitment to public education by establishing an unfair framework in which public schools will be required to accept all students while private schools will be free to reject students for a variety of reasons, including the ability to provide special education services and student noncompliance with often stricter codes of conduct.

Until recently, voucher opponents held the upper hand in this education reform battle, as there were few and isolated private school voucher programs across the United States. But the course of this issue, and perhaps the nature of public education in the United States, changed on the morning of June 27, 2002, when the U.S. Supreme Court delivered its decision for *Zelman v. Simmons-Harris*, allowing the Cleveland voucher program to continue and calling it "true public choice . . . [providing] benefits to a wide spectrum of individuals, defined only by financial need and residence in a particular district."[32]

Just days after this decision, state legislators in California, Pennsylvania, Minnesota, and elsewhere organized plans for what they believe will be a new era of school choice. However, despite the crucial Supreme Court victory, voucher programs are by no means a fait accompli. Thirty-seven state constitutions contain language that prohibits state aid from going to religious schools. Even if such provisions are not insurmountable, they are at least likely to stall voucher plans.[33]

Forces opposing vouchers also can take some comfort in the fact that provoucher state ballot initiatives have failed six times since 1972, and numerous legislative efforts have suffered the same fate. The recent downturn in the economy has many states fighting just to maintain current levels of education spending, leading to the possibility that vouchers may enjoy their best prospects during economic boom times such as the 1990s. Furthermore, teachers' unions, which have led the effort to halt vouchers, appear not the least bit discouraged in the face of the legal setback from *Zelman*. Less than one week after the ruling, NEA president Bob Chase said, "And to the voucher ideologues we make this promise: we will expose your false promises. We will lay bare your lies . . . we will defeat you!"[34]

Charter Schools

Another form of choice that exploded in popularity during the 1990s and into the 21st century was charter schools. Under the charter school concept, a group of teachers or other would-be educators applied for permission from their local education authority to open a public school, operating with taxpayer dollars just like a regular public school. The difference is that charter schools are freed from many of the rules and regulations governing regular public schools that many feel cripple learning and stifle innovation. The schools operate under a contract, or "charter," with a local school board, state, or university(ies). In exchange for exemption from most state and local regulations, the schools, usually with a smaller, limited enrollment designed to enhance attention to student needs, must educate students according to an agreed-upon standard and must prove their success in order to gain renewal of the charter.

The rise of charter schools has been rapid and influential. At the beginning of 1991 there was not a single charter school in the United States. Ten years later there were almost 2,500 serving more than one-half million students.[35] One key reason for the rapid growth of charter schools is that they are a form of school choice that most stakeholders generally embrace in a broad, bipartisan fashion. Most Republicans like the emphasis on choice, competition, and deregulation, and most Democrats appreciate the fact that they are public schools, open to all, nonreligious, and accountable to public authorities. Political disputes over charter schools usually focus on which candidate is most committed to them, rather than which candidate supports them.

Charter schools do have their critics, however. One common charge against charter schools is that they create a kind of educational balkanization by usually serving students concentrated in low socioeconomic areas. Charter boosters often respond to this by explaining that they serve the same demographic characteristics as exist in the public school community in which they are located. Further, they assert that the disproportionate percentage of minorities enrolled in charter schools is a reflection of the traditional public schools' failure to meet the needs of these groups.

Charter opponents also claim that, even after 10 years of existence, they have not demonstrably improved the achievement of their students or the performance of other public schools. Along with this, many believe that the innovations promised in charter school applications are often not delivered. Charter supporters answer this by pointing to studies that provide evidence that students and schools are improving because of the competition and accountability encouraged by charter schools. They also explain that charter schools respond to local conditions, meaning that what may be considered innovative in one area (such as block scheduling of classes, year-round schooling) may be common in another area.

Perhaps the most serious criticism of charter schools is that they need to be more accountable to the taxpayer, whose money supports their creation and maintenance. In defense of charter schools, advocates explain that in the rare cases when charter schools fail to meet their detailed goals, they can be sanctioned or even closed. Regular public schools, they argue, are the ones lacking accountability because if they fail to meet goals, which often are not articulated, they can and do remain open, continuing to poorly serve their students.

Although charter school advocates enjoy the overwhelming support of parents, businesspeople, and politicians, they often feel that teachers' unions are uncertain allies. The NEA and the American Federation of Teachers (AFT), which staunchly oppose private school vouchers, state their support of charter schools, albeit with a number of conditions. The NEA, for instance, insists that charter schools should have no negative impact on the regular public school program, hire only licensed teachers, and not contribute to racial or ethnic segregation. Both unions also favor state caps on the number of charter schools. AFT president Sandra Feldman explains, "I'm in favor of charter schools that are accountable and adhere to the same standards as all public schools. We're not for charter schools that can just go off and do their own thing."[36] Charter proponents have also charged some union leadership with seeking to weaken state charter legislation through what they view as excessive restrictions on their number, authorizer eligibility, and regulatory independence.

The passage of the No Child Left Behind Act of 2001, reauthorizing the Elementary and Secondary Education Act, included provisions for both public school choice and charter schools, further signaling the prominence of choice in current education reform. Although private school vouchers were not supported in the act, legal momentum and planned state legislation have elevated this avenue of choice to similarly high importance. Events of the near future will likely be critical in determining whether choice becomes a cornerstone or footnote in the history of education reform.

PRIVATIZATION

Closely related to aspects of school choice is the issue of privatization in public education. The notion of turning the operation of public schools over to private companies is a controversial idea based on the widely accepted premise that what makes improving public schools so hard is that they are bogged down in a bureaucratic mire.

Advocates of privatization in public schools see the move as being an opportunity to provide the best of government and business. They contend that government's oversight function and its responsiveness to the needs of its citizens can be retained while taking advantage of private enterprise's ability to be more efficient, cut costs, and maximize production—in this case, student achievement. Advocates also point out that, like other major public services such as health care and defense, public schools have been and will always be partly about business.

Opponents of privatization and public education argue that, while this appears good on paper, it will not work efficiently in reality. Through privatization they see the individual needs of students, particularly those with special and often costly requirements, being sacrificed for the needs of corporate shareholders. They worry that the pressure for profit will replace student achievement as the driving force within schools. Many skeptics also do not accept the premise upon which the privatization plans are based, pointing out that private managers can be as inefficient or incompetent as public managers, if not more so.

Privatization efforts have had the most conspicuous impact on charter schools, as entrepreneurs recognized the business opportunity in working with the teachers and community activists who founded charter schools and were running an enterprise for the first time. Data varies on the proportion of the nation's charter schools that are run by for-profit companies, though estimates are usually placed at about 10 percent.

The most prominent for-profit school management company is Edison Schools (originally named the Edison Project). It was started in 1992 by entrepreneur Christopher Whittle, whose goal was to demonstrate how the market can improve the outcomes and efficiency of the public schools. The conditions for this venture were promising, coming at the beginning of a simultaneous wave of economic prosperity and education reform activity. Whittle proceeded to raise tens of millions of dollars and hired a well-respected team, including former Yale president Benno Schmidt, to design an exemplary school model.

When the first four Edison-managed schools opened at the beginning of the 1995–96 school year, the company began implementation of "the Edison design." This 10 point framework, still used today, emphasizes fundamentals such as varied instructional programs (including project-based learning and direct instruction), a longer school day and longer school year (198 days as opposed to the standard 180 days), a focus on technology integration (including providing every teacher with their own laptop computer), and a detailed standards-based, academically oriented curriculum. By the 1999–2000 school year, Edison was managing 79 schools and could boast that it had never lost a contract. Although still controversial and opposed by many traditional educators and teachers unions, Edison was enjoying mainly favorable media coverage and looked forward to an even greater academic and fiscal future.

Some of the same market factors that led to Edison's early success, however, contributed to its recent struggles. Precipitous drops in the stock market have witnessed a plunge in Edison's stock price from $36 a share in early 2001 to as low as 14¢ a share in mid-2002, and as of December 2002, it was selling at approximately $1.70 a share.[37] Edison did demonstrate success in its mission of delivering effective education and improving academic achievement in its schools, which were overwhelmingly located in impoverished areas, but these results often did not meet initial claims of Edison's boosters. This, as well as highly publicized failures in Edison-managed schools in New York City and Philadelphia, which resulted in lost contracts, has led to a decline in Edison's impact and an increase in the questioning of the market's ability to effectively run public schools. The complaints from school districts and charter school boards lodged against Edison are familiar ones often heaped upon traditional public school management—low test scores, high teacher turnover, and unsatisfactory "bang for the buck."

Edison Schools carries on, seeking to apply lessons learned in the still lucrative and potentially expanding market of public education management. Edison and others are now involved in "cyber charters," which are typically organized around an online curriculum, often targeting homeschooling families. A key issue to watch with cyber charters is the legislative fight regarding whether such schools should receive the same per-pupil funding as "brick-and-mortar schools."

HOMESCHOOLING

The ultimate form of school choice is the decision to educate one's own child at home. The homeschooling movement, like vouchers, charters, and privatization, has grown enormously over the past 30 years. Once generally considered to be the domain of highly religious parents and those from counterculture, homeschooling has garnered steadily increasing measures of mainstream acceptance as a viable option for frustrated parents concerned that the public schools are not effectively educating or protecting their children.

Homeschooling in practice takes many different forms. For many it means duplicating school at home, complete with textbooks, report cards, and standardized tests. At the other end of the homeschooling spectrum is the practice of "unschooling," in which students pursue their studies according to their own interests and according to their own pace. Most homeschooling reflects a middle course in which parents mix methods and curricula.[38] Increasingly, homeschooling families are organizing co-ops to share resources and increase student socialization and are participating in Internet-based distance learning programs. The consensus among those who follow homeschooling is that there are at least 1 million U.S. students currently being educated at home. Reliable numbers are difficult to ascertain because states define and track homeschoolers in different ways and some parents do not comply with state rules requiring them to register their homeschooled children.

Homeschooling's appeal emanates from spiritual, financial, academic, and social concerns. Many of the earliest homeschooling families were seeking a way out from secularized public schools, which following legal and social development of the 1960s and 1970s were viewed as increasingly intolerant of religious expression. Enrollment in religious schools usually remained an option for such families, but many have decided that schooling their children at home makes too much financial sense to refuse, as the cost of supplies for a home school curriculum is consistently significantly less than the average cost of tuition at a private school.

Academic considerations also play a crucial role in homeschooling's growth. Many of the criticisms found in *A Nation at Risk* are echoed by homeschooling families: frustration with inefficient school bureaucracies, lack of time for quality academic instruction, and declining standards of achievement and discipline in schools.

Related to this is the well-established concern among homeschooling parents that schools are simply not a safe environment. This trend in thought spiked dramatically following a spate of school shootings by students, including the 1999 murder of 12 students and one teacher at Columbine High School in Littleton, Colorado.

Despite the rising popularity of homeschooling, the movement has many critics. In the view of many professional educators and others, homeschooling remains a dangerously deregulated enterprise with an unacceptable lack of quality control. A resolution passed by the NEA argues that, "homeschooling programs cannot provide the student with a comprehensive education experience."[39]

Another concern is that some parents may be keeping their children out of school not because of the commonly stated reasons but rather because they do not want them to mix with children of other races or backgrounds or even so that they can work in a family business. In line with this argument is the contention that homeschooling seriously undermines the social development of a young person. Homeschooling supporters often counter that students too often develop poor and sometimes dangerous socialization traits in public schools. Critics respond however that the skills required to deal with the real world are rarely acquired within the walls of a home and that the sheltered isolation of homeschoolers may ultimately be detrimental to them and society.

The academic merits of homeschooling have received national attention following the victories of homeschooled students in recent national spelling bee competitions. In addition, most studies of homeschoolers' academic performance suggest that they generally achieve above national norms on standardized tests and in postsecondary academic endeavors. However, such studies cannot examine how those students would have performed had they stayed in public school, and they usually are unable to provide credible data regarding homeschoolers' social and emotional development.

By 1986, homeschooling had graduated from a fringe movement to a legally recognized activity practiced in all 50 states.[40] Disputes still often occur, nonetheless, between parents and state or local education officials about enforcement of homeschooling laws, which vary considerably across the country. Most states do not require parents to have specific qualifications for teaching their children at home, but most states do have provisions requiring that homeschooled students have regular evaluations or take standardized tests.

Recent trends in homeschooling have featured the evolution of the homeschooling industry, with the proliferation of for-profit companies and nonprofit organizations providing curricular materials specifically designed for homeschooling families. As the homeschooling movement has become larger and more accepted, relationships with public schools, such as homeschooled students' participation in public school extracurricular activities, have increased, seemingly benefiting both the homeschooled and the public school system. Whether such relationships also threaten these educational stakeholders remains to be seen.

ACCOUNTABILITY

Accountability—the concept of holding schools, districts, teachers, and students responsible for academic achievement—has become the most essential element affecting the variety of current education reform efforts. Across the

United States, policymakers have moved decisively toward rewarding achievement and punishing failure in an effort to ensure that students receive a high-quality education and that the public's tax money is used efficiently.

All 50 states test students to determine what they have learned, and 45 states publish report cards on individual schools, based largely on test scores. More than half of the states publicly rate their schools, or at least identify low-performing ones, and 15 states have the legal authority to close, take over, or replace the staff and schools that have been identified as failing.[41]

This recent push for accountability is a modern manifestation of the history of education reform battles, in this case specifically seeking to prove what needs to be taught and how to measure whether this material has been effectively learned. This pursuit, combined with the back-to-basics sensibility of *A Nation at Risk,* has led to the formation and influence of accountability measures, the two most relevant of which are standards and assessments.

Standards

The underlying assumption of standards-based reform is one that harkens back to the early 20th-century conception of the educational ladder that offered all students the opportunity to meet high goals. For many supporters of standards, they represent the most effective means by which glaring gaps in student performance and expectations can be addressed, leading to a foundation of excellence and equity throughout the public school system.

Within this framework are different types of standards. Academic standards describe what students should know and be able to do in the core academic subjects at each grade level. Content standards describe basic agreement about the body of education knowledge that all students should know. Performance standards describe what level of demonstrated skill is sufficient for students to be ranked advanced, proficient, or below basic.

Public support for standards are strong, although an *Education Week* survey conducted in 2000 found higher levels of approval for the adaptation of standards among business leaders than among teachers. This popular support of academic standards has led states to put them into place. Every state but Iowa has some form of formal academic standards and 48 states have academic standards in the core subjects of English/language arts, math, science, and social studies.

Despite this widespread setting of academic standards, significant obstacles stand in the way of making them effective tools for educational progress. Standards advocates and critics often worry that standards are too vague to be truly meaningful. Many are also concerned about a "Goldilocks phenomenon," which often finds educators thinking that standards are set properly while many parents, business leaders, policymakers, and others find them to be either too easy or too difficult.

Assessments (Testing)

The role of standards and the accountability discussion is inexorably linked to the more controversial issue of assessments. The testing policies established in every state are designed largely to find an accurate way to measure students' success as well as to hold schools accountable for results. The implementation and far-reaching implications of these tests are at the heart of accountability, and they have become an increasingly essential feature of education reform.

Assessment advocates often view statewide testing as a way to raise expectations and to help guarantee that students are held to the same high standards. Critics respond that testing too often narrows student learning to what is tested, leading instructors to "teach to the test" and cover only a sample of what students should know. In addition, they lament how tests tend to focus on what is easiest to measure rather than assessing the critical thinking skills students need to develop.

One of the key issues in the assessment debate concerns alignment, or how well state tests match state standards. Developing a clear and meaningful alignment between state standards and state assessments requires time, expertise, and money. Some states have invested in developing tests designed for alignment, while others have opted for partial alignment or "off the shelf" tests that do not necessarily reflect state standards. Since 1969, the National Assessment of Educational Progress (NAEP) has administered periodic national tests in reading, math, science, writing, history, and geography, providing data on the achievement of students over time and across the country.

Another area of concern is the quality of state assessments. Many reform-minded testing experts are aiming to create assessments that elicit higher order critical-thinking, problem-solving, and communications skills rather than or in addition to the traditional multiple-choice approach that is considered effective at measuring more basic content knowledge. Assessments that measure the higher order skills are typically more open ended, with teachers judging students on written essays, on the process they used to solve a problem, and in some cases on a portfolio of their work over the course of the school year. Currently, almost all states include multiple-choice items in their assessments, most states include short answer items, approximately one-third include performance-based assessments in subjects other than English, and only two use portfolio assessments.

State assessments, particularly following the increased reliance on them in recent years, have brought to the surface another contentious aspect that has been associated with testing for years—bias. Although African Americans and most other minorities have recently demonstrated relative and absolute gains in standardized test scores, they still score much lower than whites as a group. Many educators and parents believe that it is partially, if not largely because the embedded cultural bias of standardized tests that draw primarily upon the experiences and sensibilities of middle-class white students. Critics also question what they consider to be the emphasis on these tests and the high stakes attached to them.

Social Promotion

State assessments are increasingly being applied to determine whether students advance to the next grade, attend summer school, and in some cases graduate. Led by reform efforts in the Chicago public schools during the mid-1990s, many school systems and states are implementing policies designed to restrict or end the practice of social promotion, instead basing student advancement to the next grade on whether he or she meets predetermined assessment benchmarks. Supporters of such policies argue that this is a way to raise expectations and convey the importance of academic achievement. Detractors claim that these policies are unfair because the schools implementing them often do not provide the held-back students with the tools they need to succeed, such as high-quality instruction, a strong curriculum, and support services. Further, they argue that retention, while perhaps successful in sending a message, does not actually help the student grow academically or socially.

Reconstitution

Procedures are also in place for schools that fail to meet collective assessment goals. One such method growing in frequency is reconstitution, in which a governing authority, usually a state, though sometimes a district, can replace any or all of a low-performing schools' staff. This drastic strategy to improve persistently failing schools has been explicitly endorsed in the No Child Left Behind Act of 2001.[42] Under this law, districts must implement corrective actions, such as replacing staff members if a school fails to make adequate progress for four consecutive years. After five consecutive years of inadequate progress, a district would be required to set up an alternative governance structure, such as reopening the school as a charter school or turning operation of a failing school over to the state.

Supporters of reconstitution hail its intolerance for the culture of failure within many schools and its recognition of the inability of such schools to help themselves without severe intervention. Opponents of reconstitution worry that the approach wrongly blames teachers and school staff for conditions largely out of their control. Further, they argue that deficiencies in some school communities are so endemic that changing the staff in an attempt to improve a school will do little good and may in fact cause harm.

Because reconstitution is such a recent measure, it is unclear whether it has been an effective approach to strengthening the weakest of America's public schools. What is clear is that reconstitution represents another of the dramatically increased efforts to ensure accountability that have taken hold over the past 20 years.

Bilingual Education Programs

Adding to the complexity of this issue is the issue of how to properly address standards and assessments for students enrolled in bilingual education programs. The original objective of bilingual education was to ensure that students would not fall behind academically because of a poor command of the English language and to gradually teach them English as a second language. Proponents claimed that if language minority students were taught some subjects in their native tongue, they potentially could learn English without sacrificing content knowledge. The bilingual education's critics disagreed, arguing that this approach keeps students in a cycle of native language dependency and inhibits their progress toward English-language mastery.

Bilingual education programs gained traction in the 1970s and expanded into the 1990s. However, public sentiment against bilingual education has been growing and may threaten its existence as previously practiced. In 1998, California voters overwhelmingly approved Proposition 227 (Organized by software entrepreneur Ron Unz), which largely eliminated bilingual education from the public schools. Similar campaigns have also succeeded in Arizona and Massachusetts, and more are planned.

TEACHER QUALITY

In the final analysis, any effective education reform will need to positively influence the instruction that occurs inside a classroom. With this in mind, many recent education reform efforts have been focused on strengthening the background, training, and professional development of teachers.

Research consistently shows that teachers who have been trained in the subjects they teach perform better than teachers who lack subject-matter preparation. Yet on average, about one-third of teachers in public schools are assigned at least one class a day for which they have not been trained. This occurs even more frequently in low-performing schools. In addition, most research also demonstrates that teachers are more effective when they possess at least a few years of classroom experience, yet more than 20 percent of new teachers leave the profession within five years. This high rate of turnover has had a destabilizing effect on schools and the profession as a whole.

The rise in demand for effective teacher recruitment and retention strategies that has occurred over the past 15 years is reaching a critical stage. Enrollment in public schools is expected to steadily rise until 2009, with a projected student figure reaching 48 million. Meanwhile, the average public school teacher at that time is expected to be in his or her mid 40s. Because of these projections, many districts are bracing for a wave of classroom vacancies over the course of the next 10 years.[43]

To address high attrition rates, many districts have introduced induction and mentoring programs for new teachers, and as of 2001, 10 states funded and required such programs. Many states and districts are also attempting to raise teacher compensation to make the profession more attractive to new workers and experienced educators. Experiments with such practices as forgiving student loans for future teachers have not been widespread but have demonstrated some success as an incentive to attract potential teachers.

Another way that states and districts have sought to improve teacher quality is by establishing stronger minimum requirements for initial licensure. Part of this approach has included increasing student teaching experience for prospective teachers. Currently, more than 20 states require a least 12 weeks of student teaching prior to the completion of a teacher preparation program. States have also turned to testing as a measure to ensure teacher quality. As of 2001, 37 states require prospective teachers to pass a basic skills test, 29 states require candidates to master a test of subject knowledge, and 24 states require passing a subject-specific pedagogy exam in order to be able to teach.[44]

Among all the teacher-quality reforms, none is more controversial within the education community as alternative certification, which allows teachers into the classroom without the traditional teacher training usually required. Proponents of alternative certification explain that Albert Einstein would not have been able to teach a high school physics class in a U.S. public school because he had not completed the pedagogical coursework required by state certification agencies. This mindset, they assert, is not only foolish but also a luxury that schools cannot afford, particularly in light of the anticipated teacher shortage.

One program leading the way in alternative certification has been Teach for America (TFA). Founded in 1990 by recent Princeton graduate Wendy Kopp and based on the Peace Corps model, TFA is a national corps of recent college graduates from a variety of academic backgrounds who commit to two years of teaching in public schools in low-income communities struggling with persistent teaching shortages. TFA, a largely privately supported organization, narrowly survived fiscal crises in the mid 1990s and as of 2002 had placed more than 8,000 teachers in U.S. classrooms where they have taught more than 1 million students.[45]

The federal government has recently become more vocal in advocating alternative certification programs as well as speaking out in favor of a de-emphasis on pedagogy in traditional teacher training programs. Commenting on his 2002 *Annual Report on Teacher Quality,* Secretary of Education Rod Paige stated:

> *Many schools of education have continued business as usual, focusing heavily on pedagogy ... when the evidence cries out that what future teachers need most is a deeper understanding of the subject of the teaching, of how to monitor student progress, and how to help students who are falling behind.[46]*

The report also complained that while 45 states have set up alternative routes into the profession, many do not allow prospective teachers to skip "burdensome" education courses or student teaching, leading Paige to insist that, "we must tear down barriers preventing talented men and women from entering the teaching profession."

Representatives of teachers and teacher preparation programs took exception to the secretary's comments, claiming that his plans would lower the quality of teachers without addressing the root causes of existing teacher shortages, such as inadequate salaries and unappealing working conditions. The NEA's director of teacher quality, Gayla Hudson, said, "We see this as an insult to the teaching profession. . . . we have a nursing shortage, and nowhere is there any recommendation for six week courses for nurses."[47]

The coming years promise to be active ones in the teacher-quality debate, particularly regarding teacher-related provisions in the No Child Left Behind Act that require certification and demonstration of subject-matter competence for all new teachers in Title I programs receiving federal compensatory money. This reform, and many others, will likely go a long way in determining what kind of teachers will be working in tomorrow's classrooms.

SCHOOL FINANCING

It is often said that schools would function more effectively and improve more consistently if only they had access to more money. This common notion has led to a recent emphasis in the education reform field of school financing.

The manner in which school budgets are financed varies from state to state. Although the federal government has had an increasingly influential role in public schools over the past 40 years, it accounts for less than 10 percent of the more than $600 billion spent on public schools annually. States generally use a combination of income taxes, corporate taxes, sales taxes, and fees to provide about half of public schools' budgets. Local districts typically contribute between 40 to 55 percent, drawn mostly from local property taxes, and the remaining portion of the budget comes from the federal government. However, every state creates school budgets slightly differently, and the amount of funding tends to vary dramatically, depending on fluctuating property values.

Critics of the commonly applied property tax–based system of school financing argue that it is inherently inequitable, saddling the poorest areas with the fewest financial resources. Supporters contend that it is fair as wealthier residents pay more for higher-quality public schools and that even in states with the greatest funding gaps the difference accounts for only about a $10 a day difference in per-pupil spending.

However, attacks on the funding gap are accelerating. In 1993, Michigan replaced a property tax–based system with one financed largely by an increase in state sales taxes. Currently, there are more than 20 lawsuits seeking reform of state financing of public education. Among these is the closely watched *Williams v. State of California*, in which the plaintiffs cite the deplorable conditions in school districts across the state and ask the court to require the state to ensure the provision of certain educational basics such as qualified teachers, safe facilities, and textbooks.[46]

Related to the reform of school financing is the issue of school construction. This is the focus of many educational reformers because of the burden shouldered by local districts to pay for repairs to and construction of school buildings, particularly in this era of rising student enrollment.

Advocates in this discussion often argue for a greater state role in contributing to much-needed repairs and construction of schools. They point to a 2000 NEA report placing a whopping $268 billion price tag on the cost of needed school repairs and construction. In the mid- to late 1990s the number of bills passed by state legislatures increased significantly as did the number of states making meaningful changes to their school construction financing system toward equalized funding.

SCHOOL ENVIRONMENT

A great deal of recent education reform activity has focused on factors affecting the culture of learning. In an effort to create schools in which students' academic, emotional, and social needs are respected and nurtured, many policies have been implemented to reduce class size and ensure safety.

Class-size Reduction

In recent years, reducing class size has become a leading school improvement strategy. More than 40 states now have class-size reduction initiatives in place. The reasoning behind such initiatives is rather direct: With fewer students, teachers will be able to provide each of them with more individual attention that will result in greater interest in achievement in school.

Class-size reduction has a wide range of supporters including teachers' unions and the federal government, which in 2000 created a federal class-size reduction program, giving states funding to recruit, hire, and train new teachers. Under the No Child Left Behind Act of 2001, that program was consolidated into a more general teacher-quality block grant program funded by almost $3 billion for 2002.

Research has tended to find consistent benefits of small class size, particularly for students living in poverty. However, reducing class size is more expensive than many other school improvement ideas. Another concern is that, with many districts already facing shortages of qualified teachers, the additional classes created will be filled by unprepared teachers.

Such a situation was experienced in California following its class-size reduction initiative, which began in 1996. In the first year of implementation, more than 20 percent of the new teachers hired in that state had only emergency credentials. Hit especially hard were schools serving predominantly poor and minority students. To further complicate matters, the ensuing search for new instructional space led administrators to carve classrooms out of closets and to erect portable classrooms on playgrounds.

California's experience has led some researchers to investigate other potentially more cost-effective strategies, such as improved professional development for teachers. An ominous note for class-size reduction advocates was sounded by the economic downturn of 2001 and 2002, which has led several California districts facing budget shortfalls to consider eliminating part or all of these programs.

School Safety Policies

Another set of reforms intended to improve the school environment has focused on ensuring students' protection from violence and threats of violence. Installing metal detectors, practicing hostage drills, and conducting anger management training were certainly not imagined by Horace Mann or John Dewey when they helped build the U.S. public school system, but they are often a reality in the public schools of today.

The tragic rash of school shootings across the United States during the 1990s led to a public perception that school violence was on the rise. An April 2000 Gallup poll found 63 percent of parents with children in school believing that it was very likely or somewhat likely that a Columbine-style shooting could occur in their community. Although recent studies by the U.S. Department of Education and Justice indicate that overall violent crime rates in schools actually dropped throughout the 1990s from their peak in 1993, many schools and districts have added policies designed to ensure students' safety.

Among these measures are zero-tolerance policies for students who engage in violent acts, students found with weapons on school grounds, or students who have made threats of violence against teachers or other students. Supporters of such policies appreciate the straight, no-nonsense approach that conveys the seriousness of infractions. However, several cases of zero-tolerance policy implementation have struck many in the public as clearly running counter to common sense.

An example is a 2002 Texas case in which a 16-year-old honors student with no disciplinary record was found with a bread knife in the back of his truck. His explanation that it belonged to his grandmother and must have fallen out when he was transporting boxes for her was vouched for by his parents and believed by school administrators. Nevertheless, under the zero-tolerance policy, the student was expelled for one year and ordered to attend a juvenile education program for one year. Although the student's penalty was later reduced to a five-day suspension, the case illustrated the complex intersection of confusing legal mandates, fear of liability, and fair and effective means of protecting students.[49]

Many educators, administrators, and students feel that preventive measures can be effective in creating a healthier learning environment. Among the methods often implemented are service learning and character education curriculum, conflict resolution programs, and other support systems that seek to address the root causes of school violence including student isolation, disengagement from learning, and home stress.

A highly publicized approach to create secure and orderly learning environments centers on the implementation of dress codes, often requiring school uniforms. In 1996, President Bill Clinton endorsed the idea in his State of the Union address, and the popularity of such policies jumped. School uniforms appeal to many because they bring to mind visions of more orderly public schools of the past, and in areas of high gang activity, they may help avoid conflicts that arise over opposing colors or symbols. School uniform advocates cite reports from Long Beach, California, the first large urban school district in the nation to institute a mandatory uniform policy. Studies there indicate that between 1994, when uniforms were first required for all students up to ninth grade, and 1998, there was a significant drop in school crime, assaults committed on school property, and incidents of school vandalism, and a surge in average attendance to an all-time district high. Critics decry the way that school uniform policies repress freedom of expression and dispute data, including findings from studies of Long Beach's policy in the 1990s, linking these policies to a reduction in school violence.

They claim that such data is overblown in significance and may be the result of many other factors.

THE FUTURE OF EDUCATION REFORM

The era of education reform sparked by the publication of *A Nation at Risk* shows few signs of retreating in activity. In fact, recent events suggest that the debates about the future of education reform will continue to be contentious and increasingly influential in determining the scope and nature of elementary and secondary schooling in the United States.

The 2002 Supreme Court decision in *Zelman v. Simmons-Harris* has definitively moved the issue of vouchers into the center of current education reform issues. The Court's 5-4 decision allowing the use of public money for private schools was described by President George W. Bush as "just as historic" as the 1954 Supreme Court decision in *Brown v. Board of Education* ending legalized segregation in public schools.[50] The ruling has mobilized advocates on each side of the issue nationally and will likely lead to a significant increase in activity in state legislatures to implement and restrict voucher programs. Voucher advocates have already initiated lawsuits in Maine and Washington challenging the Blaine Amendments and compelled-support clauses of state constitutions, which have served as legal barriers to state support of religious institutions. Voucher supporters are encouraged that the prejudicial history of the Blaine Amendments leave them especially vulnerable to legal attack. Many antivoucher strategists, including teacher union leaders, maintain that the legal issue involving vouchers is no longer salient, indicating that voters and elected officials will ultimately decide whether voucher programs will be enacted.

Another emerging issue in the voucher movement is whether state funds earmarked for disabled children should be able to be used by parents to enroll those children in any school. This is one recommendation of the 2002 President's Commission on Excellence in Special Education. If accepted by the Bush administration, the proposal, which does not require congressional approval, would, according to Stanford political science professor Terry Moe,

- Use federal special education funds to help support services in public charter schools and private schools in districts that offer the same services in the traditional public schools, so long as the charter or private schools are held to the same accountability and standards.

- Use special education funds to pay for private services such as speech therapy when parents of traditional public school special education students are not satisfied with the academic progress of their children.[51]

Critics warn that the commission's recommendation may divert funding from current special education programs offered by traditional public schools. But popular and legal momentum currently and clearly suggests that implementation of such policies will be enacted.

The voucher movement is also moving ahead with advocacy of giving parents tax credits to compensate them for private school tuition (and perhaps books, transportation, and other expenses). A few states, such as Minnesota and Illinois, have adopted such measures. Moe notes the more recent development of allowing tax credits to business firms for allocating money toward specially constituted scholarship foundations, which would then distribute vouchers to qualified children on the basis of need. Pennsylvania and Florida have already adopted such programs; business firms, often preferring to earmark their money for deserving education programs rather than see it dumped into the general fund, have responded by pouring many millions of dollars into their states' scholarship funds.[52]

It will also be interesting to observe whether the voucher debate continues to forge uncommon alliances and perhaps unintended consequences. Political champions of vouchers are usually Republicans, often with a very conservative orientation. Many of their greatest allies in this debate have been the poor families in struggling urban schools who otherwise generally overwhelmingly reject them in the voting booth. In addition, many expect that if future voucher programs propose to extend into more suburban and white areas with broader, more expensive, and increasingly religious educational options, support for the movement will dwindle.

The 2004 presidential election may also provide a great deal of insight into the relevance and potential impact of school vouchers as a political issue. President Bush, a strong advocate of vouchers, will likely run against one of the current field of declared and expected Democrat candidates, all whom have declared varying degrees of opposition to school vouchers that allow the use of public funds at private and religious schools.

One area of education reform that generally has had bipartisan support is charter schools. The dramatic and consistent growth in charter schools since their inception in the early 1990s, received a significant federal boost with provisions in the No Child Left Behind Act. However, battles in state legislatures are increasing and could potentially obstruct or even derail charter school growth.

A key issue of contention at the center of much state level charter school discussion is how much money is spent and how this money is spent. In March 2002, the California State Board of Education reduced funding to 46 charter schools after an audit found the schools failed to follow state spending guidelines. Charters that contract with private educational maintenance organizations, such as Edison Schools, also have come under increased scrutiny because of concerns about their financial future and academic achievement.

In addition, California policymakers are also looking at the proliferation of nonclassroom-based charter schools, including home study schools, independent study programs, and distance learning schools (sometimes labeled "cyber charters") to ensure that financial concerns are being addressed. Other states, including Pennsylvania and Wisconsin, have experienced legal battles involving cyber charters, with opponents claiming that because such schools do not physically enroll students, they are ineligible for state funding. Legislative and legal outcomes of these cases will be examined across the United States as cyber charters develop and perhaps grow in prominence.

Like the charter school movement, homeschooling exploded in popularity during the 1990s and also faces hurdles to potential growth. The slumping U.S. economy since 2000 may make parents of homeschoolers unable to stay home and may cause the financial commitment to educating their own children at home to become prohibitive. Recent legislative challenges to homeschooling, particularly on grounds of accountability, have also popped up in California and Illinois, though they have not developed much political traction. A more daunting challenge to homeschooling may be the result of the movement's success, namely the growth in overall school choice, including vouchers and charter schools, that could lead many families to keep their children in or return their children to the public schools.

Accountability has established strong footing on the education reform landscape and will likely continue to grow in importance, particularly in the wake of mandates of the No Child Left Behind Act that allow children in schools deemed to be failing an option to attend better-performing ones. Among the recent accountability measures that will attract attention, particularly in large urban districts, is New York City's new transfer policy announced in December 2002. This new transfer process will feature letters describing transfer options mailed to parents of students in failing schools in the early spring of 2003, a May 2003 deadline for parents to request transfers, and notification to parents of new school assignments for children whose transfers have been approved effective for the 2003–4 school year. The Department of Education of New York City plans to address the widespread ignorance of and confusion surrounding the No Child Left Behind Act's transfer options by launching an advertising campaign via local newspapers, posters, and the Internet describing parents' rights and options.[53]

Some school officials have circumvented these transfer provisions claiming that a lack of space in good schools and a dearth of qualified teachers hamper implementation. In July 2002, Chicago unveiled a plan in which pupils in 50 of the federally identified 179 failing elementary in the district would be allowed to move into higher-performing schools. But they could choose from a list of only 90 schools and could not pick a school more than three miles away. Chicago public schools CEO Arne Duncan explained that, "We fully support the spirit of the law, but there is a practical reality here that we have to deal with. If every student in every school exercised choice, there would be a great deal of chaos in the system. We simply don't have enough space for the students, and we do not think busing kids across the city is the answer to better schools."[54] Such attitudes concern the federal government and portend conflict. In November 2002, Undersecretary of Education Eugene Hickok addressed the failure of states and school systems to implement provisions of the No Child Left Behind Act by stating, "Watch us. We are going to get pretty aggressive. . . . You will see much activity in pushing states to implement the law."[55]

Central to future discussions of accountability is how to define the term *failing school*, which has significant consequences. Under the federal No Child Left Behind Act, "failing schools" are those failing to make "adequate yearly progress" as defined by each state. To those who favor state and local control of school standards, leaving standards to each state is a welcome feature of the legislation, designed to prevent the federal bureaucracy from interfering in local schools. But to those who do not trust state and local school boards to properly administer effective intervention, allowing the states to set standards in effect allows them to evade the intent of the No Child Left Behind Act.

The *failing school* label is expected to become a pressing issue as more of the No Child Left Behind Act's provisions take effect, with stakeholders seeking to reach some consensus as to what a "failing school" actually is. Tied closely to this designation is the growing emphasis across the United States on standardized assessments. The increased reliance on these tests continues to attract criticism from opponents of policies seeking to end social promotion of students. The most prominent district with an anti-social-promotion policy, the Chicago public schools, released figures in September 2002 showing that of the 32,838 students in the third, sixth, and eighth grades who were required to attend summer school in 2002, 13,308—nearly 41 percent—did not qualify for promotion to the next grade. Most of those children failed the end-of-summer test; some never showed up to take it or never enrolled in summer school as required. The numbers were the highest since the inception of the program in 1997 and represented a sharp upward spike from 2001.[56]

District leaders defend the program, saying the higher retention rates were produced by raising the bar that students must meet to move on to the next grade. That bar combines standardized-test scores with factors such as grades, classroom tests, homework completion, and attendance. But opponents counter that the figures show that this and similar policies do not achieve their goal and in fact harm those who are being held back. How Chicago deals with this issue will be closely watched in cities with similar programs, such as Baltimore and Boston, as well as many other districts and states around the nation.

The trend toward the dismantling of bilingual education programs established in ballot initiatives in California in 1998 and Arizona in 2000 experienced mixed results in two key state measures during the 2002 elections. Massachusetts voters overwhelmingly approved a measure making it more difficult for a child to receive a waiver of exemption from mandatory bilingual education and also giving English-learning students only one year in English immersion, after which they are to be placed in a mainstream classroom. A similar ballot measure in Colorado was decisively defeated. Advocates on each side of this issue are mobilizing for future state ballot initiatives, though momentum appears to be on the side of those wishing to increase English immersion programs, who take heart in surveys such as the 2003 report published by the nonpartisan opinion-research group Public Agenda that indicate that immigrants are no more likely than the general public to support bilingual education in public schools.

The attention given to school choice, homeschooling, and accountability over the past decade has somewhat overshadowed a critical and simmering struggle over ensuring teacher quality. This issue will likely rise in prominence with the expected departure of a high percentage of experienced teachers nationally over the next five to 15 years. Although teacher certification is primarily the responsibility of the states, the George W. Bush administration has recently increased the federal voice in the matter through portions of the No Child Left Behind Act that require all teachers in core academic subjects be "highly qualified," defined in the act as having full state certification and possessing solid content knowledge of the subjects taught, by the end of the 2005–6 school year. This provision has many critics worried that an anticipated teacher shortage will worsen if this part of the law is strictly enforced. Additionally, the Bush administration's outspoken support of alternative certification programs designed to increase the quantity and diversity of the teacher candidate pool could also grow in relevance and opposition, particularly if the 2004 presidential election features President Bush against a Democrat candidate with strong backing from the generally anti–alternative certification teachers' unions.

Voucher proponents argue that teacher quality will be enhanced through changes induced by competition, including better salary, teaching freedom, strengthened classroom discipline and control, and innovative methods that could give teachers increased stature and compensation as skilled and respected professionals. However, in the limited voucher programs that do currently exist, significant changes in these areas have not been prominent.

The most significant education reform developments over the next few years may occur in the field of school financing. On December 11, 2002, the Supreme Court of Ohio declared the way the state funds its education system as unconstitutional. The court's ruling in *DeRolph v. State* found that the current school funding system violates Ohio's constitution, a complete systematic overhaul of school funding is needed, and the General Assembly of Ohio must enact a new school funding system that is thorough and efficient. Other states have had similar rulings in the recent past, and others, including California, have lawsuits challenging various aspects of state funding polices pending.

The finance-related education reform issue of class-size reduction will also likely be a focus of increased scrutiny, as reports begin to trickle in relating to class-size reduction initiatives of the 1990s. While some reports, such as the 2002 California Class Size Reduction Research Consortium report, indicate that there is not a strong association between student achievement and class-size reduction, class-size reduction advocates are encouraged by a major victory in November 2002's Amendment 9 ballot initiative of Florida that will provide $20–$27.5 billion of state money over nine years for the construction of classrooms. Provisions of Amendment 9 require that there will be no more than 18 students in kindergarten to third-grade classrooms, 22 students for grades 4 through 8, and 25 students for grades 9 through 12.[57]

Two other strategies intended to improve the school safety environment popular during the 1990s have slowed in recent years. District adoption of zero-tolerance measures appear to have plateaued, partially as a response to the numerous local stories of what many feel are their unfair and illogical implementation. However, another highly publicized violent school tragedy would likely increase calls for stricter and more indiscriminate treatment of discipline offenses. Policies requiring students to wear school uniforms or to adhere to dress codes, while still in place in many schools and districts around the country, also have diminished in frequency, and there is little evidence that such policies will soon regain the popularity they enjoyed in their heyday of the mid-1990s.

The movements of education reform's past and present have reflected a steadfast hope and faith in public schools' ability to ensure promises of equity, opportunity, prosperity, and excellence. Perhaps the most secure prediction that can be made about the future of education reform is that the outcomes resulting from the current debates will, in the final analysis, profoundly affect the educational experience for future generations and will determine whether that hope and faith in public schools will be redeemed.

---

[1] L. Dean Webb, Arlene Metha, and K. Forbis Jordan. *Foundations of American Education.* Upper Saddle River, N.J.: Merrill, 2000, p. 147.

[2] Sir William Berkeley, quoted in John D. Pulliam and James Van Patten. *History of Education in America.* Englewood Cliffs, N.J.: Prentice Hall, 1995, p. 24.

[3] Pulliam and Van Patten. *History of Education in America,* p. 28.

[4] Pulliam and Van Patten. *History of Education in America,* p. 31.

[5] Webb, Metha, and Jordan. *Foundations of American Education,* p. 181.

[6] Pulliam and Van Patten. *History of Education in America,* p. 52.

[7] Diane Ravitch. *Left Back: A Century of Battle over School Reform.* New York: Simon & Schuster, 2000, p. 41.

[8] Pulliam and Van Patten. *History of Education in America,* p. 99.

[9] Henry Barnard, quoted in Webb, Metha, and Jordan. *Foundations of American Education,* p. 167.

[10] John Dewey, quoted in Ravitch. *Left Back: A Century of Battle over School Reform,* p. 57.

[11] Webb, Metha, and Jordan. *Foundations of American Education,* p. 209.

[12] Ravitch. *Left Back: A Century of Battle Over School Reform,* p. 60.

[13] Theodore Roosevelt, quoted in Ravitch. *Left Back: A Century of Battle over School Reform,* p. 79.

[14] See Appendix A for extract from the CRSE's *The Cardinal Principles of Secondary Education.*

[15] William Bagley, quoted in Ravitch. *Left Back: A Century of Battle over School Reform,* p. 147.

[16] Ravitch. *Left Back: A Century of Battle over School Reform,* p. 239.

[17] Webb, Metha, and Jordan. *Foundations of American Education,* p. 211.

[18] *Time,* January 21, 1938, quoted in Ravitch. *Left Back: A Century of Battle over School Reform,* p. 237.

[19] Tom Lehrer, quoted in *That Was the Year That Was,* Reprise Records (1965).

[20] Hyman Rickover, quoted in Ravitch. *Left Back: A Century of Battle over School Reform,* p. 362.

[21] Ravitch. *Left Back: A Century of Battle over School Reform,* p. 399.

[22] See Appendix C for extract from *A Nation at Risk.*

[23] See Chapter 8 for contact information about the Coalition of Essential Schools.

[24] E. D. Hirsch, quoted in Ravitch. *Left Back: A Century of Battle over School Reform,* p. 419.

[25] Ravitch. *Left Back: A Century of Battle over School Reform,* p. 434.

[26] Richard Riley, quoted in Ravitch. *Left Back: A Century of Battle over School Reform,* p. 435.

[27] Ulysses Grant, quoted in "School: The Story of American Public Education." Available online. URL: http://www.pbs.org/kcet/publicschool/roots_in_history/choice.html.

[28] Austin Cline. "Supreme Court Decisions on Religious Liberty." Available online. URL: http://atheism.about.com/library/decisions/religion/bl_l_MuellerAllen.htm.

[29] Lynn Olson. "Redefining 'Public' Schools." *Education Week*, April 26, 2000, p. 1.

[30] Linda Jacobson. "Polls Find Growing Support for Publicly Funded Vouchers." *Education Week*, September 4, 2002, p. 7.

[31] Matthew Miller. "A Bold Experiment to Fix Public Schools." *Atlantic Monthly*, July 1999, p. 15.

[32] See Appendix F for an extract from the U.S. Supreme Court ruling of *Zelman v. Simmons-Harris.*

[33] John Gehring. "Voucher Battles Head to State Capitals." *Education Week*, July 10, 2002, p. 1.

[34] Bob Chase, quoted in "Statement of Bob Chase, President of the National Education Association on the U.S. Supreme Court Decision on Private School Tuition Vouchers." June 27, 2002. Available online. URL: http://www.nea.org/nr/nr020627.html.

[35] See Appendix E for a state charter school legislation and enrollment chart (2001).

[36] Sandra Feldman, quoted in Lynn Olson. "Redefining 'Public' Schools." *Education Week*, April 26, 2000, p. 1.

[37] Morningstar web site. Available online. URL: http://quicktake.morningstar.com/stock/Price 2.asp?Country=USA & Symbol=EDS Downloaded May 28, 2003.

[38] Kathy Ishizuka. *The Unofficial Guide to Homeschooling.* Foster City, Calif.: IDG Books, 2000, p. 22.

[39] NEA resolution, quoted in "Homeschooling." January 15, 2003. *Education Week on the Web.* Available online. URL: http://www.edweek.com/context/topics/issuespage.cfm?id=37.

[40] See Chapter 2 for a detailed description of homeschooling state legislation.

[41] "Assessment." January 16, 2003. *Education Week on the Web.* Available online. URL: http://www.edweek.com/context/topics/issuespage.cfm?id=41.

[42] See Chapter 2 for a detailed description of the No Child Left Behind Act of 2001.

[43] "Teacher Quality." January 6, 2003. *Education Week on the Web.* Available online. URL: http://www.edweek.com/context/topics/issuespage.cfm?id=50.

[44] "Teacher Quality." January 6, 2003. *Education Week on the Web.* Available online. URL: http://www.edweek.com/context/topics/issuespage.cfm?id=50.

[45] Wendy Kopp. *One Day All Children: The Unlikely Triumph of Teach for America and What I Learned Along the Way.* New York: Public Affairs, 2001, p. 182.

[46] Rod Paige, quoted in Bess Keller and Michelle Galley. "Paige Uses Report As a Rallying Cry to Fix Teacher Ed." *Education Week*, June 19, 2002, p. 25.

[47] Gayla Hudson, quoted in Bess Keller and Michelle Galley. "Paige Uses Report As a Rallying Cry to Fix Teacher Ed." *Education Week*, June 19, 2002, p. 25.

[48] ACCESS web site. Available online. URL: http://www.accessednetwork.org/litigation/lit_ca.html.

[49] "Violence and Safety." *Education Week on the Web.* Available online. URL: http://www.edweek.com/context/topics/issuespage.cfm?id=39.

[50] Internet Education Exchange. "News and Data: Comments on the Court's School Vouchers Decision." Available online. URL: http://www.iedx.org/news/news.asp#News1147. Downloaded January 28, 2003.

[51] Terry M. Moe, quoted in Paul E. Petersen. *The Future of School Choice*. Stanford, Calif.: Hoover Press, forthcoming.

[52] Moe, quoted in Petersen. *The Future of School Choice*, forthcoming.

[53] Abby Goodnough. "Policy Eases the Way Out of Bad Schools." *New York Times*, December 9, 2002, p. B1.

[54] Arne Duncan, quoted in Stephanie Banchero and Michael Martinez. "Federal School Reform Stumbles." *Chicago Tribune*, July 30, 2002, p. B1.

[55] Eugene Hickok, quoted in Stephanie Banchero and Diane Rado. "Chicago Restricts Transfer Options." *Chicago Tribune*, August 28, 2002, p. A1.

[56] Catherine Gewertz. "More Chicago Pupils Flunk Grade." *Education Week*, October 9, 2002, p. 1.

[57] Internet Education Exchange. "News and Data: 2002 Elections—The Education Measures." Available online. URL:http://www.iedx.org/news/news.asp#News1266. Downloaded January 29, 2003.

CHAPTER 2

THE LAW AND
EDUCATION REFORM

This chapter describes federal, state, and local laws and court cases that have significantly influenced education reform. Extracts for some of these laws and court decisions appear in the appendices.

FEDERAL LEGISLATION

ELEMENTARY AND SECONDARY
EDUCATION ACT OF 1965

Background

In the early 1960s, momentum increased for government programs designed to aid those who did not share in the post–World War II economic prosperity. As a result of this growing concern with poverty, the administrations of Presidents John Kennedy and Lyndon Johnson successfully supported federal legislation to subsidize low-income housing, improve access to health care, expand welfare services, and provide job training.

In his 1964 State of the Union address, President Johnson, a former teacher, announced, "This administration today, here and now, declares unconditional war on poverty in America." Central to this War on Poverty were programs specifically intended to strengthen U.S. public schools, particularly those in poor areas. Among the early measures passed during Johnson's presidency was the Economic Opportunity Act of 1964. Included in this legislation was the creation of Project Head Start, which Johnson claimed would "strike at the basic cause of poverty" by boosting the disadvantaged preschool child.

The Law and Education Reform

Key Aspects of Legislation

On April 11, 1965, President Johnson signed the Elementary and Secondary Education Act (ESEA) of 1965. The ESEA was the most far-reaching piece of federal education legislation in the history of the United States, providing more than $1 billion in federal funds to education.

The ESEA consisted of five major sections, or titles, which provided financial assistance for

- Title I—Local Educational Agencies to Educate Students from Low-Income Families
- Title II—School Library Resources and Instructional Material
- Title III—Supplementary Education Centers and Services
- Title IV—Educational Research and Training
- Title V—Strengthening of State Departments of Education

Among these, by far the most influential on public schools was Title I. The purpose of Title I was to give schools with the highest concentrations of poverty the funds to provide special aid for students who are not achieving well academically or who are at risk of educational failure. Title I's key provisions included an expansion of Head Start, creation of bilingual education programs, establishment of guidance and counseling programs, and a significant increase in the number and scope of reading instruction programs.

Title I has been reauthorized by Congress many times, including in 1981 when it became known as Chapter I. Since its inception, Title I and Chapter I funding has eclipsed more than $100 billion spent by the federal government in an effort to support the education of the poorest Americans.

Impact

The implementation of the ESEA was the seminal event in the history of federal involvement in education. Although the funds were largely controlled by state and local agencies, the financial resources allocated by this act and the more than two dozen other major pieces of legislation affecting education passed later in the 1960s represented a significant increase in federal involvement in public education.

In 1963–64, federal funds for elementary and secondary education schools totaled almost $900 million, and by 1968–69, that amount jumped to $3 billion. In addition, the federal government's share of the financing of education rose from 4.4 percent to 8.8 percent during that time period.

The ESEA has been consistently reauthorized by Congress, including the 1966 addition of Title VI for programs for Native American children, children of migrant workers, and the disabled and the 1968 addition of Title VII for programs addressing students with limited English-speaking ability. The Goals 2000: Educate America Act of 1994 and No Child Left Behind Act of 2001 are also reauthorizations of the original ESEA.

GOALS 2000: EDUCATE AMERICA ACT OF 1994

Background

Following the 1983 publication of *A Nation at Risk*, political leaders became more vocal in advocating education reform efforts. This was evident during the presidential campaign of 1988, in which Republican candidate George H. W. Bush promised that, if elected, he would be the "education president."

Soon after his inauguration in 1989, Bush organized the National Education Summit in Charlottesville, Virginia, the first-ever gathering of all 50 state governors, convening for the sole purpose of improving U.S. elementary and secondary education.

Bush articulated his vision at the summit, explaining, "From this day forward let us be an America of tougher standards, of higher goals . . . and our goals must be national, not federal." To this end, the president and the governors, led by then Arkansas governor Bill Clinton, crafted the National Education Goals.

Goal number one stated that by the year 2000, "all children in America will start school ready to learn." This emphasis on the concept of school readiness was further delineated by a 1991 National School Readiness Task Force report that highlighted the educational importance of physical health, self-confidence, and social competence, in addition to academic knowledge and skills. The report also noted the relationship between school readiness and developmentally and culturally appropriate instruction, class size, access to technology, and staff development.

Key Aspects of Legislation

The National Educational Goals established at the 1989 summit provided the framework for the GOALS 2000: Educate America Act, signed into law with broad bipartisan congressional support on March 31, 1994, by President Bill Clinton. The language of GOALS 2000 recognized that education is a state and local responsibility, but that it must also be a national priority.

GOALS 2000 encouraged states to develop challenging standards for students and provided grants for schools, communities, and states to support their own approach to student achievement. It also sought to promote flexibility by providing authority for the secretary of education to waive certain regulations to states and communities implementing school improvements.

Six original education goals were codified into law by GOALS 2000. These concerned school readiness, school completion, student academic achievement, leadership in math and science, adult literacy, and safe and drug-free schools. Two additional goals supporting teacher professional development and parental participation were included in 1996.

GOALS 2000 also established a National Education Standards and Improvement Council to examine and certify national and state content, student performance, opportunity-to-learn standards, and assessment systems voluntarily submitted by states. A National Skill Standards Board was also established to facilitate development of occupational standards. The goal of the board was to identify broad occupational clusters and standards that would lead to portable, industry-recognized credentials indicating mastery of skills in specific occupational areas.

Impact

The precise impact of GOALS 2000 is somewhat difficult to determine, owing to its relatively brief existence. Supporters of the legislation point to some improving academic bright spots, including climbing graduation rates and percentages of students taking a core of academic subjects. Many also note how the passage of GOALS 2000 demonstrated a genuine bipartisan effort to make improving education a top-priority issue. Parental participation and professional development initiatives have expanded nationally and are generally well received by those across the education reform philosophy spectrum.

Detractors, however, often describe GOALS 2000 as a bold, overly ambitious piece of legislation that failed to bring about its intended change. Low proficiency results on standardized assessments continue, particularly in comparison to many other industrialized nations. Standards and assessments often remain an area of contention and stagnation, with advocates upset with the slow pace of change and opponents discouraged with the growing emphasis on test taking. Perhaps GOALS 2000's most enduring legacy will be is vision of where Americans hope to take its public education system, even if specific dates and benchmarks are achieved later than originally hoped.

NO CHILD LEFT BEHIND ACT OF 2001

Background

In the 2000 presidential election, the Republican candidate, Texas governor George W. Bush, touted his record as a leader able to usher in bipartisan and successful education reform laws that strengthened the academic performance of Texas schools. Three days after taking office, Bush announced the plans for the No Child Left Behind Act (NCLBA). Describing the legislation as "the cornerstone of my administration," the president noted that despite the nearly $200 billion in federal spending since the passage of the Elementary and Secondary Education Act of 1965, "too many of our neediest children are being left behind." The title of the act was taken from the slogan of the ideologically left-leaning Children's Defense Fund, but its measures were largely popular within the Republican Party, particularly provisions for accountability and choice. The bill was approved with broad bipartisan support by the Congress and was signed by President Bush less than a year after his inauguration.

Key Aspects of Legislation

Significant provisions of the NCLBA include

- **Student Assessment:** Title I assessment provisions are significantly expanded by the NCLBA. Participating states are required to implement standards-based reading and math assessments for students in each of grades 3–8 by the 2005–6 school year. In addition, states will have to develop and implement assessments at three grade levels in science by the 2007–8 school year. All states are required by the NCLBA to participate in National Assessment of Educational Progress (NAEP) reading and math tests for fourth and eighth grade, to be administered every two years, with the costs paid for by the federal government. The bill requires students who have been in U.S. schools for at least three years to be tested for reading in English, and it requires states to annually assess the English-language proficiency of their limited English proficient (LEP) students. Assessment results and other data for individual public schools, local educational agencies (LEAs) or districts, and states must be reported to parents and the public through "report cards." These report cards are to include information on student performance, broken down by race, ethnicity, gender, disability status, English proficiency, and status as economically disadvantaged.

- **Adequate Yearly Progress Requirements:** Requirements for state-developed standards of adequate yearly progress (AYP) are substantially increased under the NCLBA. These standards will be applied to all students in each public school, district, and state and will be specifically applied to students who are economically disadvantaged, LEP, and disabled. Each state must define what constitutes AYP in increasing student achievement toward the goal of all students reaching proficient levels on the state assessments by 2014. Each state must establish a "starting bar," or measuring point, for the percentage of students who must be at the proficient level, which may be based upon the lowest achieving schools or lowest achieving demographic subgroup in the state (whichever is higher). Once the starting bar and target year are set, the state must "raise the bar" in gradual but equal increments to reach 100 percent of students performing at the proficient level by the target year, which must be 2014.

- **Corrective Actions:** Schools that fail to meet AYP for two consecutive years must be identified as needing improvement. For such schools, technical assistance is to be provided and public school choice must be offered to their students by the next school year, unless prohibited by state law. Districts are generally required only to offer public school choice options within the same district. However, if all public schools in the district to which a student might transfer have been identified as needing improvement, then districts "shall, to the extent practicable," establish cooperative agreements with other districts to offer expanded public school choice options. If a school fails to meet the state AYP standard for three consecutive years, students for low-income families must be offered the opportunity to receive instruction for a supplemental services provider of their choice. States are to identify and provide lists of approved providers of such supplemental services, which may include public or private schools or commercial firms, and monitor the quality of services they provide. Schools that fail to meet AYP for four consecutive years must undergo at least one of the noted "corrective actions," including replacing school staff, implementing a new curriculum, decreasing management authority at the school level, appointing an outside expert to advise the school, extending the school day or year, or changing the internal organizational structure of the school. "Restructuring" will occur for schools that fail to meet AYP standards for five consecutive years. Such restructuring must consist of one of more of the following "alternative governance" actions: reopening as a charter school, replacing all or most school staff, or state takeover of school operations (if permitted by state law). Similar procedures are set to be applied in the NCLBA for districts that fail to meet AYP requirements.

- **Staff Qualifications:** Each state receiving Title I funds must develop a plan to ensure that all teachers teaching core academic subjects are "highly qualified" by the end of the 2005–6 school year. Teachers hired and teaching in a program supported with Title I, Part A funds had to be "highly qualified" starting the first day of the 2002–3 school year. All paraprofessionals hired and working in a program supported with Title I, Part A funds are required by the NCLBA to have completed at least two years of college or to have met a "rigorous standard of quality."

- **Flexibility Measures:** Under the NCLBA, states may transfer up to 50 percent of the funds received for state-level activities for specified Title I programs including preparing, training, and recruiting high-quality teachers and principals; technology; safe and drug-free schools; 21st-century community learning centers; and innovative programs. Districts may also transfer up to 50 percent of the funds received for local activities for specified programs. However, if a district is in school improvement, it may transfer only 30 percent of its funds, and these funds must be used for school improvement. If the district is in corrective action, it may not transfer funds.

- **Performance Bonuses and Sanctions:** The NCLBA includes provisions for the U.S. secretary of Education to establish a peer review process to determine whether states are meeting their AYP standards and to report the results of this review to Congress. The Department of Education would provide technical assistance to states that fail to meet their AYP requirements for two consecutive years.

- **Voluntary School Choice Programs:** As a means of achieving education reform through school choice, states may use specified funding for the planning, design, and implementation of charter schools. Districts may use specified funding to support school choice by using it for magnet schools and for the planning, design, and implementation of charter schools. Districts may also apply specified funding to promote, implement, or expand public school choice and for supplemental educational services, including transportation supporting public school choice, tuition transfer payments, enhancements in schools receiving transfer students, and for public education campaigns about public school choice.

- **Mandatory School Choice Provisions:** Each state receiving NCLBA funding will be required to allow students who attend chronically unsafe schools and those who are victimized on the grounds of an elementary or secondary school to transfer to a safe public school.

- **Reading Initiatives:** The Reading First program (Title I, Part B) of the NCLBA provides funds to help states and districts implement comprehensive reading instruction. It replaces the Reading Excellence Act and is designed to help teachers identify students at risk of reading failure in order to provide them with effective early instruction leading to reading proficiency. Funds are allocated according to a poverty-based formula. Although states must apply to the U.S. Department of Education for funding, every state with a satisfactory application will receive a grant. States may retain up to 20 percent of their allocations to develop and implement professional development for teachers of kindergarten through third grade, provide technical assistance, administer the program, and fund eligible, alternative providers of reading instruction chosen by parents. States must use at least 80 percent of the funds to make five-year grants on a competitive basis to local school districts, with a priority to school districts with at least 15 percent of families in poverty.

Funded districts may only serve schools that have a high percentage of students in grades K–3 below the poverty line or schools that have a high percentage of students reading below grade level. Funds may be used to provide eligible services including identifying students who have difficulty with reading, providing research-based reading instruction, providing professional development for teachers, and expanding access to engaging reading material. The Reading First program is funded at $900 million, compared to $286 million for the Reading Excellence Act in the 2001–2 school year. Funds for the Early Reading First program are distributed directly to local school districts and public and private organizations that serve children aged three to five (such as Head Start and family literacy programs).

- **School Library Programs:** The NCLBA's Improving Literacy Through School Libraries program awards grants to states in order to provide students with access to up-to-date and technologically advanced school library media resources and well-trained, professionally certified school library media specialists.

- **Teacher and Principal Training and Recruiting Funding:** Title II, Part A of the NCLBA, the Teacher and Principal Training and Recruiting Fund, replaces the Eisenhower Professional Development program and the Class Size Reduction program with a new state formula grant program authorizing a broad array of teacher-related activities for states and local school districts.

  Among the state activities included in the more than $3 billion appropriation for this program are supporting teacher and principal professional development, reforming teacher and principal certification requirements, assisting local districts in recruiting and retaining highly qualified teachers and principals, reforming tenure systems, helping teachers use state standards and assessments to improve instruction and student achievement, helping teachers meet certification and licensure requirements, and training educators in integrating technology into instruction. To receive these funds from the state, districts must submit a plan that addresses a range of key issues, including a description of the professional development that will be made available to teachers and principals. Districts may use funds for permitted activities, including hiring highly qualified teachers; providing professional development for teachers, principals, and paraprofessionals, including training for improving classroom behavior and teaching students with different learning styles; developing and implementing educator recruitment and retention strategies; testing teachers in their subject area; establishing partnerships with institutions of higher learning; developing teacher advancement plans to emphasize multiple career paths and pay differentiation; and establishing programs for exemplary teachers.

- **Technology Programs:** The NCLBA's Title II, Part II Enhancing Education Through Technology program consolidates several technology programs authorized under prior law. Participating states and districts must have new or updated long-range technology plans, and districts must use at least 25 percent of its funding for professional development in the integration of advanced technologies into curriculum and instruction. Other authorized activities for districts include using technology to connect schools and teachers with parents and students, preparing teachers to serve as technology leaders in their schools, and acquiring, expanding, implementing, repairing, and maintaining technology. States may use funds for such activities as supporting innovative strategies to deliver courses and curriculum through technology including distance learning and developing performance measures to determine the effectiveness of educational technology programs.

- **Safe and Drug-Free Schools and Communities:** State and local agencies are funded for programs to prevent student violence in and around schools and the illegal use of alcohol, tobacco, and drugs. Funding is available for many new purposes, including permitting states to require expelled or suspended students to perform community services during their time away from school, assisting districts to improve school security by creating a school security center, establishing school hot lines and other safety procedures, and allowing eligible groups to assist in creating and supporting mentoring programs for students in need.

- **Twenty-First-Century Community Learning Centers:** The NCLBA provides grants for districts, community-based organizations, and other public and private groups to conduct after school activities for students and their families, although activities are narrower in scope than previously permitted.

Impact

It is far too early to assess the impact of the No Child Left Behind Act. The bill's advocates and detractors have nonetheless been active in speaking out about it. Supporters of the No Child Left Behind Act claim that it represents a sincere and commonsense commitment to public school improvement on the part of President Bush. They often note the legislation's emphasis on stronger accountability for results, greater flexibility and local control, expanded options and choice for parents, and early literacy as evidence of its strengths. Those displeased with the bill often cite its confusing mandates and unreasonable implementation requirements, a shortsighted emphasis on standardized testing in determining the academic progress of students and schools, as well as an insufficient financial allocation for included programs.

Regardless of one's view on the wisdom or effectiveness of the No Child Left Behind Act, it is significant that the bill was passed with overwhelmingly bipartisan support in the Congress and was among the first major pieces of legislation passed during the administration of President Bush. These facts suggest that federal involvement in public education continues to hold an increasingly prominent place in U.S. domestic policy.

STATE AND LOCAL LEGISLATION

CHICAGO SCHOOL REFORM ACT OF 1988 (AND AMENDMENTS OF 1995)

Background

In 1987, U.S. secretary of education William Bennett pronounced the Chicago public schools to be "the worst in the nation," and there was much evidence to support his claim. The poor performance of the Chicago public schools, including a fiscal crisis that required a financial bailout, chronically low test scores, a high dropout rate, and consistent labor strife, led a coalition of parents, activists, and business leaders to press the Illinois legislature to pass the Chicago School Reform Act of 1988. The law shifted significant powers and responsibilities from the central administration to local school communities.

Key Aspects of Legislation

Among the important provisions of the Chicago School Reform Act were

- **Creation of Local School Councils (LSCs):** LSCs consisted of the principal, six parents, two community members, two teachers, and, in high schools, one student. Responsibilities of the LSCs included writing and approving the principal's contract, evaluating the principal's performance, and helping to create the school's budget and school improvement plan.
- **Reorganization of Central Authority:** The 11-member Board of Education was abolished and replaced with a 15-member board nominated by a community-driven nominating commission and approved by the mayor.

- **Revision of Principal's Authority:** The principal became able to fill vacant educational positions with the applicant of his or her choice, regardless of seniority. The principal's authority was also extended to allow him or her to keep a set of keys to the building and reduce remediation time for unsatisfactory teachers from one year to 45 days.
- **Implementation of Accountability Procedures:** Subdistrict councils were established to propose actions to remedy low-performing schools, including drafting remediation plans and placing schools on probation.
- **Use of State Chapter I Funds:** This required the distribution of money directly to schools based on their enrollment of poor children only for programs that supplement the basic curriculum, including reduced class size, early child education, and enrichment activities
- **Expansion of School Choice:** Students were able to attend schools within the district based on a lottery admissions process, providing busing for low-income students and complying with desegregation regulations. Magnet schools were exempted from this provision.

In 1995, Democratic Chicago mayor Richard M. Daley, teamed up with primarily Republican leaders in the Illinois legislature to pass many amendments to the Chicago School Reform Act of 1988. Focusing on finding an effective way to deal with chronically underperforming schools, these reforms have come to be known as "the Chicago Model" and have recently been emulated in many large cities throughout the United States. As a result of the 1995 amendments:

- The mayor was allowed to appoint a five-person Chicago School Reform Board of Trustees without needing city council approval, as well as a seven-member regular board to serve four-year overlapping terms. Together these entities would be known as the superboard. In addition, the mayor became responsible to appointing a chief executive officer (CEO) to assume the powers of the superintendent.
- The CEO was given the duty to appoint a chief operating officer, a chief financial officer, a chief purchasing officer, and a chief educational officer, with approval of the new superboard. The CEO also took over all powers of the subdistricts and subdistrict councils. These included initiating action against failing schools, breaking LSC deadlocks over principal selection, and evaluating principals in conjunction with LSCs.
- School board policies were revised to allow the hiring of outside, privatized contractors to do work currently done by board employees. Policies placing restrictions on nepotism and conflicts of interest were also adopted.

- LSCs were endowed with new powers to approve receipts and expenditures for schools' internal accounts. They also were required to undergo three days of training within six months of taking office or be removed.
- The teacher and principal dismissal process was streamlined, although principals were still required to document cases against teachers and LSCs needed to document cases against principals. Written warnings were no longer required for conduct that is "cruel, immoral, negligent, or criminal or which in any way causes psychological or physical harm or injury to a student.
- The Chicago Schools Academic Accountability Council was developed to carry out an evaluation system of schools. Intervention and reconstitution procedures for "chronically underperforming schools" were established, allowing the CEO to select a new principal to guide the school and select all staff. In addition, 5 percent of a school's Chapter I money was allocated for employee performance incentives.
- The principal gained the authority to supervise, evaluate, and otherwise discipline his or her school's maintenance and lunchroom staffs. The principal could also "determine when and what operations shall be conducted" within school hours and to schedule staff within those hours. Assistant principals were no longer allowed to be represented by the teachers' union, giving principals more freedom to select and change assistants.
- The board had more flexibility in the use of state Chapter I money, allowing the amount in the "general education" block grant to be used for "any of the board's lawful purposes."
- Regulations against corruption, waste, and financial mismanagement were expanded through the protection of whistle-blowers and the expansion of the powers of the district's inspector general.

Impact

The Chicago School Reform Act and its 1995 amendments had an enormous impact on Chicago's schools as well as on the education reform debate, particularly in big cities, throughout the country. In Chicago, the act gradually gave schools money that was previously controlled by the city schools' central administration. It also gave principals the ability to select teachers to fill vacancies rather than having them delivered by seniority and allowed them to choose their own vice principals.

These laws are also credited with ushering in new systems of school accountability. By 1996, more than 100 schools (about a fifth of Chicago's total) were put on probation for having less than 15 percent of its students scoring at or above national norms on the Iowa Test of Basic Skills (ITBS) for elementary students and Tests of Achievement and Proficiency (TAP) for high school students. Probation managers, usually former public school administrators and principals, were quickly recruited to work with these schools, and more than $20 million was paid to "outside partners," mainly university professors, to help these schools correct their problems. Reports on the effectiveness of the managers and partners vary, but in subsequent years the number of schools requiring such remediation dropped significantly.

Less than a year after announcing probation, the Reform Board of Trustees added the procedure of reconstitution for the schools deemed to be the most egregious failures. In some cases, reconstitution involved removing principals and teachers and reorganizing the entire structure of the school. In addition, a promotion policy was instituted requiring students in third, sixth, eighth, and ninth grades to hit test-score targets in reading and math in order to advance to the next grade. This stance against the policy of social promotion has also included sending failure warning notices to parents and requiring summer school for low-achieving students, including first graders who lag behind. Although debate and research disagree about the cause-effect relationship of these reforms, test scores in the Chicago public schools have risen steadily since the implementation of the act, particularly in elementary schools (24 percent to 34 percent at or above national norms in reading between 1989 and 2000 and 28 percent to 44 percent at or above national norms in math between 1989 and 2000).

Nationally, the Chicago School Reform Act and its amendments have been influential in framing discussion of education reform issues, particularly social promotion, school accountability, and local control. Similar reform laws, investing primary power over public schools to the mayor, have since been implemented in Boston, Detroit, Cleveland, and New York City and are being seriously considered in many other cities.

MILWAUKEE PARENTAL CHOICE PROGRAM (1990)

Background

Frustration with the struggling condition of Milwaukee's public schools led Republican Wisconsin governor Tommy Thompson and the Democratic-controlled state legislature to enact the Milwaukee Parental Choice Program (MPCP) in 1990. The program allowed a maximum of 1 percent of the Milwaukee public schools' enrollment—about 1,000 students—to attend religious schools. The cap was raised to 1.5 percent in 1993. In response to growing program support, the Wisconsin legislature and governor raised the cap to 15 percent and allowed low-income parents to choose among religious and nonreligious schools.

Opponents of the MPCP have twice challenged the constitutionality of the law and have failed both times. During the three-year challenge to the 1995 amendments to the law, the Wisconsin Supreme Court delayed the participation of religious schools in the program but ultimately upheld its constitutionality in 1998. In November 1998, the U.S. Supreme Court declined to hear an appeal of the Wisconsin Supreme Court's 1998 decision, and the expanded program was allowed to continue.

Key Aspects of Legislation

The MPCP legislation includes specific descriptions of key participation factors, including

- **Student Eligibility:** A student qualifies for the MPCP on the basis of his or her residency in the city of Milwaukee, household income, and where and if the child was enrolled in school in the prior school year. For the 2002–3 school year, the child's household income had to be at or below the specified amounts of $26,140 for a household of three and $36,932 for a household of five. Additionally, in the prior school year the child must have been enrolled in the Milwaukee public schools; participated in the MPCP; enrolled in kindergarten or first, second, or third grade in a private school in Milwaukee but not in the choice program; or not enrolled in school anywhere.

- **Admissions Procedures:** A parent or guardian must fill out a MPCP student application form and submit it to the school during the open application period(s) for the program. Parents will have to prove the child's residency in Milwaukee and their income status. Choice schools must inform parents how many choice program slots are open by grade level; the date, if necessary, of a lottery to select choice students if more applications are received than there are choice slots available; and within 60 days of receiving the student's completed application, whether the child has been accepted into the choice program.

- **Related Fees:** The private school cannot charge MPCP students tuition for instructional purposes. A student in the program can be charged reasonable fees for personal items such as gym clothes or uniforms, or social and extracurricular activities if the activity is not a part of the required curriculum.

- **Receipt of State Aid Payments:** The state issues checks payable to the parent or guardian of an MPCP student and sends the checks to the school where the child is enrolled four times a year. The parent or guardian must sign the checks over to the school and cannot cash the checks.

- **Aid-Per-Student Provisions:** In the 2002–3 school year, the state aid for a student enrolled full-time in the choice program at a particular school (defined as enrolled in the choice program on both the third Friday in September and the second Friday in January) is estimated to be $5,785 or the private school's operating and debt service cost per student, whichever is less.

- **Requirements Regarding Religious Participation:** If a choice student's parent or guardian submits to the student's teacher or the school's principal a written request that the student be excused from any religious activity, the teacher and school must honor that request.

- **Special Needs Services:** A private school may not discriminate against a child with special educational needs in the admission process for the program. However, as a private school, an MPCP school is required to offer only those services to assist students with special needs that it can provide with minor adjustments.

- **Student Suspensions and Expulsion:** State law does not require private MPCP schools to have any procedures in place regarding student suspensions or expulsions. Milwaukee public schools involved in the program must abide by a state law that describes actions punishable by suspension or expulsion and allows a pupil or the parent or guardian to appeal a suspension to the school administrator. These expulsions are determined by the school board and may be appealed to the state superintendent and circuit court. Private schools are not required to have such procedures in place.

Impact

The MPCP has been watched more closely and for a longer period of time than any other voucher program in the United States. Its leadership and survival have encouraged choice advocates across the country and spurred calls of inequity and inefficiency from opponents.

Studies by Wisconsin's Legislative Audit Bureau as well as research by Harvard and Princeton Universities have found some statistical support that the reforms brought on by the program may be positively influencing academic achievement. Fourth graders scoring at or above proficiency on the Wisconsin Knowledge and Concept Examination have increased in all core academic areas, and high school students have either demonstrated gains or smaller decreases than usually seen on standardized exams in reading and math. However, the cause-effect relationship of such results is a complex one and should not be solely attributed to individual factors such as the voucher program.

The law's impact has been clearly evident where Milwaukee's students have attended school. In 1990–91, the first year of the program, only seven schools and 341 schools participated. That number stayed relatively steady until the 1997–98 school year when 235 schools and 1,545 students took part. Following the Wisconsin Supreme Court decision allowing expansion of the MPCP, 86 schools and more than 6,000 students participated. Those figures grew to 106 schools and 10,882 students for the 2001–2 school year. For that year, 34 percent of the program's students attended nonreligious schools, and 66 percent were enrolled in religious schools.

FLORIDA A+ PLAN FOR EDUCATION (1999)

Background

Education reform as a political issue, increasingly prominent on the federal level, over the past 20 years has been even more salient on the state and local level due to the nature of funding and history of U.S. public schools. Evidence of this is seen with the evolution of the A+ Plan for Education. In 1998, Republican candidate for Florida governor, Jeb Bush, proposed the A+ Plan to be the nation's first statewide school voucher program. Bush was elected and signed the bill into law on June 25, 1999.

The A+ Plan survived the near-immediate legal challenges that followed its passage. In October 2000, the First District Court of Appeals for Florida declared the plan constitutional, and in April 2002 the Florida Supreme Court declined to review that decision. However, on August 6, 2002, a circuit court judge in Florida ruled that the A+ program's provision that allows students in failing schools to get scholarships to move into other schools, including private and religious institutions, violates the religious Establishment Clause of the state's constitution.

Key Aspects of Legislation

Florida's A+ Plan includes many measures designed to improve the academic achievement of the state's students and schools. Among the law's provisions are a revision of the state curriculum standards; expansion of student assessment requirements, including the administration of the Florida Comprehensive Achievement Test annually from third to 10th grade; and expanded funding for school safety enhancements, truancy reduction, and teacher training and recruitment initiatives. Funding is also provided to districts for the elimination of social promotion through summer school programs, after school instruction, tutoring, mentoring, and extended-day programs.

However, the most influential and controversial measures revolve around the A+ Plan's requirement that all schools receive a report card detailing how well they perform. This report card, featuring a letter grade, provides the foundation for such measures as incentives for school achievement and improvement and to the provisions of Opportunity Scholarships.

The incentives feature financial rewards of up to $100 per student for schools that receive an "A" and those that improve at least one grade based on student achievement and dropout rate. Under the plan, the highest-performing and improving schools also are deregulated and encouraged to manage their own budgets and use innovative strategies to continue their improvement.

Opportunity Scholarships are provided for students at failing schools. Under the A+ Plan, a school receiving an "F" will be given two years to improve, during which time it will receive assistance from the school district and state Department of Education. If a school fails to improve beyond an "F" in the second year, parents will have an opportunity to send their children to any public or private school with a state rating of "C" or better within or adjacent to their home district.

The amount of the voucher is based on the local district's per-pupil cost or the private school's tuition, whichever, is less. Selection of eligible transfer students must be random, though the siblings of students already enrolled are given preference. Participating private schools must be in compliance with specified civil rights laws and health and safety codes and must demonstrate fiscal soundness. Transportation for students who attend another public school inside their district can use the transportation provided by local school districts, but parents choosing to use an Opportunity Scholarship to send their child to a private school would have to make their own arrangements. Participating private schools must also administer the standardized tests given in public schools and report the results to the state.

Students with learning disabilities are also covered in A+ legislation under the McKay Scholarship, named for Republican state senator John McKay who sponsored the legislation. With a McKay Scholarship, any parent of a learning-disabled student who is dissatisfied with the progress his or her child is making in a public school can transfer the child to a participating program school.

Another closely watched, hotly debated provision of the A+ program is its plan allowing corporations to donate up to 75 percent of what they would pay in state taxes to fund low-income public school students to transfer to private schools.

Impact

Because of the A+ Plan's Opportunity Scholarships, Florida has taken the lead in state efforts to advance school vouchers. The state pays the private school tuition of more than 25,000 students, which far outnumbers the combined amount of students enrolled in the highly publicized Cleveland and Milwaukee voucher programs.

The establishment of the Opportunity Scholarship program and of the publication of many reports lauding its positive effects has led state legislators in Illinois, California, Texas, and elsewhere to begin exploring limited or statewide voucher programs. The program is continuing while voucher proponents appeal for the trial court's ruling that vouchers for private or religious schools violate the state's constitution. The Florida Supreme Court will review this decision, and many believe the case may ultimately end up in the U.S. Supreme Court, whose ruling could render far-reaching implications for the future of school choice programs.

The McKay Scholarship has also significantly influenced education reform in Florida, and its success or failure will likely affect other states as well. Many special education advocates criticize the program, arguing that those who transfer from public schools lose federal civil rights protections under the Individuals with Disabilities Education Act. Supporters of the program counter that parents are the best judges of what their children need, and if they are unhappy with the private school option, they may choose to reenroll their child at a public school.

The newest of the A+ provisions, the corporate tax program for school vouchers, has attracted enormous interest from Floridians. Under the program, students qualifying for free and reduced-price lunches can receive up to $4,500 for private school tuition. Its first-year capacity of 15,000 students was reached quickly, with more than 25,000 eligible applications rejected because the program selected students on a first-come first-serve basis. Again, the academic and legal fortunes of this program are being closely watched in many other states that have expressed interest in introducing similar programs.

Arizona Charter School Law (1994)

Background

The charter school movement traces its roots to a number of other reform ideas, from alternative schools, site-based management, and magnet schools to public school choice, privatization, and community-parental empowerment.

The term *charter* may have originated in the 1970s when New England educator Ray Budde suggested that small groups of teachers be given contracts, or "charters," by their local school boards to explore new approaches. Albert Shanker, a former president of the American Federation of Teachers, then publicized the idea, suggesting that local boards could charter an entire school with union and teacher approval.

Education Reform

In 1991, Minnesota passed the first charter-school law based on three basic values: opportunity, choice, and responsibility for results, with California following suit in 1992. By 1995, 19 states had signed laws allowing for the creation of charter schools, and by 1999, that number increased to 36 states, Puerto Rico, and the District of Columbia. Charter schools are one of the fastest-growing innovations in education policy, enjoying broad bipartisan support from governors, state legislators, and past and present secretaries of education. President Bill Clinton also supported them, calling in his 1997 State of the Union address for the creation of 3,000 charter schools by the year 2000 and delivering remarks for the 1999 Charter Schools National Conference.

Since 1994, the U.S. Department of Education has provided grants to support states' charter school efforts, from $6 million in fiscal year 1995, to almost $100 million in fiscal year 1999. President George W. Bush requested and received approval for $200 million for the creation of almost 2,000 new charter schools in fiscal year 2003.

The Arizona state legislature passed the Charter School Law on September 16, 1994. This legislation was among the earliest state charter laws and is often recognized as the strongest in the nation.

Key Aspects of Legislation

The Arizona Charter School Law is the blueprint by which all charter schools in the state operate, regardless of their sponsorship. Major provisions of the bill address the purpose of charter schools, application and maintenance requirements, academic policies, financial procedures, and employment regulations.

- **Purpose:** The expressed goal of Arizona's charter school legislation is to "provide additional academic choices for parents and pupils" through the establishment of "public schools that serve as alternatives to traditional public schools." Charter school in Arizona may consist of new schools or any portion of an existing school.

- **Application and Maintenance Requirements:** Under Arizona's charter school law, there are three types of boards that may sponsor a charter school, including the state board of education, the state board for charter schools, and any local school district governing board.

  The Board for Charter Schools consists of the following members:

  1. The superintendent of public instruction or the superintendent's designee.

  2. Six members of the general public, at least two of whom shall reside in a school district where at least sixty percent of the children who attend school in the district meet the eligibility requirements established under the national school lunch and child nutrition acts . . . for free lunches, who are appointed by the governor . . .

3. Two members of the business community who are appointed by the governor . . .

4. Three members of the legislature who shall serve as advisory members and who are appointed jointly by the president of the senate and the speaker of the house of representatives.

There is no restriction on the number of charters any of these three entities may sponsor, although since July 1, 2000, school districts may only sponsor schools located within the geographic boundaries of the district. The initial charters that are granted run for 15 years and must be reviewed by the sponsoring body every five years.

Application eligibility for potential sponsors is very open under Arizona's charter school legislation. Existing public and private schools may submit proposals. However, private schools must agree to the laws that govern charter schools in the state, including having a nonselective and nondiscriminatory admission policy as well as rules prohibiting the charging of tuition. A religious organization may organize a charter school, although the school charter must ensure that the school is "nonsectarian in its programs, admission policies, and employment practices and all other operations."

Once granted a charter, new charter school operators are required to hold a public meeting at least 30 days prior to opening, posting notices of the meeting in at least three different locations within 300 feet of the proposed school site.

- **Academic Policies:** Arizona's charter law addresses student admission by explaining:

A charter school shall enroll all eligible pupils who submit a timely application, unless the number of applications exceeds the capacity of a program, class, grade level or building. A charter school shall give enrollment preference to pupils returning to the charter school in the second or any subsequent year of its operation and to siblings of pupils already enrolled in the charter school. A charter school that is sponsored by a school district governing board shall give enrollment preference to eligible pupils who reside within the boundaries of the school district where the charter school is physically located. If capacity is insufficient to enroll all pupils who submit a timely application, the charter school shall select pupils through an equitable selection process such as a lottery except that preference shall be given to siblings of a pupil selected through an equitable selection process such as a lottery.

Other academic policy mandates include the provision of a comprehensive program of education aligned to the Arizona Academic Standards, although such instructional programs may emphasize a particular learning philosophy, style, or subject area and the annual issuance of school report cards reflecting the academic progress of a school. A charter school may have any grade configuration as long as it provides a comprehensive program of education for at least one grade from among kindergarten through 12th grade.

- **Financial Procedures:** Charter schools in Arizona are subject to the same financial requirements as a school district, including the Uniform System of Financial Records for Charter Schools, procurement rules, and audit requirements. However, exceptions to these rules may be requested by the party applying for a charter and granted by the charter's sponsor. A school district is not financially responsible for any charter school that is sponsored by the state board of education or the state board for charter schools. Arizona's charter legislation also provides a stimulus fund providing:

  financial support to charter school applicants and charter schools for start-up costs and costs associated with renovating or remodeling existing buildings and structures. The fund consists of monies appropriated by the legislature and grants, gifts, devises and donations from any public or private source. The department of education shall administer the fund.

- **Employment Regulations:** Teachers in Arizona's charter schools do not have to be certified, although federal regulations require that special-education programs be supervised by a certified teacher. The legislation protects employment benefits of teachers through a provision stating:

  A teacher who is employed by or teaching at a charter school and who was previously employed as a teacher at a school district shall not lose any right of certification, retirement or salary status or any other benefit provided by law, by the rules of the governing board of the school district or by the rules of the board of directors of the charter school due to teaching at a charter school on the teacher's return to the school district.

Impact

The Arizona Charter School Law has served as a model for other states with far-reaching charter school legislation, including Florida and Texas. Furthermore, Arizona has more charter schools (465 as of fall 2002) than any other state and represents just under 20 percent of the national charter school enrollment, despite a population that is only 2 percent of the national total.

According to the Arizona Department of Education's February 2002 report, *Arizona Public Charter School Goals: Enhancing Pupil Progress; Increasing School Choice,*

- As of February 2002, Arizona has 288 charters operating 422 school sites. Over 60,000 students were enrolled in charter schools for the 2001–2 school year.

- Arizona charter schools are among six of the top-10 scoring schools by grade in the language subtest of the spring 2001 SAT 9 test, seven out of the top 10 in the math subtest, and six out of the top-10 scoring schools in the reading subtest.

- Charter schools are drawing heavily from the state's minority communities. The percentage of Native American and African-American students in charter schools is higher than that in the total public school population according to the annual report from the superintendent of Public Instruction for the 1999–2000 school year.

- The average length of a charter school year is 186 days; the average pay for charter school teachers is roughly $2,000 higher than those in public schools.

However, problems have emerged in the implementation of the legislation. In 1996, an Arizona charter school folded following allegations that its founder spent more than $100,000 in state money on a home and jewelry. In 1998, a charter school in Mesa closed amid allegations of financial mismanagement by the operator and charges that the charter holder was located too far away to maintain effective oversight of the school.

Despite these issues, charter schools continue to expand throughout Arizona. Already the national leader in the number of charters in operation, the state has received approval to add 11 more for the 2003–4 school year, the second-largest increase in the United States.

SAMPLING OF STATE
HOMESCHOOLING-RELATED LEGISLATION

Background

Although the roots of homeschooling in the United States trace back to its founding, when most children were educated at home by parents or tutors, the surge in the popularity of the homeschooling movement is a relatively recent development.

The challenge to traditional institutions commonly seen in the 1960s extended to public schooling as well. John Holt, a former teacher and left-wing education reformer, advocated homeschooling as an alternative to conformist and failing public schools, although his views were usually viewed as fringe. Homeschooling's voice became a bit louder in the 1970s and early 1980s following the publication of additional research and books, usually from conservative activists, that supported the movement. The 1972 Supreme Court decision in *Wisconsin v. Yoder*, which struck down compulsory education laws, and the 1983 publication of *A Nation at Risk*, which portrayed the dangerous weaknesses of the U.S. public school system, also added momentum to homeschooling.

However, homeschooling remained extremely rare until the 1980s and 1990s when mainly well-organized evangelical Christians adopted it as a way to combat what they saw as the disorder and oppressive secularism of public schools. Over the past 20 years, homeschooling has emerged as perhaps education reform's most influential, if often overlooked, movement.

The most recent federal study, completed in 1999, points to almost 900,000 homeschooled students. With the current number at most likely more than 1 million students, homeschooling's population currently is easily greater than the enrollment in charter schools and voucher programs combined. Although the largest estimates place the homeschooled population at about 4 percent of the entire K–12 population, that total still outnumbers the combined enrollment of all students in Alaska, Delaware, Hawaii, Montana, New Hampshire, North Dakota, Rhode Island, South Dakota, Vermont, and Wyoming. In light of this rampant growth, home school legislation has become more prominent throughout the United States.

Key Aspects of Legislation

Provisions included in homeschooling legislation vary significantly from state to state. Following is a description of laws that cover the range of states with almost no regulation, to low, moderate, and high regulation of homeschooling.

Texas homeschooling law provides an example of a state with no requirement for parents to initiate contact with the school district, submit to visits by state authorities, gain approval of a curriculum, or have any specific teacher certification. Home schools only need to have a written curriculum, conduct it in a bone fide manner, and teach math, reading, spelling, grammar, and good citizenship. This hands-off policy followed a 1987 class-action lawsuit filed on behalf of more than 80 homeschooling families who were criminally prosecuted for truancy. The case *Leeper v. Arlington Independent School District* resulted in a key victory for homeschooling that was subsequently upheld by the Texas court of appeals and the Texas Supreme Court. The *Leeper* decision stated:

> *The evidence establishes that from the inception of the first compulsory attendance law in Texas in 1915, it was understood that a school-age child who was being educated in or through the child's home, and in a bona fide manner by the parents . . . was considered a private school.*

In 1989, the Texas legislature exempted private and parochial schools from new state requirements for schools and in the process, confirmed that the term *private school* includes home schools. Other states with similar legislation include Alaska, Idaho, Illinois, Indiana, Michigan, Missouri, and Oklahoma.

Many states have home school laws with low regulation. An example of this is California, where families interested in homeschooling their children have four options:

1. The individual home school could qualify as a private school* by filing an annual private school affidavit certifying that
   a. The instructors must be capable of teaching;
   b. The instruction must be in English;
   c. The instruction must be in the several branches of study required in public schools;
   d. Attendance must be kept in a register; and
   e. A private school affidavit must be filed with the county superintendent between October 1 and October 15 of each school year.
2. The home school could have instruction provided by a certified private tutor.
3. The child could be enrolled in an independent study program at home, using the public school curriculum. Under this option, the child is considered a public school student and has to abide by the rules and policy of the public school.
4. Homeschoolers could enroll in a private school satellite program and take "independent study" through that private school, as long as the private school independent study program (ISP) complies with Cali-

---

* The establishment of home schools as private schools was supported by the 1992 U.S. District Court of the Southern District of California decision *Institute of Creation Research v. Honig*, which ordered, "a private K–12 school is not within the jurisdiction of the State Department of Education for the purpose of approval of courses or course content or issuance of regulations, except as provided by law."

fornia law. Many home school families have organized these private ISPs, which enroll anywhere from two to several hundred families.

Under California law, teacher certification is necessary only if the home school parent chooses to qualify as a private tutor and standardized testing of homeschooled students is not required. Other states with similar low-regulation laws include Alabama, Arizona, Kansas, Kentucky, Mississippi, Montana, Nebraska, New Mexico, and Wisconsin.

Georgia is an example of a state whose homeschooling legislation reflects moderate regulation. Under Georgia law,

- Parents must submit a declaration of intent to home study to the local superintendent within 30 days after the establishment of the home study program and by September 1 every year thereafter. This declaration must include the names and ages of students, the location of the home school, and the time the parents designate as their school year.
- The home school must provide "a basic academic educational program."
- Each school day must be at least four and one-half hours long.
- Attendance records must be kept and submitted to the superintendent each month.
- Parents must write an annual progress report and retain it for three years.
- Parents or guardians may teach only their own children in the home study program provided they have a high school diploma or GED, but the parents or guardians may employ a tutor who holds at least a baccalaureate college degree.

Homeschooled students must take a national standardized test every three years beginning at the end of third grade, though these test scores are not required to be submitted to public school authorities. Other states considered moderate in their regulation of homeschooling include: Arkansas, Colorado, Connecticut, Florida, Iowa, Louisiana, Maryland, New Hampshire, North Carolina, Ohio, Oregon, South Carolina, South Dakota, Tennessee, and Virginia.

Finally, many states have homeschooling laws that require parents to provide a relatively high degree of notification to, and approval from, the state. Pennsylvania is one such state. Its home school statute requires

- Parental filing of a notarized affidavit with the local superintendent prior to the commencement of the home education program and annually thereafter by August 1. The affidavit must include
  a. The name of the parent/supervisor, name and age of children, address, and telephone number;

b. Assurance that subjects are taught in English;

c. "Outline of proposed education objectives by subject area";

d. Evidence of immunization;

e. Receipt of health and medical services required by law; and

f. A certification that the supervisor, all adults living within the home, and persons having legal custody of the children have not been convicted of certain criminal offenses within the past five years.

- Annual parental maintenance and provision to the superintendent of education with certain documentation, including

  a. A portfolio of records and materials, including a "log . . . which designates reading materials used, samples of any writing, work sheets, workbooks or creative materials used by the student."

  b. An annual written evaluation of the student's educational progress by (1) a licensed psychologist, (2) a teacher certified by the state, or (3) a teacher or administrator (who must have at least two years' teaching experience in the last 10 years in public or nonpublic schools). The evaluation shall be based on an interview and review of the portfolio and "it shall certify whether or not an appropriate education is occurring."

A 1990 federal district court decision in *Stobaugh v. Wallace* ruled that a superintendent cannot "arbitrarily choose to flout state law" by requesting to see the portfolio midyear when he has no evidence of noncompliance. If the superintendent determines an appropriate education is not taking place, the parent-supervisor has 20 days to submit additional documentation. If there is still a problem, the family has a right of appeal to an impartial hearing examiner and then to the secretary of education or the court.

Parents may also teach their children at home if they qualify as a "properly qualified private tutor," which is defined as "a person who is certified by the Commonwealth of Pennsylvania to teach in the public schools of Pennsylvania." The private tutor must file a copy of their Pennsylvania certification and the required criminal history record with the student's district of residence superintendent.

In addition, parents may teach their children at home if the home is an extension or satellite of a religious day school. Such a day school must provide a minimum of 180 days of instruction or 900 hours of instruction per year at the elementary level or 990 hours per year of instruction at the secondary level. Specific requirements regarding courses of study at the elementary and secondary levels are also noted. Other states with similarly high regulation statutes include Maine, Massachusetts, Minnesota, Nevada, New York, North Dakota, Rhode Island, Utah, Washington, and West Virginia.

Impact

One result of the rapid rise in homeschooling has been a strain on public schools' financing. For instance, in Florida the homeschooled population has quadrupled between 1991 and 2001. Although less than 2 percent of students were homeschooled, that flight from public schools represented a loss of nearly $130 million in the state's public education budget. Of course, this means that the schools have fewer students to teach, but the damage to the image of schools as well as a loss of often high academic achievers has been significant. In addition, property taxes, which provide a large chunk of most school systems' budgets, have been tougher to approve in communities whose reliance on public schools has diminished.

Homeschooling advocates often claim that the proliferation of homeschooling legislation has led to a higher academic achievement for homeschooled students, and they point to testing results for evidence. Indeed, the average homeschooled student does rank higher than the average public school student in most studies. However, not all home school students take standardized tests, and it is difficult to assess how a homeschooled student would have done in a traditional school.

One trend that has emerged from recent homeschooling legislation is an increase in crossover efforts between public schools and home schools. Some states such as California and Texas now allow homeschooled students to participate in such activities as football and advanced placement classes. Such arrangements allow homeschooled students to gain access to resources unlikely to be available to them otherwise, and school districts are able to recoup a portion of the per-pupil funding lost by counting homeschooled students in their programs. Although nearly 20 percent of homeschooled students participate in such forms of traditional school activities, the home school debate remains a highly contentious one whose future will affect millions of students and the perception of the role of public schools.

COURT CASES

BROWN V. BOARD OF EDUCATION, 347 U.S. 483 (1954)

Background

In the 1940s and 1950s, the National Association for the Advancement of Colored People (NAACP), the leading civil rights organization in the country, organized legal challenges to the "separate but equal" doctrine established by the U.S. Supreme Court in *Plessy v. Ferguson* (1896).

In *McLaurin v. Oklahoma State Regents* (1950), the Supreme Court unanimously struck down University of Oklahoma rules that had permitted a black man to attend classes but required that he be separated from his white classmates. On the same day as its *McLaurin* decision, the Supreme Court ruled in *Sweatt v. Painter* that a makeshift law school created by the state of Texas to avoid admitting blacks into the University of Texas Law School was unconstitutional.

Encouraged by these legal decisions, the NAACP and its chief legal counsel, Thurgood Marshall, brought five cases before the Court specifically designed to challenge segregation laws requiring separate public schools for blacks and whites. The case took its name from the lawsuit brought on behalf of Linda Brown, a student enrolled in the Topeka, Kansas, school system. She had been denied admission to the all-white elementary school a few blocks from her house. Instead, she had to travel 21 blocks to an all-black school.

Legal Issues

The NAACP argued that segregating students on the basis of race denied them the equal protection guarantees of the Fourteenth Amendment. Many of the arguments they presented were based on social and psychological research material gathered by professor Kenneth Clark.

The Topeka Board of Education argued in favor of the decades of law and custom, as well as the tradition of states' rights, which permitted the segregation of public schools by race. They further contended that it was not the intention of the Fourteenth Amendment to abolish segregation.

Decision

Chief Justice Earl Warren issued *Brown's* unanimous and historic ruling on May 17, 1954. In it, he reflected the growing belief in the importance of public education in American society, explaining,

> *Today, education is perhaps the most important function of state and local governments. Compulsory school attendance laws and the great expenditures for education both demonstrate our recognition of the importance of education to our democratic society. It is required in the performance of our most basic public responsibilities, even service in the armed forces. It is the very foundation of good citizenship. Today it is a principal instrument in awakening the child to cultural values, in preparing him for later professional training, and in helping him to adjust normally to his environment. In these days, it is doubtful that any child may reasonably be expected to succeed in life if he is denied the opportunity of an education. Such an opportunity, where the state has undertaken to provide it, is a right which must be made available to all on equal terms.*

Warren proceeded to address the Court's view on the legal justification for, and societal impactions of, public school segregation:

We come then to the question presented: Does segregation of children in public schools solely on the basis of race, even though the physical facilities and other "tangible" factors may be equal, deprive the children of the minority group of equal educational opportunities? We believe that it does. . . . To separate them (minority group children in public schools) from others of similar age and qualifications solely because of their race generates a feeling of inferiority as to their status in the community that may affect their heart and minds in a way unlikely ever to be undone. The effect of this separation on their educational opportunities was well stated by a finding in the Kansas case by a court which nevertheless felt compelled to rule against the Negro plaintiffs: "Segregation of white and colored children in public schools has a detrimental effect upon the colored children. The impact is greater when it has the sanction of the law; for the policy of separating the races is usually interpreted as denoting the inferiority of the negro group. A sense of inferiority affects the motivation of a child to learn. Segregation with the sanction of law, therefore, has a tendency to retard the educational and mental development of negro children and to deprive them of some of the benefits they would receive in a [racially] integrated school system." Whatever may have been the extent of psychological knowledge at the time of Plessy v. Ferguson, this finding is amply supported by modern authority. Any language in Plessy v. Ferguson contrary to this finding is rejected.

We conclude that in the field of public education the doctrine of "separate but equal" has no place. Separate educational facilities are inherently unequal.

Impact

The Supreme Court's unanimous decision in *Brown* was a landmark in constitutional history and has served as an enduring symbol for the cause of civil rights. Its more particular influence on public education is also significant. The case served as the most important catalyst leading to the end of sanctioned segregation in public education. The years immediately following the decision led opponents to resentment, delay, and occasionally conflict with legal authorities, most notably at Little Rock Central High School in 1957.

Implementation of the decision also represented the growth in judicial activism of the Supreme Court regarding education issues. Over the course of ensuing decades, education reformers of various ideological persuasions increasingly viewed the courts as an outlet for the promotion of their agendas.

The Law and Education Reform

LEMON V. KURTZMAN, 403 U.S. 602 (1971)

Background

The Supreme Court case known as *Lemon v. Kurtzman* is actually three separate cases (including *Easrley v. DiCenso* and *Robinson v. DiCenso*) that were joined together because they all concerned public assistance to private schools, some of which were religious. The cases concerned a Pennsylvania law that allowed the public payment of teachers' salaries as well as assistance for the purchase of teaching supplies and textbooks in parochial schools and a Rhode Island law that allowed state payment of up to 15 percent of private school teachers' salaries. In each of these cases, the teachers were teaching secular subjects.

Prior to being argued before the Supreme Court, a federal court upheld the Pennsylvania law and a separate district court had ruled that the Rhode Island law fostered "excessive entanglement" of church and state.

Legal Issues

The complex and controversial relationship between religion and public education had long been an area of constitutional contention, particularly in the 30 years leading up to the *Lemon* case. A clearer separation of church and state gathered momentum following Supreme Court decisions in *McCollum v. Board of Education* (1948), disallowing the practice of having religious education take place in public school classrooms during the school day, and *Abington Township School District v. Schemp* (1963), which prohibited the forced recital of Bible verses and the Lord's Prayer in public schools.

Decision

On June 28, 1971, the Supreme Court ruled unanimously that direct government assistance to religious schools was unconstitutional. Chief Justice Warren Burger wrote to the majority's decision, establishing what has become known as the "Lemon Test." This three-part analysis was established to determine whether a policy or activity violates the First Amendment's Establishment Clause. It notes:

> *Every analysis in this area must begin with consideration of the cumulative criteria developed by the Court over many years. First, the statute must have a secular legislative purpose; second, its principal or primary effect must be one that neither advances or inhibits religion; finally, the statute must not foster an excessive government Entanglement with religion.*

Education Reform

The payment of public school teachers' salaries under the control of religious officials and in a religious institution was found to be in violation of this new criteria. Further, the Court explained that to ensure that teachers play a nonideological role, the state would have to become directly involved in the management of the teachers and, hence, become entangled with the church.

Impact

The *Lemon* decision has served as the seminal case relating to government aid to religious schools. However, the trend following this case of increasing distance between church and state has narrowed recently as a result of Supreme Court decisions marginalizing or ignoring the Lemon Test.

This shift is most evident in the Supreme Court's decision in *Mitchell v. Helms* (2000), which allowed federal and state support for private and religious schools' purchase of library and media materials as well as computer software and hardware. The Court decision that aid to religious groups can be made so long as it furthers some legitimate secular purpose and is granted in the same manner to nonreligious groups could signal significantly increased government financing of religious institutions, including schools, in the future.

WISCONSIN V. YODER, 406 U.S. 208 (1972)

Background

This case concerned three Amish families who sued the state of Wisconsin over a requirement that children be enrolled in school until the age of 16. The parents refused to comply by removing their children from school after they completed eighth grade and continued their education at home, with an emphasis on domestic and farming skills. The parents also claimed that further education would present their children with too much exposure to the "evil world."

Legal Issues

The Amish families involved in the suit argued that their rights to freely exercise their religion were not being respected by the state's compulsory attendance laws. Before reaching the U.S. Supreme Court, the Wisconsin Supreme Court ruled in favor of the parents.

Decision

On May 15, 1972, the U.S. Supreme Court ruled 6-1 that the compulsory education law in Wisconsin violated the Constitution's Free Exercise Clause.

Justice Warren Burger wrote in his majority opinion that the Amish have a legitimate reason for removing their children from school prior to their attending high school, because qualities emphasized in high school, such as scientific accomplishment, are contrary to their mission and values.

The Court further determined that the beliefs of the Amish were religiously based and rejected the state's arguments that the Free Exercise Clause extends no protection because the case involved "action" or "conduct" rather than "belief." Additionally, the court asserted that the governmental interest of providing education was met, with the Amish attending public schools through the eighth grade and then continuing with the home-based, primarily vocational instruction.

Impact

The primary impact of the *Wisconsin v. Yoder* decision has been seen in the growing prominence of homeschooling over the past 30 years. In California alone, there are more than 100,000 children being homeschooled, and reliable national estimates reached to approximately 1 million.

The Court's decision prevented states from asserting any absolute right to institute compulsory high school education, as parents' rights to teach their religion were deemed more important than governmental interest in educating all children. Since this decision, legal scholars and parents have often successfully argued that people with more individualistic choices based on secular grounds should be granted the same consideration in school attendance matters, significantly expanding homeschooling options.

SAN ANTONIO INDEPENDENT SCHOOL DISTRICT V. RODRIGUEZ, 411 U.S. 1 (1973)

Background

On May 16, 1968, approximately 400 students at Edgewood High School in San Antonio, Texas, held a walkout and demonstration, marching to the district administration office to protest insufficient supplies and lack of qualified teachers in their school. The walkout induced parents to form the Edgewood District Concerned Parents Association to address the problems highlighted by the student protest. A few weeks later, one of the students' parents, Demetrio Rodriguez, and seven other Edgewood parents filed a class-action lawsuit on behalf of Texas schoolchildren who were poor or resided in school districts with low property tax bases, claiming a notable unfair disparity in the per-pupil expenditures among school districts. On

December 23, 1971, a federal district court agreed with the plaintiffs and declared the Texas school finance system unconstitutional.

Legal Issues

The primary issue of this case was inequity in school financing. The plaintiffs argued that although their school district had one of the highest tax rates in Bexar County, it was only able to raise $47 per student, while Alamo Heights, the county's wealthiest district, was able to raise $413 per student. They argued that this common public school funding strategy was unconstitutional under the Equal Protection Clause of the Fourteenth Amendment.

Decision

On March 21, 1973, the Supreme Court ruled 5–4 that the system of school finance at the center of contention did not violate the U.S. Constitution and that the issue should be resolved by the state of Texas. The Court also held that the state would not be required to subsidize poorer school districts, which produced additional legal barriers to funding equalization.

In his majority opinion, Justice Lewis Powell explained:

Wealth did not constitute a suspect class and thus the strict scrutiny test, which was appropriate when state action impinged on a fundamental right or operated to the disadvantage of a suspect class, was not applicable in this case. The financing method employed did not impinge on any fundamental right so as to call for the application of the strict judicial scrutiny test. In addition, the Court did not view education as a fundamental right which afforded explicit or implicit protection under the Constitution.

The Court then applied the traditional standard of review which requires a showing that the state's action had a rational relationship to legitimate state purposes. It found that the financing method used satisfied this test, namely in the areas of fiscal policy and educational requirements. This result was achieved despite the inherent and somewhat obvious imperfections in the current system. However, it was not up to the Court to measure the quality of system, only its constitutionality.

Impact

The Supreme Court's decision in the *Rodriguez* case allowed states a more relaxed standard for justifying their funding policies. In addition, it asserted that the fourteenth Amendment's Equal Protection Clause permits any kind of school finance system as long as it provides a minimum education for every student. As a result, the issue of per-pupil expenditure has been the frequent focus of challenges in state courts, which often rule against the funding policies established by state legislatures.

LAU V. NICHOLS, 414 U.S. 563 (1974)

Background

In the early 1970s, parents of Chinese-speaking students in the San Francisco Unified School District (SFUSD) filed a class-action lawsuit alleging that the district's failure to provide equal educational opportunities for students who did not speak English was a violation of the Fourteenth Amendment to the U.S. Constitution.

A federal district court and the ninth court of appeals denied the plaintiffs' claims before the case came to the U.S. Supreme Court. The Court was not asked to determine a specific remedy but rather to direct the SFUSD to apply its expertise to the problem.

Legal Issues

The Supreme Court avoided addressing the arguments relating to the Fourteenth Amendment's Equal Protection Clause, instead relying on the much narrower grounds of the regulations issued under Title VI of the Civil Rights Act of 1964, which prohibits federally funded programs from discrimination on the basis of race or national origin.

Decision

On January 21, 1974, the Supreme Court ruled in favor of the plaintiffs; however, the Court carefully refrained from dictating a particular methodology, leaving the pursuit of remedies for the local level. Writing for the majority, Justice William Orville Douglas noted:

> *Where inability to speak and understand the English language excludes national origin minority group children from effective participation in the educational program offered by a school district, the district must take affirmative steps to rectify the language deficiency in order to open its instructional program to these students.*

While concurring the decision, Justice Harry Andrew Blackmun (joined by Justice Warren Burger) added a caveat that has proven to be significant as school districts confront increasingly diverse student populations:

> *Against the possibility that the Court's judgment may be interpreted too broadly, I stress the fact that the children with whom we are concerned here*

number about 1,800. This is a very substantial group that is being deprived of any meaningful schooling because the children cannot understand the language of the classroom. We may only guess as to why they have had no exposure to English in their preschool years. Earlier generations of American ethnic groups have overcome the language barrier by earnest parental endeavor or by the hard fact of being pushed out of the family or community nest and into the realities of broader experience.

I merely wish to make plain that when, in another case, we are confronted with a very few youngsters, or with just a single child who speaks only German or Polish or Spanish or any language other than English, I would not regard today's decision . . . as conclusive upon the issue whether the statute and the guidelines require the funded school district to provide special instruction. For me, numbers are at the heart of this case and my concurrence is to be understood accordingly.

Impact

Lau v. Nichols is the most important Supreme Court case concerning students with limited English proficiency. Key words and phrases in the decision have led to heated debate and varying interpretations among educators and policymakers, particularly "effective participation," "affirmative steps," "rectify the language deficiency," and "open its instructional program."

The volatile dispute over the best approach to educating limited-English-proficient students was left unresolved by *Lau*. The Office of Civil Rights set forth a series of principles, known as the Lau Guidelines, outlining procedures to follow for districts enrolling 20 or more limited-English-language-proficient students. However, it soon became apparent that these guidelines did not have the force of law.

In the decades since the *Lau* decision, California has been the primary battleground over the issue of bilingual education. Its leadership in implementing the far-reaching Chaco-Mosconi Bilingual Bicultural Education Act of 1976, which mandated bilingual education, was emulated in many states throughout the country. However, by the mid-1990s, criticism of these programs became widespread. Prominent reports suggested that bilingual education programs had done little to boost the academic achievement or competitiveness of a limited-English-proficient students.

In June 1998, California's Proposition 227, designed to all but end the state's bilingual education programs, passed with more than 60 percent support from the state's voters. The proposition, headed by software mogul Ron Unz, has survived legal challenges and has led to similar efforts across the country.

GOSS V. LOPEZ, 419 U.S. 565 (1975)

Background

The student protests that broke out on many college campuses in the 1960s spread to many high schools by the early 1970s. In February and March 1971, race-related student riots at Columbus, Ohio's Central High School led to the suspensions of 75 students for disruptive behavior and damage to school property.

One of the suspended students, Dwight Lopez, insisted that he was an innocent bystander, but he was not allowed to get a hearing to tell his side of the story. Lopez and eight other students, through their parents, sued the school board for violation of their civil rights.

Legal Issues

At issue in the *Goss* case were two provisions of the Fourteenth Amendment: the Equal Protection Clause and the Due Process Clause, requiring states to recognize the rights of all citizens facing legal action. Specifically, the Supreme Court examined whether these protections necessarily extend past the schoolhouse doors.

Decision

On January 22, 1975, the Supreme Court ruled 5-4 in favor of the plaintiffs, striking down the Ohio law as a violation of students' limited rights to due process.

In his majority opinion, Justice Byron White noted:

Among other things, the State is constrained to recognize a student's legitimate entitlement to a public education as a property interest which is protected by the Due Process Clause and which may not be taken away for misconduct without adherence to the minimum procedures required by that Clause. The Due Process Clause also forbids arbitrary deprivations of liberty. "Where a person's good name, reputation, honor, or integrity is at stake because of what the government is doing to him," the minimal requirements of the Clause must be satisfied. School authorities here suspended appellees from school for periods of up to 10 days based on charges of misconduct. If sustained and recorded, those charges could seriously damage the students' standing with their fellow pupils and their teachers as well as interfere with later opportunities for higher education and employment. It is apparent that the claimed right of the State to determine unilaterally and without process whether that misconduct has occurred immediately collides with the requirements of the Constitution.

The decision explained that students were entitled to the following due-process rights: oral or written notice of the charges; if a student denies the charges, an explanation of the evidence the school will use against him or her; and an opportunity for the student to present his or her side of the story. The Court ruled that in an emergency situation, students could be sent home immediately and a hearing held at a later date. The Court did not rule, however, that students had a right to an attorney, to cross-examine witnesses, to call witnesses in their defense, or to a hearing before an impartial person.

Impact

More than 25 years of law or court case rulings have elaborated these procedural protections for a wide range of situations, from short-term suspensions in interscholastic athletics to lengthy expulsions from school.

In recent years, rulings have tended to favor public school officials, particularly in the wake of the Columbine High School murders committed by two students in Littleton, Colorado, in 1999. The subsequent spread of zero-tolerance policies for certain types of student conduct have proliferated as have legal challenges to them.

HONIG V. DOE, 484 U.S. 305 (1988)

Background

On November 6, 1980, a 17-year-old student (referred to in the case as Doe) at the Louise Lombard School in San Francisco, a developmental center for learning disabled students, responded to the taunts of a fellow student by choking the student to the degree that abrasions were left on the student's neck. Doe then kicked out a school window as he was being escorted to the principal's office.

Doe admitted his misconduct and the school suspended him for five days. The principal referred the matter to the San Francisco Unified School District (SFUSD), recommending expulsion. The district agreed and notified Doe's mother that he would not be allowed to come to school until the expulsion hearing was held. Doe's family sued, alleging that the suspension and proposed expulsion violated the Individuals with Disabilities Education Act (IDEA). A district judge granted an injunction, and Doe reentered school.

A similar incident within the SFUSD occurred almost simultaneously involving another student, who was expelled for stealing, extorting money from fellow students, and making sexual comments to female classmates. The student's family joined in the Doe family suit.

A district judge agreed with the students' families and prevented the school district from taking any disciplinary action other than a maximum five-day suspension against any disabled student for disability-related misconduct or from effecting any other change in the educational placement of any such students without parental consent pending completion of any IDEA proceedings.

The ninth circuit court of appeals affirmed the orders of the district judge with slight modifications. The case was referred to as *Doe v. Maher* at the district and appeals levels. When California superintendent of education Bill Honig petitioned the Supreme Court for review of the case, it became known as *Honig v. Doe.*

Legal Issues

Honig v. Doe provided the intersection of two critical education-related constitutional issues: the rights of the disabled and the protection of the student population by school authorities. Honig argued that a "dangerousness" exception exists in the "stay-put" provision of IDEA though not explicitly noted in the law, explaining that Congress either excluded it because it was too obvious to be included or inadvertently failed to provide such authority.

Decision

On January 20, 1988, the Supreme Court in a unanimous decision ruled that suspensions of disabled students, particularly those with emotional disabilities, was a form of exclusion and therefore a violation of the student's right to a "free and appropriate education" guaranteed by IDEA. The Court ruled that such students could not be suspended for more than a total of 10 days in one school year and that such suspensions should be reviewed by multidisciplinary teams to determine if they constituted a change in the placements prescribed in the student's individualized educational plan (IEP).

Justice William Brennan's majority opinion explained:

Our conclusion that 1415(e)(3) means what it says does not leave educators hamstrung. The Department of Education has observed that, "[w]hile the [child's] placement may not be changed [during any complaint proceeding], this does not preclude the agency from using its normal procedures for dealing with children who are endangering themselves or others." Such procedures may include the use of study carrels, time-outs, detention, or the restriction of privileges. More drastically, where a student poses an immediate threat to the safety of others, officials may temporarily suspend him or her for up to 10 school days.[8] This authority, which respondent in no way disputes, not only ensures that school administrators can protect the safety of others by promptly removing the most dangerous of students, it also provides a "cooling down" period during which officials can initiate IEP review and seek to persuade the child's parents to agree to an interim placement. And in those cases in which the parents of a truly dangerous child adamantly refuse to permit any change in placement, the 10-day respite gives school officials an opportunity to invoke the aid of the courts . . .

Impact

The 15-year period following the *Honig* decision has been a turbulent one in the area of student discipline. Initially, lower courts were reluctant to grant preliminary injunctions. In 1997, Congress passed amendments to IDEA to clarify what constitutes removal of students and offered schools other options for dealing with disruptive behavior.

The generally hands-off approach to offenses committed by special education students runs counter to the recent wave of zero-tolerance policies for rules infractions within public schools. This perceived double standard in treatment of special education and regular education misconduct has come under increased scrutiny following highly publicized school shootings that followed the kinds of taunting that Doe responded to a generation earlier.

DAVIS V. MONROE COUNTY BOARD OF EDUCATION, 97 U.S. 843 (1999)

Background

LaShonda Davis was a fifth-grade student at Hubbard Elementary School, in Monroe County, Georgia, during the 1992–93 school year. She claimed that a male classmate, referred to as "G.F.," repeatedly tried to touch her in a sexual manner and made sexual comments despite her reporting of the incidents to her mother, principal, teacher, and other teachers at the school. G.F. was subsequently charged with sexual battery, which he did not deny.

Frustrated with the failure to effectively respond to this harassment, Davis's mother sued the Board of Education of Monroe County. The U.S. District Court for the Middle District of Georgia dismissed the suit for failing to state a claim upon which relief could be granted. Davis appealed and a panel for the Court of Appeals for the Eleventh Circuit reinstated the claim but then rejected it. Davis then filed a petition for certiorari, asking the Supreme Court to review the decision of the lower courts.

Legal Issues

The salient issue of the *Davis* case concerned whether Title IX of the Education Amendments of 1972 covers peer sexual harassment and if so, what the standard of liability is for school districts. Specifically, Title IX provides that "no person in the United States, shall, on the basis of sex be excluded from participation in, be denied the benefits of, or be subjected to discrimination under any education program or activity receiving federal financial assistance."

Decision

On May 24, 1999, the Supreme Court in a 5-4 ruling reversed the lower court's decision and remanded the case to the district court.

Justice Sandra Day O'Connor explained in the majority decision:

A private Title IX damages action may lie against a school board in cases of student-on-student harassment, but only where the funding recipient is deliberately indifferent to sexual harassment, of which the recipient has actual knowledge, and that harassment is so severe, pervasive, and objectively offensive that it can be said to deprive the victims of access to the educational opportunities or benefits provided by the school.

The decision went on to assert:

Applying this standard to the facts at issue, the Eleventh Circuit erred in dismissing petitioner's complaint. This Court cannot say beyond doubt that she can prove no set of facts that would entitle her to relief. She alleges that LaShonda was the victim of repeated acts of harassment by G.F. over a 5-month period, and allegations support the conclusion that his misconduct was severe, pervasive, and objectively offensive. Moreover, the complaint alleges that multiple victims of G.F.'s misconduct sought an audience with the school principal and that the harassment had a concrete, negative effect on LaShonda's ability to receive an education. The complaint also suggests that petitioner may be able to show both actual knowledge and deliberate indifference on the part of the Board, which made no effort either to investigate or to put an end to the harassment.

Impact

The *Davis* decision established that lawsuits can be filed against school officials who knowingly and deliberately ignore student-on-student harassment. This has resulted in a dramatic increase in harassment in school litigation. Fearing liability, many schools and districts have developed polices and procedures mandating intervention in such cases, including the highly publicized and legally contentious enactment of zero-tolerance policies.

Education Reform

ZELMAN V. SIMMONS-HARRIS, 200 U.S. 321 (2002)

Background

In the early 1990s, the Cleveland public schools were in dismal condition. Most of the more than 75,000 students enrolled in the system performed below proficiency on state exams, and more than two-thirds of high school students dropped out or failed before graduation. In 1995, the city's school system was placed under state control.

In 1995, the Ohio legislature adopted the Ohio Pilot Scholarship Program, which provided two kinds of assistance: tuition aid for kindergarten through third-grade students to attend a participating public or private school of their parents' choosing and tutorial aid for students who chose to remain in public school. Provisions for school participation included location within district boundaries and nondiscrimination on the basis of race, religion, or ethnic background. Tuition aid was distributed to parents according to financial need.

The program began at the start of the 1996–97 school year. In the 1999–2000 school year, 56 private schools participated in the program, and 46 of these (82 percent) had a religious affiliation. None of the adjacent public schools eligible to participate chose to do so.

In January 1996, Doris Simmons-Harris, a parent of a public school student, and others challenged the program in state court on the grounds that it violated both the state and federal constitutions. The case eventually reached the Ohio Supreme Court, which determined that the voucher program violated Ohio's "one subject" rule because the voucher bill was an addition to a state budget bill.

In June 1999, the Ohio legislature reenacted the voucher program as a freestanding measure. A month later, Simmons-Harris and others sued the state department of education in federal court alleging violation of the First Amendment's Establishment Clause. Some parents and religious schools then intervened in the suit to defend the program.

In December 1999, a federal district court ruled in favor of the plaintiffs' claim that the voucher program was unconstitutional. The state's appeal to the Court of Appeals for the Sixth Circuit was denied, and the state then appealed the case to the U.S. Supreme Court, which agreed to hear the case.

Legal Issues

The central legal issue of the *Zelman* case was the major conflict embroiling advocates of each side of the voucher issue. Does the First Amendment's Establishment Clause prohibit a voucher plan in which participating students in the program attend religiously affiliated schools?

The Law and Education Reform

Decision

On June 27, 2002, the Supreme Court ruled in a 5-4 decision that the Ohio Pilot Project Scholarship Program did not violate the Establishment Clause of the First Amendment, reversing the decisions of the lower courts.

Writing for the majority, Justice William Rehnquist noted:

> We believe that the program challenged here is a program of true private choice, . . . and thus constitutional. As was true in those cases, the Ohio program is neutral in all respects toward religion. It is part of a general and multifaceted undertaking by the State of Ohio to provide educational opportunities to the children of a failed school district. It confers educational assistance directly to a broad class of individuals defined without reference to religion, i.e., any parent of a school-age child who resides in the Cleveland City School District. The program permits the participation of all schools within the district, religious or non-religious. Adjacent public schools also may participate and have a financial incentive to do so. Program benefits are available to participating families on neutral terms, with no reference to religion. The only preference stated anywhere in the program is a preference for low-income families, who receive greater assistance and are given priority for admission at participating schools.

Rehnquist then elaborated on the issue of government endorsement of religion by explaining,

> We further observed that "[b]y according parents freedom to select a school of their choice, the statute ensures that a government-paid interpreter will be present in a sectarian school only as a result of the private decision of individual parents." Our focus again was on neutrality and the principle of private choice, not on the number of program beneficiaries attending religious schools. Because the program ensured that parents were the ones to select a religious school as the best learning environment for their handicapped child, the circuit between government and religion was broken, and the Establishment Clause was not implicated.

Impact

The impact of this recent decision is not entirely clear, though the proliferation of similar voucher programs seems to be a likely outcome. It seems that, despite the court's decision, the intensity of this critical education reform debate will not subside, as evidenced by the words of the justices who rendered this decision. Referencing the historic importance of this issue,

Justice Clarence Thomas wrote, "If society cannot end racial discrimination at least it can arm minorities with the education to defend themselves from some of discrimination's effects." Justice John Paul Stevens reasoned, "Whenever we remove a break from the wall that was designed to separate religion and government, we increase the risk of religious strife and weaken the foundation of our democracy."

CHAPTER 3

CHRONOLOGY

This chapter provides a chronology of important events in the history of education reform. It focuses primarily on events that have occurred since 1920.

360 B.C.

- Plato writes *The Republic*, expressing benefits of state support of an educational system.

FIRST CENTURY A.D.

- Roman educator Quintilian expresses the importance and benefits of a broad public education system.

LATE 13TH CENTURY

- Dominican monk, philosopher, and scholar Thomas Aquinas establishes the foundation of Roman Catholic education.

1511

- Dutch humanist Desiderius Erasmus writes *Upon the Method of Right Instruction*, proposing the systematic training of teachers.

1516

- Erasmus publishes *Of the First Liberal Education of Children*.

1635

- The Boston Latin School becomes British North America's first secondary school and later the model for similar schools throughout New England.

Education Reform

1642

- The passage of the Massachusetts Law requires that the selectmen of each town determine that parents and masters of apprentices are providing for the education of children.

1647

- The Education Law is passed in Massachusetts ordering every township of 100 or more households to establish a grammar school.

1683

- The Pennsylvania Assembly enacts a law providing that all children be instructed in reading, writing, and a useful trade, yet formal education remains primarily a private or denominational endeavor largely owing to the diversity of religious groups in the colonies.

1690

- *The First New England Primer,* featuring an English-language guide and biblical content, is published and quickly becomes the main instructional text of the pre-Revolutionary period.

1762

- French philosopher Jean-Jacques Rousseau writes the novel *Emile*, providing early description of the benefits of child-centered education.

1776–81

- Many British Colonial schools close or are abandoned due to the Revolutionary War.

1779

- Thomas Jefferson's Bill for the More General Diffusion of Knowledge, proposing tax-supported education for three years to all white children, is defeated in the Virginia legislature.

1783

- Noah Webster publishes the *Elementary Spelling Book*, often referred to as the "Blue-Back Speller," which includes distinctively American spelling, grammar, and content.

Chronology

1787

- *July 13:* The Northwest Ordinance is adopted proclaiming, "religion, morality, and knowledge being necessary to good government and the happiness of mankind, schools and the means of education shall forever be encouraged."
- *September 17:* The U.S. Constitution is adopted making no mention of education.

1812

- New York becomes the first state to appoint a superintendent of education.

1821

- Boston English Classical School, later named Boston English High School, becomes the nation's first high school.

1828

- Catherine Beecher founds the Hartford Female Seminary, a key forerunner in the training of teachers.

1837

- Massachusetts legislator Horace Mann becomes the first secretary of the nation's first state board of education, significantly contributing to increased support for public education.
- Buffalo, New York, becomes the first major city to appoint a local superintendent whose major duty is to develop a uniform course of study.

1846

- Horace Mann's *Tenth Annual Report* asserts that education is the right of every child and that it is the state's responsibility to ensure that every child is provided with an education.

mid-1800s

- Enrollment in private secondary academies reaches more than 250,000 students at more than 6,000 schools throughout the United States.

1852

- The first compulsory school attendance law is approved by the Massachusetts legislature.

Education Reform

1861

- Twenty-eight of 34 states have established state boards of education and have chief state school officers whose responsibilities include distributing school funds and organizing the state's system of common schools.

1865

- More than 50 percent of the nation's children are enrolled in public schools, with the lowest rate of enrollment in the South.

1870

- Massachusetts congressman George Hoar's bill to establish a federal school system in the South is defeated.
- The National Education Association (NEA) is founded.

1873

- The Maine legislature enacts the first law providing state aid for public high schools.

1874

- The Michigan Supreme Court rules in the Kalamazoo School Case *(Stewart et al. v. School District No. 1 of the Village of Kalamazoo)* that the state legislature can tax for the support of both elementary and public schools.

1875

- Sales of Noah Webster's "Blue-Back Speller" reach 75 million copies, making it the most influential book in U.S. schools.

1876

- The U.S. Supreme Court decision in *Plessy v. Ferguson* establishes the legal foundation for racial segregation in education.

1890

- Rapid industrialization and increased immigration lead to the establishment of more than 2,500 high schools, whose enrollment doubles that of private academies.

1892

- The Committee of Ten is formed by the National Education Association and recommends uniform subject matter and instruction for all high school students.

- New York College for the Training of Teachers, later known as Teachers College, becomes part of Columbia University.

1896

- Professor and philosopher John Dewey establishes the University of Chicago Laboratory School as a center of progressive educational practice emphasizing learning through experience and the preparation of children for full participation in democratic society.

1900

- More than 300 normal schools designed to train teachers exist throughout the United States.

1907

- W. E. B. DuBois cofounds the National Association for the Advancement of Colored People (NAACP) and advocates for expanded educational opportunity for blacks.

1909

- The cities of Columbus, Ohio, and Berkeley, California, establish the nation's first junior high schools.

1910

- The illiteracy rate among Americans over age 10 drops to 7.7 percent, compared to 20 percent in 1870.

1916

- John Dewey publishes *Democracy and Education*, which describes his progressive educational philosophy for a generation of educators.
- The measurement movement, featuring the increased use and application of intelligence and aptitude tests, grows in schools following its pervasive use in the World War I–era military.

1917

- Congress passes the Smith-Hughes Act, the first federal program for education of any kind, establishing federal aid for vocational education.

1918

- All states enact laws requiring full-time school attendance until the child reaches a certain age or grade.

- The Commission on the Reorganization of Secondary Education issues *The Cardinal Principles of Secondary Education*, which counters much of the Committee of Ten's recommendations.

1919

- The Progressive Education Association forms, giving organizational strength to the burgeoning progressive movement.

1932

- The Progressive Education Association begins an eight-year study of 3,000 high school students, which results in a report showing the academic and social benefits of progressive education.

1933

- Depression-era New Deal programs, including the Civilian Conservation Corps (CCC) and the National Youth Administration (NYA), provide many out-of-school youth with employment and signify the increase in the federal role for education.

1935

- A liberal wing of progressive educators begins the publication of the journal the *Social Frontier*, which argues in favor of the social reconstruction role of schools and signifies a division within the movement.

1938

- Education professor William Bagley publishes support for the educational theory of essentialism, which criticizes social reconstructionsists and argues in favor of an emphasis on the school's role in developing fundamental knowledge.

1940

- The National Teachers Exam is administered for the first time.

1953

- Professor Arthur Bestor publishes *Educational Wastelands*, criticizing progressive education's influence on U.S. schools.

1954

- The U.S. Supreme Court rules 9-0 in *Brown v. Board of Education* that segregated educational facilities are inherently unequal and orders an end to racial segregation in education.

Chronology

1955

- The motion picture *Blackboard Jungle*, portraying a chaotic urban public high school, is released.
- Rudolph Flesch publishes *Why Johnny Can't Read*, setting off national debate about quality of reading instruction and school curriculum.

1957

- President Dwight Eisenhower sends federal troops to ensure the safe passage of black students integrating Little Rock, Arkansas, Central High School.

1958

- Largely in response to the previous year's Soviet launch of the *Sputnik* satellite, President Dwight Eisenhower signs the National Defense Education Act, which increases funding for science, math, and foreign language curricula and significantly raises the federal role in elementary and secondary education.

1959

- Former Harvard president James Conant publishes *The American High School Today*.

1963

- The Vocational Education Act more than quadruples federal funds for vocational education.

1964

- John Holt publishes *How Children Fail*, establishing the foundation for the homeschooling movement.
- Congress passes the Civil Rights Act, including the Title VI provision that prohibits discrimination against students based on race, religion, and national origin and provides federal financial assistance to school districts attempting to desegregate.

1965

- *April 11:* President Lyndon Johnson signs the Elementary and Secondary Education Act (ESEA), providing more than $1 billion in federal funds to education and representing the most significant education contribution of his Great Society legislation.

1966

- Under Title VI, the Elementary and Secondary Education Act (ESEA) expands to include programs for Native American students, children of migrant workers, and the disabled.

1967

- Title VII of the Elementary and Secondary Education Act (ESEA) adds programs for students with limited English-speaking ability.
- President Lyndon Johnson signs the Education Professions Development Act to provide funding for expanded in-service training for teachers.

1968

- The Vocational Education Act expands, doubling its funding authorization.

1969

- Federal funding for education reaches $3 billion, a threefold increase from 1964.

1970s

- The open education movement grows in popularity.

1971

- The U.S. Supreme Court determines in *Lemon v. Kurtzman* that direct government aid to religious schools is unconstitutional.

1972

- Title IX of the Elementary and Secondary Education Act (ESEA) prohibits sex discrimination against students in educational programs receiving federal funds.
- The U.S. Supreme Court strikes down many state compulsory attendance laws as a violation of the Constitution's Free Exercise Clause in *Wisconsin v. Yoder.*

1973

- In *San Antonio School District v. Rodriguez*, the U.S. Supreme Court upholds the use of property taxes in determining school financing.

Chronology

1974

- U.S. Supreme Court rules in *Lau v. Nichols* that schools must provide special language programs for non-English-speaking students.

1975

- The Education for All Handicapped Children Act establishes the right of the disabled to a free and appropriate education.

1979

- President Jimmy Carter establishes the Department of Education as a cabinet-level part of the executive branch.

1981

- President Ronald Reagan signs the National Education Consolidation and Improvement Act, which combines federal education aid into several large block programs.

1983

- *A Nation at Risk*, a report released by the National Commission on Excellence in Education, blasts the "rising tide of mediocrity" in schools and sparks the current education reform movement.
- Theodore Sizer publishes *Horace's Compromise*, advocating a new wave of progressive education including increased local control, parental involvement and a de-emphasis on standardized tests. Sizer also starts the Coalition of Essential Schools to help promote his ideas of education reform.

1987

- E. D. Hirsch's book *Cultural Literacy*, which emphasizes the importance of creating a common, explicit curriculum in schools, is published and becomes a best-seller.

1988

- The Illinois state legislature approves the Chicago School Reform Act, which shifts significant powers and money to the local schools. Elected local school councils are created with the authority to hire principals and approve local education and spending plans.
- Vice President George H. W. Bush campaigns for (and will win) the presidency promising to be the "Education President."

- Retired teacher Ray Budde writes *Education by Charter: Restructuring School Districts*, proposing charter schools as a method of providing schools with greater flexibility and accountability for student performance.
- American Federation of Teachers president Albert Shanker endorses the idea of charter schools in speeches and editorials.

1989

- President Ronald Reagan concludes his two terms in office with a 17 percent drop in federal funding for elementary and secondary education compared to the beginning of his administration.

1990

- Recent Princeton graduate Wendy Kopp founds Teach For America to attract noneducation majors to teach with alternative certification in areas with persistent teaching shortages.
- The National Governors Association and the Bush administration approve six national educational goals, known as America 2000, to be accomplished by 2000.
- The Milwaukee Parental Choice Program is enacted, allowing up to 1 percent (approximately 1,000) economically disadvantaged students in the Milwaukee public schools to use their state share of education funds as full payment of tuition on participating nonsectarian private schools.

1991

- Minnesota enacts the nation's first charter school legislation.

1991

- School management company the Edison Project (later named Edison Schools) is founded.

1994

- President Bill Clinton signs the GOALS 2000: Educate America Act.
- The Republican takeover of Congress includes the "Contract with America," featuring prominent support for choice and privatization in education.
- Congress approves creation of the Public Charter Schools Program (PCSP) to help charter schools defray some of the costs associated with school planning and implementation.
- President Clinton signs the bipartisan Safe and Drug-Free Schools Act and the Gun-Free Schools Act.

- National History Standards are released by the University of California, Los Angeles's Center for History in the Schools and are immediately met by protest.

1995

- The Milwaukee choice program is expanded to include religious schools among the options. Following a suit on separation of church and state grounds, the Wisconsin Supreme Court allows nonsectarian expansion of the program but prohibits inclusion of religious schools.
- The Ohio legislature enacts the Pilot Project Scholarship Program allowing Cleveland students to use tuition scholarships and assistance grants to attend participating private schools within Cleveland or public schools in participating adjacent districts.

1998

- Congress passes the Charter School Extension Act, which reauthorizes the Public Charter Schools Program (PCSP) and creates grants to operate charter schools.
- Wisconsin Supreme Court upholds publicly funded vouchers in religious schools. Plaintiffs appeal the decision to the U.S. Supreme Court, which declines to hear the case.
- California voters overwhelmingly approve ballot initiative that effectively eliminates that state's bilingual education programs.

1999

- Ohio Supreme Court overturns Cleveland voucher program on a legal technicality. The Ohio legislature reauthorizes the program, which is then halted under a judicial injunction, during which current students in the program return to their school of choice.
- Florida enacts the nation's first statewide voucher program as part of the A+ Plan for Education, for students in "chronically failing" schools (defined as failing to meet minimum state standards two out of four years).
- *April 30:* Two high school students murder 12 students and a teacher at Columbine High School in Littleton, Colorado, leading to increased calls for zero-tolerance policies that will impose mandatory suspensions for a variety of offenses including making verbal threats.
- The Michigan legislature approves a law to remove the elected Detroit school board from power and give Detroit's mayor the authority to appoint a new reform school board. The measure allows Detroiters to vote on restoring the elected board in 2004.

2000

- Florida's voucher program is ruled unconstitutional by a state circuit judge in *Bush et al. v. Holmes et al.* but the program is allowed to continue while the decision is appealed to the Florida Supreme Court.
- U.S. Supreme Court rules that Louisiana private school students are entitled to benefits of the federal Chapter II program, allowing the provision of computers, software, and other educational materials to all schools regardless of their affiliation.
- The Board of Education of Cincinnati and the district's teachers' union adopt an incentive-based merit pay system, including the use of peer evaluators.
- *December 11:* Cleveland voucher program is rejected by federal appeals panel on the grounds that it violates the separation of church and state. The ruling is later appealed to the U.S. Supreme Court, which accepts the case *Zelman v. Simmons-Harris.*

2001

- Homeschooled population is estimated at 1 million students.

2002

- *January 8:* President George W. Bush signs the No Child Left Behind Act.
- *June 27:* In a 5–4 decision that provides major support for full school choice advocates, the U.S. Supreme Court rules in *Zelman v. Simmons-Harris* that the Cleveland voucher program does not infringe on the constitutional separation of church and state.
- *August 6:* A Florida circuit court judge rules that the Florida A+ Education Plan's provision allowing children in failing schools to receive vouchers to attend private schools violates the state's constitution. The decision is appealed by voucher supporters.
- *Fall:* The number of charter schools operating reaches an all-time high of 2,699.

2003

- *January 15:* New York City mayor Michael Bloomberg announces major overhaul of nation's largest school system, featuring increased administrative centralization, adaptation of unified curriculum for most schools, and expanded parent involvement initiatives.
- *January 27:* First lawsuit filed seeking rights provided by the No Child Left Behind Act of 2001 filed in New York City charging that

students have been denied transfers and guaranteed supplemental educational services.

- *February 19:* Colorado State House passes first voucher law allowing public funding for private school tuition since the U.S. Supreme Court decision in *Zelman v. Simmons-Harris.*
- *May 19:* The U.S. Supreme Court agrees to hear *Davey v. Locke* to consider Washington's Blaine Amendment prohibiting state scholarship aid for religious instruction.

CHAPTER 4

BIOGRAPHICAL LISTING

This chapter briefly profiles key individuals in the history of U.S. education reform, including activists, writers, educators, and legal and political leaders.

Mortimer Adler, professor and founder of the Great Books curriculum, which was created to counter many progressive education measures seen as inhibiting academic achievement.

Jeanne Allen, president of the Center for Education Reform, a Washington, D.C.–based advocacy organization she founded in 1993. Allen is a frequent contributor to media examinations of education reform issues, speaking out in favor of school choice, charter schools, and the standards movement.

Thomas Aquinas, 13th-century Dominican monk, philosopher, and scholar who established the foundation of Roman Catholic education by explaining reason and faith as complementary sources of truth.

William Chandler Bagley, early 20th-century professor of education, well known for his critique of popular reforms of that era. Bagley emphasized the importance of a general liberal education, which he viewed as crucial in equipping individuals with skills to confront new situations.

Henry Barnard, late 19th-century Connecticut legislator and editor of the *American Journal of Education.* He was famed for his philosophy "schools good enough for the best and cheap enough for the poorest," and is considered the Father of American School Administration.

Roland Barth, a former Massachusetts teacher and principal. His popular and influential book, *Open Education and the American School,* described his enthusiasm and ultimate disillusionment with the open education movement in the United States during the 1960s–1970s.

Catherine Beecher, founder of the Hartford Female Seminary, a leading institution for teacher training in the late 19th century. Her leadership was key in providing support for the role of women as teachers in U.S. schools.

William Bennett, secretary of education 1985–88, during the Reagan administration. He has been an influential conservative critic of the failure of U.S. public schools and prominent supporter of the school choice and standards movements. Bennett became editor of the best-selling Book of Virtues series, designed to provide children with examples of moral behavior.

Arthur Bestor, a history professor and author of the influential 1953 book *Educational Wastelands*, which attacked progressive education's de-emphasis on intellectual disciplines.

John Franklin Bobbitt, author of *The Curriculum*, the earliest and widely used textbook on the theory of curriculum construction. Bobbitt's view that educators could use schools to precisely address deficiencies in the social order was particularly influential in the 1920s.

John Boehner, Republican (Ohio) chairman of the House Committee on Education and the Workforce. He has been a consistent supporter of President George W. Bush's educational initiatives, including the No Child Left Behind Act and expansion of school choice programs.

Clint Bolick, litigation director for the Institute for Justice. Bolick is a leading legal advocate in the nationwide effort to defend school choice programs and he has played a key role in recent voucher victories in Milwaukee, Wisconsin, and Cleveland, Ohio.

Carl Brigham, professor of psychology at Princeton in the first half of the 20th century who is credited with the creation of the Scholastic Aptitude Test (SAT) in the 1920s. Brigham's work was very influential in the spread of intelligence testing throughout U.S. schools.

George H. W. Bush, 41st president of the United States. Bush won the election of 1988 campaigning as "the Education President" and organized the 1989 Education Summit with all 50 governors to establish national education goals.

George W. Bush, 43rd president of the United States. One of the first major legislative accomplishments of his administration was his signing of the No Child Left Behind Act (2001). As governor of Texas in the 1990s, Bush advocated accountability measures for districts, schools, teachers, and students.

Nicholas Butler, a founder of what later became known as Columbia's Teachers College in 1887 and president of Columbia University 1902–45. Butler's leadership in professional teacher training strengthened the progressive movement in education and influenced the formal study of pedagogy and curriculum.

Hollis Caswell, dean of Columbia's Teachers College in the 1930s–40s. Caswell's expertise in curriculum reform emphasized teacher leadership through the creation of in-service trainings.

Bob Chase, president of the National Education Association (NEA) 1996–2002. During his tenure, Chase led union opposition to many controversial proposed education reforms, particularly private school vouchers, and advocated for such measures as class-size reduction.

Lynne Cheney, former chairwoman of the National Endowment for the Humanities (NEH) and frequent conservative critic of U.S. public schooling. Cheney's vocal opposition to the proposed National History Standards in 1994 helped lead to increased debate about the role and composition of academic standards.

Kenneth Clark, influential City College of New York professor and psychologist. Clark's research demonstrating that segregation adversely affected the self-image of African-American children played a pivotal role in the movement to desegregate public schools.

Bill Clinton, 42nd president of the United States. He signed the GOALS 2000 legislation that provided funds for states to develop standards and assessments. Clinton supported the expansion of charter schools and public school choice, though he consistently opposed vouchers that would allow public funds to be used for public education.

James Conant, former president of Harvard and author of the 1959 book *The American High School Today.* The highly praised and popular book supported the elimination of small high schools that could not offer a full array of services, but otherwise supported the common practices of schools and refuted critics who called for widespread strengthening of academic standards.

George Counts, educational sociologist at Columbia's Teachers College. His progressive era journal the *Social Frontier* reflected his view that schools can and should lead the way in creating a new social order.

Elwood Cubberley, teacher, superintendent, and professor of education at Stanford. Cubberley was a major figure in the early 20th-century progressive education movement, advocating for the introduction of vocational education, professional management of public schools, and the use of schools as a tool to assimilate immigrants.

Richard M. Daley, mayor of Chicago since 1989. Daley obtained unprecedented control over the Chicago public schools from the Illinois General Assembly in 1995 and handpicked a management team that pursued academic performance through the reduction of the budget deficit, construction of new schools and building improvements, restriction of social promotion, and expansion of summer and early education programs.

John Dewey, philosopher and professor whose educational theories broke new ground in the first half of the 20th century and remain the foundation for modern advocates of progressive education. Dewey rejected the formalized drill-and-recitation methods of early U.S. public education, arguing in favor of a child-centered education based on experience, reflection, and the world outside the classroom. His creation of the University of Chicago Laboratory School in 1896 emphasized project-based learning that sought to appeal to children's interests and served as a model for the burgeoning progressive education movement.

W. E. B. DuBois, scholar, educator, writer, and leading African-American voice in the late 19th and early 20th centuries. He was a cofounder of the National Association for the Advancement of Colored People (NAACP) and used his position as editor of the organization's newspaper, the *Crisis,* to advocate for increased educational opportunity for African Americans.

Dwight Eisenhower, 34th president of the United States. In 1958, Eisenhower signed the National Defense Education Act in response to Soviet advancements in technology. The act sent for the first time massive amounts of federal money to aid public education.

Desiderius Erasmus, Dutch humanist and writer who proposed the systematic training of teachers in *Upon the Method of Right Instruction.* He later advocated for the abolition of corporal punishment and advanced the necessity of understanding individual needs and abilities in education in *Of the First Liberal Education of Children.*

Sandra Feldman, president of the American Federation of Teachers since 1997 and former head of New York City's teachers' union, the largest local labor organization in the United States.

Rudolph Flesch, author of the 1955 book *Why Johnny Can't Read.* Flesch's primary contention that education professors were responsible for the diminished use of phonics in reading instruction touched off a national debate about literacy and intensified the national discussion of curriculum reform.

Milton Friedman, professor and prominent U.S. economist of the 20th century. In 1955, Friedman first proposed vouchers as an education reform.

Louis Gerstner, business executive and former chairman and CEO of IBM. Gerstner is a leading proponent of business-education relationships that seek to improve student performance and school accountability.

Jay Heubert, professor at Columbia University and a nationally recognized expert in the law of education reform. Much of Heubert's research has assessed the equity and efficiency of standardized testing as well as issues of discrimination.

E. D. Hirsch, English professor at the University of Virginia and author of the 1987 best-selling book *Cultural Literacy.* In it, Hirsch urged schools to emphasize specific knowledge of basic information and adoption of explicit curriculum to promote social justice and help increase opportunities for disadvantaged children.

John Holt, former teacher and author whose book *How Children Fail* and magazine *Growing Without Schooling* have led many to consider him the Father of Modern Homeschooling.

John Hughes, Catholic archbishop of New York City 1850–64. Hughes led protests against anti-Catholic bias in U.S. public schools and became known as the Father of Parochial Schools following his role in creating a privately funded national system of Catholic schools.

Thomas Jefferson, third president of the United States and author of the Declaration of Independence. Jefferson's opinions linking the health of a democracy to the establishment of education for common people helped provide the foundation for the early formation of the U.S. school system.

Lyndon Johnson, 36th president of the United States. During Johnson's administration upward of 60 education bills were passed, more than in any other administration. A former teacher before becoming involved in politics, Johnson explained the landmark Elementary and Secondary Education Act of 1965 by stating, "No measure I have signed, or will ever sign, means more to the future of America."

Isaac Kandel, prominent critic of the progressive education movement during the 1930s–40s. Kandel's advocacy for common, rigorous standards led to his influential support for the National Teacher Examinations.

Edward Kennedy, Democratic senator from Massachusetts since 1962 and chairman of the Senate's Committee on Health, Education, Labor, and Pensions. Kennedy led the bipartisan congressional support for President George W. Bush's 2001 No Child Left Behind Act but has sought more funding for the plan than proposed by the White House.

William Heard Kilpatrick, a key figure in the U.S. progressive education movement in the first quarter of the 20th century. Kilpatrick helped popularize and extend ideas such as project-based learning, curriculum integration, and whole child education.

Wendy Kopp, founder and director of Teach for America (TFA), a national teaching corps created to recruit, train, and place top college graduates in school districts with persistent teaching shortages. Kopp's senior thesis at Princeton University served as the model for TFA, which has been a leader in the drive for alternative certification for new teachers, as well as a target of that movement's critics.

Jonathan Kozol, author of the popular school-themed books *Death at an Early Age* (1967) and *Savage Inequalities* (1991), which reflect on the oppressive educational conditions among urban poor of the United States. Kozol remains a frequent critic of conservative school reforms.

John Locke, 17th-century English philosopher. His explanation of the value of experience and truth's relationship to objective reality helped establish a foundation for early American practical education.

Horace Mann, Father of the Common School, established America's first board of education in Massachusetts and left his position as a state senator to serve as its first secretary. Mann fought for reforms that resulted in the creation of training institutes for teachers and an increase in funding for teacher salaries, books, and school construction.

William Henry Maxwell, New York City schools superintendent in the early 20th century. His support of traditional instructional methods, including a general education curriculum and opposition to many of the progressive movement's ideas, such as vocational education and junior high schools, placed him in the minority of education leaders of the time.

Thurgood Marshall, lawyer arguing against school segregation in the landmark U.S. Supreme Court case *Brown v. Board of Education* (1954). In 1967, Marshall became the first African–American Supreme Court justice. During his 24-year tenure on the bench, he played a critical role in education reform decisions, including his strong dissent against the property tax system's impact on school financing.

Deborah Meier, founder and former principal of Central Park East School in the Harlem section of New York City and current principal of Mission Hill School in Boston. Meier's success in raising student achievement through an emphasis on active learning, parent/community involvement, and teacher autonomy has served as a model for many urban charter schools. She is a prominent opponent of the movement for standards-based reform.

Rod Paige, U.S. secretary of education since 2001. Prior to taking his role in the Bush administration, Paige served as a teacher, college dean of education, and superintendent of the Houston schools.

Plato, ancient Greek philosopher and author of *The Republic*. He expressed the belief that the state should operate an educational system with the aim to discover and develop abilities of the individual and prepare the individual for a role in society.

Quintilian, first-century A.D. Roman educator who advocated broad instruction with an emphasis on public education's advantages for socialization.

Diane Ravitch, a leading education historian and author of many books related to school reform. Ravitch was an assistant secretary of education during President George H. W. Bush's administration and is currently a senior fellow in education policy at the Brookings Institution.

William Rehnquist, chief justice of the U.S. Supreme Court since 1986. Rehnquist wrote the majority decision in the 2002 Cleveland school voucher case and has provided key support of other conservative positions on education reform issues.

Jean-Jacques Rousseau, 18th-century French philosopher and author. Rousseau's ideas about education profoundly influenced supporters of progressive education, particularly his emphasis on learning by experience over book-based, rote memorization practices.

Albert Shanker, president of the American Federation of Teachers, the nation's largest teachers' union, from 1974 until his death in 1997. He was an influential voice in favor of national standards and assessment through his frequent op-ed pieces in the Sunday edition of the *New York Times*, arguing that social promotion offered students few incentives to excel.

Charles Silberman, journalist and author of the 1970s best-selling book *Crisis in the Classroom.* Silberman's book decried the "grim, joyless" conditions in public schools and extolled the advantages of open education, which encouraged increased informality in schools and student freedom in course selection and instructional time.

Ted Sizer, education professor, author, and founder and chairman of the Coalition of Essential Schools, a national network of schools and centers engaged in restructuring and redesigning schools to promote student learning and achievement.

Adam Smith, Scottish economist and author of the 1776 book *Wealth of Nations.* Smith expressed the belief that the state should give parents money for the education of their children, providing a philosophical foundation for supporters of school vouchers.

David Snedden, early 20th-century progressive education advocate. As Massachusetts commissioner of education and later as a Teachers College professor, Snedden helped lead efforts to implement aspects of social efficiency into public high schools.

David Souter, associate justice of the U.S. Supreme Court since 1990. Souter wrote the lead dissent in the Cleveland school voucher case, expressing a deep concern for the protection of the separation of church and state.

Paul Vallas, CEO of the Philadelphia school district and former CEO of the Chicago public schools. In the mid- to late 1990s, Vallas led the effort to implement provisions of the Chicago School Reform Act, and he is often credited with helping turn around that city's struggling schools.

Booker T. Washington, founder of Tuskegee Institute in 1881 and a prominent voice for educational and economic advancement for African Americans in the late 19th and early 20th centuries. Washington supported the application of vocational education to help African Americans gain skills that would raise their status in U.S. society.

Noah Webster, early 19th-century lexicographer and advocate for widespread, systematic, and publicly supported education. Webster's books, *Grammatical Institute of the English Language* and the *Compendious Dictionary*, were enormously successful textbooks that helped define and popularize U.S. education practices.

Chris Whittle, founder and chief executive officer of Edison Schools, the United States's leading private, for-profit manager of public schools. Since its creation in 1995, Edison Schools has grown to operate more than 100 schools serving more than 70,000 students. Whittle's prominence has led to increased debate over the privatization of schools, school choice, and school financing.

Ella Flagg Young, teacher, principal, superintendent, and professor of pedagogy at the University of Chicago in the early 20th century. Flagg was the first female superintendent of schools, in Chicago 1907–15. In 1910, she became the first female president of the National Education Association.

CHAPTER 5

GLOSSARY

This chapter presents definitions of the most significant terms related to education reform and provides descriptions of their significance.

accountability   A policy that holds districts, schools, and/or students responsible for performance. School and district accountability systems generally include public reporting and apply rewards or sanctions according to performance or improvement on assessment exams over time. Student accountability typically requires students to pass a test to be promoted from grade to grade or to graduate from high school.

alternative assessment   Any form other than traditional standardized tests of measuring what students know and are able to do. Popular types include portfolios and performance-based assessments.

alternative certification   The effort to expand entries into the teaching profession beyond the traditional path of taking pedagogy courses before entering the classroom. Programs require a bachelor's degree and a demonstration of knowledge in the subject area but allow intensive or compressed training while practice teaching or teaching students.

alternative school   A public school that is set up by a state or school district to serve populations of students who are not succeeding in the traditional public school environment. While there are many different kinds of alternative schools, they are often characterized by their flexible schedules, smaller teacher-student ratios, and modified curricula.

assessment   An exercise, such as a standardized exam, written test, portfolio, or experiment, that seeks to measure a student's knowledge or skills in a subject area.

at risk   Term used to describe a student facing socioeconomic challenges, such as high poverty or teen pregnancy rates and exposure to violence, that may place him or her at a greater risk of failing, dropping out, or not achieving academic, social, and career goals.

Glossary

bilingual education An instructional program for students whose native language is not English in which students are taught for some portion of the day in their native language to allow them to keep up academically while they learn English.

Blaine amendments Provisions of state constitutions restricting government aid to religious schools beyond those noted in the U.S. Constitution. They are named for late 19th-century Speaker of the House and proponent James Blaine and they are currently a key focus of legal challenge by advocates of school vouchers.

business-education partnership A school-reform coalition formed by private businesses and schools or school districts. Such partnerships include resource support for individual schools, the introduction of management principles into public schools, and often advocacy of school choice and performance standards reforms.

character education A national movement advocating specific instruction in basic virtues or morals as a means of combating concerns about the values and behavior of students.

charter school A school that receives public funding but is run independently of the traditional public school system. Charter schools are often organized and established by groups made up of teachers, parents, or foundations, are free of many district regulations, and are often tailored to community needs.

Chicago School Reform Act Sweeping legislation passed by the Illinois legislature in 1993 (with amendments in 1995) that includes a wide range of measures to improve public school performance, including **reconstitution, local control,** and opposition to **social promotion.**

child-centered curriculum Pedagogical approach designed with the child's interests and needs at the center of the learning process, with an emphasis on experiential and problem-solving activities. Popular among educational progressives, it is also known as student-centered curriculum.

class-size reduction initiatives A series of measures designed to improve the quality of classroom instruction by allowing teachers to focus on fewer students. The broad popularity of such laws has recently been undercut by concerns over cost and teacher availability.

Commission of the Reorganization of Secondary Education (CRSE) A 1918 group composed mainly of professors of education that redefined curricula in high schools to reflect notions of social efficiency, including providing different curricula for different groups of students based on their interests and likely future occupation. The CRSE's published plan, which shaped comprehensive high school instructional practice, was lauded by progressives for its inclusive nature and criticized by others for its lack of academic rigor.

Committee of Ten A panel dominated by college presidents that published a report in 1893 expressing the belief that every high school student should have a solid liberal education regardless of the student's ultimate occupation. The committee's findings were very influential in shaping the academically oriented nature of secondary education through the early 1900s.

common school A publicly supported school started during the mid-1800s that was open to all students.

compensatory education Programs established to overcome the academic deficiencies associated with the socioeconomic, cultural, or minority group disadvantages of students.

core curriculum A curriculum that stresses the required minimum subjects and topics that all students are expected to learn.

criterion-referenced test A standardized test that is aligned with a state's academic standards and intended primarily to measure students' performance related to those standards rather than to the performance of their peers nationally.

dame school Colonial and early national period low-level primary school usually conducted by an untrained woman in her own home. Instructors taught only basic fundamentals for which they were paid small fees.

decentralization The breakup and distribution of power from a central governing authority, most frequently applied in education to describe the transfer of school policymaking authority from the federal to the state level, or the transfer of decision-making authority from the state level to districts or schools (*see also* **local control**).

desegregation The reduction of racial isolation in schools and improvement of racial balance by eliminating the separation of groups of people along racial lines.

dress code School or district policy that requires school uniforms or restrictions on the color and type of clothing allowed in school in an effort to curb the presence of gangs and to reduce disciplinary conflicts.

drug-free and gun-free school zone An area around a school in which people caught or convicted of possession or use of illegal drugs or guns are subject to increased penalties under the law.

Edison Schools The United States's largest private manager of public schools. Founded in 1992 as the Edison Project by Christopher Whittle, Edison has implemented its school design in 150 public schools, including many charter schools, operating under management contracts with local school districts and charter boards.

educational management organization (EMO) A company that provides curriculum, facility, financial, special education, technological, and other services to schools. Most EMOs are privately run and contract with charter schools.

Eight-Year Study   An evaluation undertaken by progressive educators in the 1930s designed to demonstrate that students educated according to progressive philosophies were capable, adaptable learners who could excel even in postsecondary settings.

Elementary and Secondary Education Act (ESEA)   Legislation of 1965 representing the federal government's single largest investment in elementary and secondary education. The ESEA focuses on children from high-poverty communities and students at risk of educational failure and authorizes several well-known federal education programs including Title I, Safe and Drug-Free Schools, and Bilingual Education.

English-only movement   Advocates English as the official and only language used in the United States. Proponents generally view bilingual education as detrimental to the social mobility and economic advancement of immigrants.

Establishment Clause   The constitution's First Amendment prohibition against government regulation or endorsement of religion. This has been a common battleground in education as groups argue over the meaning of the U.S. Supreme Court's requirement that public school students never be given the impression that their school officially sanctions religion in general or prefers a specific faith in particular.

experiential education   Curriculum and instruction that stresses hands-on experience through such activities as field trips, internships, and service learning projects as opposed to traditional classroom learning.

Florida A+ Plan   An education reform law passed in 1999 that includes the United State's first statewide voucher program allowing public funds to be used at private and religious schools, provisions for special education vouchers, and corporate tax incentives to support vouchers. The law has survived legal challenges, though appeals are pending.

GOALS 2000: Educate America Act   A federal program signed by President Bill Clinton in 1994 that provides grants to states and school districts in exchange for the establishment of challenging academic content standards and accompanying assessments.

Head Start   A federal program established in 1965 that provides economically deprived preschoolers with education, nutrition, health, and social services at special centers based in schools and community settings throughout the country.

high stakes testing   Assessments, typically standardized exams, that carry serious consequences for students or for educators. Schools gain public praise or financial rewards for high scores, and low scores may bring public embarrassment or heavy sanctions. For individual students, high scores may bring recognition of exceptional academic accomplishment and low scores may result in students being held back a grade or denied a high school diploma.

homeschooling   The educating of a student at home instead of in a public or private school setting. Legal in all 50 states, with regulations, the movement grew in the 1990s following parents' dissatisfaction with the quality of curricula, moral instruction, and school safety.

inclusion   The practice of educating children with disabilities alongside their nondisabled peers, often in a regular education classroom. Inclusion has become more prominent since the 1975 passage of the Individuals with Disabilities Education Act (IDEA) and subsequent amendments.

Kalamazoo School Case   An 1874 legal decision by the Michigan Supreme Court that supported public financial support for high schools in Michigan, influencing similar decisions and legislation across the United States.

in-service training   The lectures and workshops (often referred to as professional development) designed to keep teachers informed of the latest developments in their field. The training is called "in-service" to distinguish it from "pre-service" training, which means undergraduate coursework taken by those intending to teach.

local control   District or school flexibility and decision-making authority in the use of federal education funds for the unique needs of that community's students.

magnet school   A school that places special emphasis on academic achievement or on a particular field such as science, math, or performance arts. Such schools are designed to attract students from any part of a school district.

Massachusetts Act of 1642 and Massachusetts Law of 1647   Laws that established government influence on education. The 1642 law stated that parents and masters of those children apprenticed to them were responsible for their basic education and literacy. The 1647 law required the establishment of elementary schools in all towns of 50 or more families and the establishment of secondary schools in towns of more than 100 families.

merit pay   A plan to pay teachers on the basis of their demonstrated competence in teaching and academic achievement of their students. Difficulty in objectively identifying good teaching and concern about how such a plan would be fairly administered have slowed its progress.

Milwaukee Parental Choice Program   The first voucher legislation in the United States, passed in 1990, that allows students to attend private, nonreligious schools at taxpayer expense. The program originally allowed up to 1 percent of economically disadvantaged pupils in the Milwaukee,

Wisconsin, public schools to use their state share of education funds as full payment of tuition in participating private schools.

multicultural education   A curriculum that seeks to highlight subjects from diverse cultural, ethnic, racial, and gender perspectives beyond the traditional white, western European tradition.

National Assessment of Educational Progress (NAEP)   Known as "the nation's report card," the NAEP is a national testing program administered by the U.S. Department of Education. Since 1969, NAEP tests have been conducted periodically in reading, math, science, writing, history, and geography and have provided comparable data over time on the achievement of fifth, eighth, and 10th graders across the nation.

National Defense Education Act   Legislation of 1958 from the Eisenhower administration that responded to the fear of Soviet technological gains with a major federal influx of money for school construction, improved math and science curricula, and calls for higher academic standards.

A Nation at Risk   This 1983 Reagan administration report has played a key role in initiating education reform efforts over the last 20 years. It warned that U.S. schools were lagging dangerously behind changes in society and the economy and that lax academic and behavioral standards needed to be dramatically improved.

No Child Left Behind Act   The reauthorization in 2001 of the **Elementary and Secondary Education Act** signed by President George W. Bush. The act contains many education reform–related measures reflecting an emphasis on **accountability,** state flexibility and **local control,** public school choice, and teaching methods.

norm-referenced test   A standardized test designed primarily to compare the performance of students with that of their peers nationally. Such tests do not generally measure how students perform in relation to a state's own academic standards.

Ohio Pilot Project Scholarship Program (Cleveland voucher program)   A law adopted in 1995 that provides school vouchers for public school students to attend private and religious schools and to receive tutorial aid for students who chose to remain in public school. Legal challenges to the program led to the U.S. Supreme Court's 2002 decision *Zelman v. Simmons-Harris* that upheld the legality of the program.

open education   A popular movement in the late 1960s and 1970s that emphasized student initiative to pursue their own interests in learning, teachers as facilitators rather than transmitters of knowledge, and large learning environments without walls. The movement faded, but its effects remained including increased course electives and reductions in graduation requirements.

outcome-based education An education theory that guides curriculum by setting goals for students to accomplish rather than mastering subject content.

parochial school A school that is affiliated with a religious denomination, most commonly associated with Roman Catholicism.

pay equity The common form of teacher compensation that pays teachers based on a single-salary schedule according to how many years they have been teaching and how many educational credits or degrees they have accumulated.

private scholarship program A funding source from foundations or individuals intended to provide low-income families with money to pursue educational opportunities. Such programs are popular among supporters of school choice.

privatization The transfer of the management of public schools of private or for-profit education organizations that emphasize common business-oriented concepts such as cost-effectiveness and customer satisfaction in running schools.

progressive education movement An influential period in the history of U.S. schools that sought to make schools an instrument of social reform by focusing on instruction becoming more practical and centered on the interests of students. Supporters also increased the professionalization of teaching and school administration. It grew in prominence in the late 19th century and the first half of the 20th century largely due to the leadership of philosopher and professor John Dewey.

reconstitution School accountability measure in which a governing authority can disband a low-performing school's faculty following an intervention process and reopen the building with a new staff, structure, and curriculum.

school-based management A form of decentralization, also known as site-based management, in which decision-making authority shifts from school districts to individual schools. Such proposals usually give control of a school's operation to a school council composed of parents, teachers, and local administrators.

school choice A broad term that refers to proposals that allow students to attend schools outside their local district boundaries, with public funding for all or some of the tuition costs. The controversy over school choice largely revolves around the concern with using public funds for private or parochial schools.

school financing A term broadly used to describe the mechanisms that fund the construction and maintenance of schools as well as the expenses associated with personnel, instruction, and student services. Typically, local property taxes make up the most significant portion of school financing, leading many to argue for a more equitable system.

Glossary

school reform   The variety of efforts to improve schools. Reform encompasses issues of curriculum, instruction, financing, governance, discipline, and other factors in education.

school survey movement   The period between 1911 and 1930 in which nearly 200 cities and states were surveyed by experts from the major schools of education to determine school efficiency. The findings usually included recommendations for more curricular differentiation, increased intelligence testing to properly place students in programs, new vocational programs, and more power to administrators.

separation of church and state   *See* **Establishment Clause.**

service learning   Programs that incorporate citizenship values into education by requiring students to perform community service, which in some districts is a mandatory requirement for graduation.

Smith-Hughes Act   A 1917 act passed by the U.S. Congress that established federal aid for vocational education. It was the first federal program of any kind for public education.

social efficiency   The popular early 20th century progressive education movement that emphasized curriculum and instruction that served purposes outside the classroom. Many supporters of this movement believed that many academic subjects, or at least the traditional approaches to them, lacked relevance for the great majority of students.

social promotion   The practice of schools and districts allowing students to proceed to the next grade, even if they are not performing at grade level. Opposition to this grew with the popularity rise in the standards movement.

special education   Programs designed to serve children with mental and physical disabilities. Special education students are entitled to individualized education plans that detail the services needed to reach their educational goals. Traditionally, special education has taken place in separate classrooms, though increasingly, the services may also be offered in regular schools and classrooms (*see* **inclusion**).

standardized curriculum   Instructional content that specifies in detail the carefully selected topics that will be covered in every subject area at every grade level at the school, district, state, or national level. Strict adherence to such curricula suggests that teachers should not have the option of disregarding or replacing that content.

standards   Subject-matter benchmarks that measure students' academic achievement. Although most agree that public schools' academic standards need to be raised, there is national debate over the construction and content of such standards and whether they should be national or local, voluntary or mandated.

state board of education   A state agency charged with adopting regulations and monitoring local school districts to ensure implementation of the constitutional and statutory mandates related to the operation of the state system of schools.

Teachers College   The leading education institution in the nation during the progressive education movement. Located at Columbia University in New York City, its professors and graduates have been among the most influential voices in school reform since its founding in 1887.

Title I   Also known as Chapter I, this is the nation's largest federal education program, with a 1995 funding level of $7.2 billion. Created in 1965 as part of President Lyndon Johnson's War on Poverty, Title I of the **Elementary and Secondary Education Act** serves remedial education programs to poor and disadvantaged children in nearly every school district in the country. Amendments to the law in 1994 have linked the program to schoolwide and districtwide reforms based on academic standards.

tuition tax credits   A mechanism that refunds expenses made toward education, including tutoring, texts, and computers, and, in the states that have them so far, private school tuition, up to a fixed figure. State legislation determines the amount of credit and what can be included in the deductions.

vocational education   Instruction that prepares a student for employment immediately after the completion of high school. Traditionally, the curriculum has focused on manufacturing industries, though recently it has expanded to include computer-related fields.

voucher   A document that can be used by parents to pay tuition at an out-of-district public school, a private school, and/or a religious school. The term is also used to describe school choice proposals in which states would help pay tuition for children attending private or religious schools (*see* **school choice**).

year-round education   A modified school calendar that offers short breaks throughout the year, rather than the traditional summer vacation. Reasons for switching to a year-round schedule include to relieve crowding and to prevent students from forgetting much of the material covered in the previous year.

zero tolerance   School discipline policies that specify mandatory and strict punishment for breaking rules, usually relating to guns, drugs, or violence. These policies are designed to serve as a deterrent and protect the school population, but critics suggest they are often illogically applied.

PART II

GUIDE TO FURTHER RESEARCH

CHAPTER 6

HOW TO RESEARCH EDUCATION REFORM ISSUES

The explosive growth of the Internet, particularly the World Wide Web, has allowed students, teachers, and advocates of education reform to gain research access to relevant and specific information more efficiently than ever before. Despite the Internet's expansive reach, good old-fashioned library research remains an essential component to finding information on education reform. This chapter explains what is available to the education reform researcher via the Internet, bibliographical resources, and in the area of legal research. It also describes strategies for their effective use.

ONLINE RESOURCES

The ability to explore the vast expanse of information found on the Internet is a critical skill needed to conduct efficient research projects. The Internet provides a kind of library that never closes and can serve as an excellent starting point for education reform researchers, particularly those seeking the most recent articles and developments. Understanding how to navigate online can help the researcher find the information he or she is seeking and lead to many other useful web sites that contain even more relevant information.

APPROACHING THE WEB

Whether one is an experienced computer user or new to this style of research, searching for information online can be an exhilarating and exasperating experience. In order to avoid the frustrations that can accompany online searching, a few approaches are helpful. First, understand that the specific research being sought may be found quickly or may be uncovered only after investigating other usually related and often interesting links. With discipline and focus, the initial search will usually prove fruitful, if longer than anticipated, and may very well yield additional rewarding information.

During the course of Web searching, one can easily get distracted and lose track of a particularly useful site previously encountered. In these situations, there are two critical online allies that can help lead the researcher back to the intended site. The "Back" button directly retraces all the sites previously viewed all the way to the beginning of the search, allowing the researcher to view any of the sites along the way. The "History" button provides a similar function. It allows the researcher to review all of the sites previously viewed and can track these by order visited on that particular day, the previous day, the previous week, and even as far back as many weeks prior to the current search.

Added to this celebration of the Internet's use for education reform researchers is an important caveat: Some material posted on web sites may be inaccurate or unreliable. In conducting research, one will likely encounter sites created by credible and well-known individuals and groups as well as those created by unknown origin. The material on such sites may be valuable but should be checked scrupulously. Exposure to the variety of web sites will allow the researcher to sharpen his or her instincts regarding the quality of information presented, and it will also help the researcher to properly interpret and use it.

RESEARCH ORGANIZATIONAL TOOLS

The greatest benefit of conducting online research, access to the volume of diverse information, can also be its greatest pitfall. Strategies and tools to keep this research organized are critical.

A web browser's "Favorites" menu (sometimes called "Bookmarks") allows the education reform researcher to create a folder (and subfolders) for key topics. A web browser also provides the user with the option of creating links that can be organized in a conspicuous space on the user's computer screen, allowing even quicker access to commonly viewed sites.

Utilizing the Favorites or Bookmarks links is often more efficient than downloading a copy of an entire web page or web site because of the large amount of disk space that downloading requires. One may wish to download an entire site or page to guard against the unlikely event that it will disappear from the Web. To archive the entire site, a program such as Web Whacker is helpful but, again, can use up a large chunk of the computer's memory.

Another online method allowing researchers to stay informed of recent information is to subscribe to web sites. This usually does not involve any monetary transaction but rather simply requires providing contact information. The person or group administering the web site can then send notifications of important information.

WEB DIRECTORIES AND SEARCH ENGINES

The potentially daunting task of searching for information on the Web is made manageable thanks to web directories and search engines. A web directory is similar to a library's subject catalog. Web directories attempt to organize the seemingly limitless amount of information on the Web into topics and subtopics, such as News, Health, Business, Entertainment, Sports, and Education. A leading web directory is Yahoo! (http://www.yahoo.com). This is an excellent site to start a search if one has a good sense of how to find the intended subjects within a hierarchy of larger subjects.

For instance, the education reform researcher can go to Yahoo! and find the topic heading Education. A click on the Education link leads to multiple categories including Reform. Clicking "Reform" leads the researcher to more category links including Books, Organizations, and School Choice, as well as a direct link to many of the most popular sites about education reform on the World Wide Web.

This top-down organization of Web content allows the researcher to search for a particular subject while simultaneously reviewing other related issues and links. In addition, Yahoo! employs indexers who evaluate sites for quality, which for many raises confidence that the information retrieved is accurate.

In addition to Yahoo!, other top web directories include

- About.com (http://www.about.com)
- Open Directory Project (http://www.dmoz.org)

A search engine, like a library's card catalog, serves as an index enabling the researcher to seek out specific words or phrases. With the assistance of a search engine, one can locate individual appearances of such words in all documents throughout the Web, allowing the researcher to scan quickly the millions of sites and billions of words on the Web for the precise information desired.

Search engines use software programs known as robots, spiders, or crawlers that automatically follow hyperlinks from one document to the next. Because documents change so regularly, these robots also update previously cataloged sites. How quickly and comprehensively search engines carry out these tasks varies.

Directions for using search engines are usually straightforward and reliant on the use of keywords. Those wishing for more specific instruction may investigate the many Web tutorials available online. To find one, simply type in "Web search tutorial" into the keyword section of any of the search engines listed at the conclusion of this section.

Following are some tips for the effective use of search engines:

- When searching for a broad topic, simply enter keywords that are as descriptive as possible (for example, "zero tolerance policies in schools"). Most search engines will then return a list of web sites that match those terms.

- To narrow a search, use "AND" in the keyword box. For example, "charter schools AND Michigan" will match only links that include both terms.

- To broaden a search, use "OR" in the keyword listing. For example, "bilingual programs OR limited English proficiency" will match any page that has either term.

- To exclude unwanted results use "NOT" as part of the keyword instruction. For example, "school voucher cases NOT Zelman" finds sites that include information about school voucher cases but not the *Zelman v. Simmons-Harris* case.

Recently, many search engines have built large subject catalogs, minimizing the difference between them and web directories. There are scores of commonly used search engines, but among the most popular and efficient are

Alta Vista (http://www.altavista.com)
Excite (http://www.excite.com)
FAST (http://www.alltheweb.com)
Google (http://www.google.com)
HotBot (http://www.hotbot.com)
Lycos (http://www.lycos.com)
WebCrawler (http://www.webcrawler.com)

Because search engines and web directories have different orientations and strengths, one may wish to use a metasearch site, which automatically processes the query to multiple search engines. Among the top metasearch sites are

AskJeeves (http://www.ask.com)
Dogpile (http://www.dogpile.com)
Metacrawler (http://www.metacrawler.com)
Search (http://www.search.com)

EDUCATION REFORM SITES

While web directories and search engines will lead the education reform researcher to useful sites, there are many sites that are particularly helpful because of their thorough organization, detailed information, and numerous links to other resources.

Among these especially content-rich sites are the following:

- The Education Resources Information Center (ERIC) (http://www.askeric.org) is a personalized Internet-based service providing education information through 16 subject-specific clearinghouses, including assessment and evaluation and teacher education. This site also includes a link to the ERIC database, the world's largest source of education information, with more than 1 million abstracts of documents and journal articles on education research and practice.

- Yahoo! has an Education Curriculum and Policy page (http://news.yahoo.com/fc?tmp1=fc&in=us&cat=education_curriculum_and_policy) that includes daily updates of news stories about education, links to education news sources including *Time* and the *Washington Post,* and links to opinion and editorial pieces relating to education reform.

- The Center for Education Reform (http://www.cer.org) offers thorough sets of links relating to issues, analysis, and resources of education reform. This advocacy organization is a strong supporter of school vouchers and charter schools.

- The American Federation of Teachers web site (http://www.aft.org) features positions of the nation's largest teachers' union on many of the key education reform issues. The site also includes archives of more than 1,000 articles from the organization's Where We Stand series.

- *Education Week's* web site (http://edweek.com) offers links to current and archived articles, daily news, special reports, and a Hot Topics section featuring a wealth of information on education reform issues, including accountability, charter schools, homeschooling, school finance, standards, violence and safety, and vouchers.

- The North Central Regional Educational Laboratory, a provider of research-based expertise for educators and policymakers, has a site (http://www.ncrel.org) that includes links to policy issues and sources of research with guidelines for its interpretation and application.

- The U.S. Department of Education's web site (http://www.ed.gov) provides an extensive range of links related to the federal role in public education, including policy and research statistics. It also includes links to the complete text of key federal education legislation.

FINDING ORGANIZATIONS AND INDIVIDUALS

The education reform sites listed and the myriad others that exist on the Web may lead the researcher to seek more information about particular groups or people. The simplest method to finding this additional information is to enter the group's or person's name into a search engine's keyword space. This should lead to web sites and possibly contact information.

Guessing what an organization's web address is, though seemingly a short-cut, can often take longer than working through a search engine. For example, one might think that Teach For America's address would be http://www.tfa.org, but it is actually http://www.teachforamerica.org. Conversely, the Committee for Education Funding uses an acronym for its site, http://www.cef.org.

Finally, it is important to note the suffix that is used for particular sites. In general, most advocacy groups use the suffix ".org," government sites employ ".gov," educational institutions use ".edu," and commercial and many personal sites use ".com."

BIBLIOGRAPHIC RESOURCES

Any printed resource that identifies and lists books, periodical articles, and other published works that deal with education reform can also be an enormously useful tool in conducting research. Among these resources are library catalogs, bookstore catalogs, and periodical databases.

LIBRARY CATALOGS

The ubiquitous card catalogs of yesteryear's public and academic libraries have largely been replaced or complemented by online catalogs that often allow researchers remote access via the Internet.

The Library of Congress has the largest library catalog, and online access to it is available (http://catalog.loc.gov/). A subject search at this site for "education reform" leads to a notation that the Library of Congress uses the term *educational change* for "works on alterations in the scope of the total educational endeavor, including modification of curricula, teaching methods, enrollment patterns, etc."

Once the record for a book or other item is found, the education reform researcher may wish to investigate what other subject headings are assigned to it, as these headings may be useful in future research. In the case of "educational change," the heading is subdivided by place (United States, an individual state, a foreign nation) and then organized into many important sublistings, including

- academic achievement
- accountability
- bibliography

- case studies
- citizen participation
- Congress
- evaluation
- finance
- history
- periodicals
- statistics

In addition to the Library of Congress's online library catalog, most public and academic libraries now offer online access, which in many cases, allows the researcher to check an institution's holdings from any computer with Internet capability. Directions for using the online catalogs at local, school, and university libraries are usually similar to those noted for the Library of Congress.

BOOKSTORE CATALOGS

The impact of the Internet on research is also evident in another bibliographic resource: the bookstore catalog. A growing number of bookstores, such as Borders and Barnes and Noble, have rich online catalogs (http://www.borders.com and http://www.bn.com). The prominent bookseller Amazon provides only an online catalog, although it is the world's largest (http://www.amazon.com).

Many researchers find these online bookstore catalogs attractive because of their ease of use and their inclusion of publisher's information, available excerpts, book reviews, and readers' commentary about a particular book. Although the education reform researcher can find great benefits in exploring the online bookstores, visiting "brick-and-mortar" bookstores and personally holding and reviewing a book remains a valuable experience.

PERIODICAL DATABASES

Database services such as Info Trac are commonly found in most public libraries. Such subscription-based services index articles from hundreds of general interest and some specialized periodicals. The database can be searched by author, words in the title, subject headings, and occasionally words found anywhere in the text. Depending on the database used, "hits" can result in a bibliographical description (featuring author's name, title, pages, periodical name, issue date, etc.), a description plus an abstract (a paragraph summarizing the contents of the article), or the full text of an article.

Many libraries also provide dial-in, Internet, or telnet access to their periodical databases as an option in their catalog menu. Licensing restrictions, however, usually mean that only researchers who have a library card for that particular library can access the database. In such cases, the researcher need only type in his or her name and card number.

Another avenue that may lead to useful database information is to find the web sites for periodicals likely to cover the topic of interest. Some scholarly publications put all or most of their articles online, while the more popular publications tend to offer a more limited selection. Some publications of both types offer archives of several years' back issues that can be searched by author or keyword.

LEGAL RESEARCH

Education reform issues continue to occupy an increasingly prominent place in public debate. This focus has led to a growing body of legislation and court cases. Because legal research is so often heavy with specialized terminology, it can be more difficult to conduct than bibliographical or general research.

Again, the Internet has provided a variety of helpful tools to combat this potential research roadblock. The Internet offers a variety of ways to look up local laws and court cases without having to delve into the often intimidating bound volumes in law libraries, which may not be accessible to the general public.

FINDING LAWS

When federal legislation is approved, it becomes part of a massive legal compendium known as United States Code. Laws in the U.S. Code can be referred to either by their popular name or by a formal citation. The U.S. Code can be searched online (http://uscode.house.gov/) and via Cornell Law School's web site (http://www4.law.cornell.edu/uscode/).

Many states also have their codes of law online. The Internet Law Library provides a link to state laws that can be accessed (http://www.lect.law.com/inll/1.htm). Cornell Law School's web site also provides links to this information (http://www.law.cornell.edu/state/index.html).

TRACKING LEGISLATION

Congress and state legislatures regularly debate education reform–related bills. The Library of Congress's catalog site includes files that summarize legislation by the number of the congressional session (every two-year session of Congress is designated a consecutive number; for example, the 107th

Congress was in session in 2001–2). Legislation can be searched for at this site by the name of its sponsor, the bill number, or by keywords.

The Library of Congress's THOMAS site (http://thomas.loc.gov/) provides a clearer and easier resource for keeping up with legislative developments. At THOMAS, the education reform researcher can search for summaries of legislation considered by each Congress by name, bill number, or keyword. For example, the No Child Left Behind Act can be found by its name or under its bill number, H.R. 1. If one has heard about a bill increasing parental choice in where a child attends school but does not know the bill's number, a keyword search for "school choice" may produce useful listings. Clicking on the bill number of a particular listing leads to a screen with links to a summary, legislation text, current status, floor actions, and other related information.

FINDING COURT DECISIONS

Legal decisions are also organized using a system of citations. The general form for citation is *Party 1 v. Party 2, volume and court reporter (year)*. An example of this is *Zelman v. Simmons-Harris*, 200 U.S. 321 (2002). Here the parties are Zelman (plaintiff) and Simmons-Harris (defendant), the case is in volume 200 of the U.S. Supreme Court Reports, beginning on page 321, and with the case was decided in 2002. (For the Supreme Court, the name of the court may be omitted, though it would be included for other cases.)

Finding federal court decisions involves determining the level of the court involved: District courts are the lowest level and are where trials are normally held, circuit courts are the main courts of appeals, and the Supreme Court is the nation's highest court. Once this is ascertained the education reform researcher can visit sites on the Web to find cases by citation and often the names of the parties. Among the most useful sites for locating court decisions are

- The **Legal Information Institute** web site (http://supct.law.cornell.edu/supct/), which features all Supreme Court decisions since 1990 as well as more than 600 other influential, earlier decisions. It also provides links to other databases with early court decisions.
- The **Washburn University School of Law** web site (http://www.washlaw.edu), which provides links to a variety of court decisions, including those from state courts, and includes information about many important topics in legal research.

More information about conducting legal research online can be gained by visiting a reliable search engine and typing "conducting legal research online tutorial" into the keyword bar and then visiting the selected sites listed.

141

CHAPTER 7

ANNOTATED BIBLIOGRAPHY

This chapter provides bibliographic information and brief content descriptions of books, periodicals articles, Internet articles, and other media relating to education reform issues. This bibliography lists a representative sample of sources, primarily those published since 1999. It also includes some earlier materials that have particular historical relevance. Listings are categorized as books, periodicals (including magazines, newspapers, and journals), Internet articles (some of which also appear in print), and other media (including videos and web casts). Sources have been selected to present clear and useful research from a variety of viewpoints.

BOOKS

Apple, Michael W. *Educating the "Right" Way: Markets, Standards, God, and Inequality.* New York: RoutledgeFalmer, 2001. Explores what the author calls the "conservative restoration" that has been successful in influencing U.S. education policy and seeks pragmatic approaches to build alternative coalitions that are more democratic.

Armacost, Michael H., and Gary Burtless, eds. *Does Money Matter? The Effect of School Resources on Student Achievement and Adult Success (Brookings Dialogues on Public Policy).* Washington, D.C.: Brookings Institute, 1996. Presents essays and numerous tables on performance-based incentive programs, school choice, and allocation of funds, from leaders in economics, educational policy, and political science.

Armacost, Michael H., and Helen F. Ladd, eds. *Holding Schools Accountable: Performance-Based Reform in Education.* Washington, D.C.: Brookings Institute, 1996. Offers options for policymakers to ensure school accountability for improved academic achievement.

Ayers, William, ed. *Zero Tolerance: Resisting the Drive for Punishment.* New York: New Press, 2001. Criticizes the implementation of zero-tolerance policies in schools, claiming they are ineffective, racially biased, and constitutionally unsound.

Barth, Roland Sawyer. *Improving Schools from Within: Teachers, Parents, and Principals Can Make the Difference.* New York: Jossey-Bass, 1991. Concentrates on the role of the principal in bringing about education reform, stressing the job's importance in creating an active community of teacher leaders.

————. *Open Education and the American School.* New York: Schocken Books, 1974. Analyzes the initial growth and subsequent difficulties of the open education movement in the early 1970s.

Bell, James, Bruce J. Biddle, and David C. Berliner. *The Manufactured Crisis: Myths, Fraud, and the Attack on America's Public Schools.* Cambridge, Mass.: Perseus Publishing, 1996. Debunks statistics about public schools and proves that SAT scores are rising for many groups, investments in education pay off in greater student achievements and earnings, and many private schools are not better than public schools.

Bennett, William. *The Book of Virtues: A Treasury of Great Moral Stories.* New York: Simon & Schuster, 1993. Supports character instruction in schools through stories and poems relating to such moral themes as compassion, responsibility, courage, and faith.

Bensman, David. *Central Park East and Its Graduates: Learning by Heart.* New York: Teachers College Press, 2000. Applauds the approach and success of Harlem's Central Park East Elementary School, renowned for its bottom-up reforms.

Berube, Maurice R. *American School Reform: Progressive, Equity, and Excellence Movements, 1883–1993.* Westport, Conn.: Praeger Publishing, 1995. Analyzes three great education reform movements in U.S. history and describes their evolution, relationships, and common characteristics.

Bestor, Arthur. *Educational Wastelands: The Retreat from Learning in Our Public Schools.* Reprint, Champaign: University of Illinois Press, 1988. Criticizes progressive education's anti-intellectual effect on schools and advocates for a rigorous and well-defined curriculum. This influential book was first published in 1953.

Betts, Julian R., Anne Darenberg, and Kim S. Rueben. *Equal Resources, Equal Outcomes: The Distribution of School Resources and Student Achievement in California.* San Francisco: Public Policy Institute of California, 2000. Examines the effects that centralizing funding of California's public schools has had on resource allocation and student achievement, taking into account students' socioeconomic status and school location.

Bonilla, Carlos A., Alan Bonsteel, John E. Coons, and Milton Friedman. *A Choice for Our Children: Curing the Crisis in America's Schools.* Oakland, Calif.: Institute for Contemporary Studies, 1997. Criticizes the role government has played in public education and advocates for increased power for parents.

Bracey, Gerald W. *The War Against America's Public Schools: Privatizing Schools, Commercializing Education.* Boston: Allyn & Bacon, 2001. Criticizes individuals and organizations that have promoted politically conservative and market approaches to school reform.

Bracey, Gerald W., Denise Bradby, and Karen Levesque. *At Your Fingertips: Using Everyday Data to Improve Schools.* Washington, D.C.: MPR Associates, 1998. Offers tips for collecting, organizing, analyzing, and disseminating data for school leaders addressing such accountability issues as instruction and student achievement.

Braden, Jennifer S., and Thomas L. Good. *The Great School Debate: Choice, Vouchers, and Charters.* Mahwah, N.J.: Lawrence Erlbaum Associates, 2000. Examines education reform over the past 50 years and states that voucher plans and charter schools have yet to fulfill the expectations of their advocates.

Busch, Carolyn, and Allan Odden. *Financing Schools for High Performance: Strategies for Improving the Use of Educational Resources.* New York: Jossey-Bass, 1998. Examines methods of ensuring effectiveness of public schools in various socioeconomic areas through changes in funding procedures.

Caldwell, Brian, and Don Hayward. *The Future of Schools: Lessons from the Reform of Public Education.* New York: Routledge Falmer, 1997. Charts the move from dependence on a highly centralized and bureaucratized structure to one that values local decision making and the creation of a system of self-managing schools.

Campbell, Christine, James Harvey, Paul Herdman, and Paul T. Hill. *It Takes a City: Getting Serious About Urban School Reform.* Washington, D.C.: Brookings Institute, 2000. Profiles six major urban school systems to show the importance of mayors, civic leaders, and school board members in implementation of school reform.

Carini, Patricia F., and Joseph Featherstone. *Starting Strong: A Different Look at Children, Schools, and Standards.* New York: Teachers College Press, 2001. Counters critics of public schools and proponents of high stakes testing by describing the learning capacity of young students.

Carter, Samuel Casey. *No Excuses: Lessons from 21 High-Performing, High Poverty Schools.* Washington, D.C.: Heritage Foundation, 2000. Examines the common practices of principals in low-income schools who have had success in the struggle to improve academic achievement.

Casella, Ronnie. *At Zero Tolerance: Punishment, Prevention, and School Violence.* New York: Peter Lang Publishing, 2001. Argues against the proliferation of "get-tough" policies in schools and offers methods of violence prevention including school restructuring and vocational education.

Celio, Mary Beth, and Paul Thomas Hill. *Fixing Urban Schools.* Washington, D.C.: Brookings Institute, 1998. Identifies key elements of education reform strategies that can improve school performance in big cities beset by poverty, social instability, and racial isolation.

Center for Education Reform. *National Charter School Directory.* 7th ed. Washington, D.C.: Center for Education Reform, 2002. Provides comprehensive listing of charter schools including school addresses, telephone numbers, contact names, enrollment figures, grades served, date opened, and a brief synopsis of each school's philosophy and educational mission.

Chalk, Rosemary, Helen F. Ladd, and Janet Hansen, eds. *Equity and Adequacy in Education Finance: Issues and Perspectives.* Washington, D.C.: National Academy Press, 1999. Focuses on impact of court decisions and politics on reforming school finance systems in a collection of eight papers.

Chubb, John E., and Terry M. Moe. *Politics, Markets and America's Schools.* Washington, D.C.: Brookings Institute, 1990. Recommends a new system of public education, built around parent-teacher choice and school competition, that would promote school autonomy and academic achievement.

Codding, Judy B., and Marc S. Tucker. *Standards for Our Schools: How to Set Them, Measure Them, and Reach Them.* New York: Jossey-Bass, 1998. Proposes "internationally benchmarked certificate standard that students could pass at any age that they are capable" as a means of ensuring excellence in education.

Cohen, David K., and Heather C. Hill. *Learning Policy: When State Education Reform Works.* New Haven, Conn.: Yale University Press, 2001. Argues that effective state reform depends on conditions that most reforms ignore: coherence in practice as well as policy and opportunities for professional learning.

Cole, Ardra L., ed. *The Heart of the Matter: Teacher Educators and Teacher Education Reform.* San Francisco: Caddo Gap Press, 1998. Focuses on the important role played by those who train teachers and includes a collection of responses from university administrators.

Conant, James. *The American High School Today: A First Report to Interested Citizens.* New York: McGraw-Hill, 1959. Recommends replacing small high schools with larger, comprehensive schools offering broader services and rejects calls for popular school reform strategies of the late 1950s.

Corbett, H. Dickson, and Bruce L. Wilson. *Listening to Urban Kids: School Reform and the Teachers They Want.* Albany: State University of New York Press, 2001. Presents the voices and perspectives of urban middle school students, who explain how to make school more relevant and meaningful.

Coulson, Andrew J. *Market Education: The Unknown History.* Somerset, N.J.: Transaction Publishers, 1999. Presents the historical case for competitive, free-market education reform and describes how education for low-income children might be funded under a market system and how the transition from monopolistic public education to market education might be achieved.

Cuban, Larry, and David B. Tyack. *Tinkering Toward Utopia: A Century of Public School Reform.* Cambridge, Mass.: Harvard University Press, 1997. Suggests that reformers must remember the democratic purposes that guide public education and focus on ways to help teachers improve instruction from the inside out instead of expecting change by decree.

Darling-Hammond, Linda. *The Right to Learn: A Blueprint for Creating Schools That Work.* New York: Jossey-Bass, 2001. Describes learner-centered schools that work for students in all kinds of communities and outlines the policies and practices that are needed to create these schools on a systemwide basis.

Dewey, John. *Democracy and Education: An Introduction to the Philosophy of Education.* Reprint, Washington, D.C.: Freer Gallery of Art, 1997. Describes strategies for training students to become socially responsible adults and conscientious citizens concerned with the rights of others and the common good, while developing the knowledge and technical skills to be productive members of society. This landmark book in the progressive education movement was first published in 1916.

DiConti, Veronica Donahue. *Interest Groups and Education Reform: The Latest Crusade to Restructure the Schools.* Lanham, Md.: University Press of America, 1996. Examines the impact of interest groups on the education reform debate, focusing on the movements for public school choice and school-based management.

Digiulio, Robert C. *Educate, Medicate, or Litigate? What Teachers, Parents, and Administrators Must Do About Student Behavior.* Thousand Oaks, Calif.: Corwin Press, 2001. Explores bullying and other antisocial behavior in schools, analyzes common myths about school violence and its origins, and prescribes methods of prevention.

Dwyer, James G. *Vouchers Within Reason: A Child-Centered Approach to Education Reform.* Ithaca, N.Y.: Cornell University Press, 2001. Advocates vouchers for private schools as a fair, child-centered approach for good schooling and proposes a plan that would restrict vouchers to secular aspects of school programs, sidestepping legal issues relating to the separation of church and state.

Engel, Michael. *The Struggle for Control of Public Education: Market Ideology vs. Democratic Values.* Philadelphia: Temple University Press, 2000. Argues that the battle of school control is an ideological one and urges increased openness, social awareness, and idealism in community-controlled schools over vouchers, charter schools, and standards.

Evans, Robert. *The Human Side of School Change: Reform, Resistance, and the Real-Life Problems of Innovation.* New York: Jossey-Bass, 2001. Adopts a holistic approach to education reform, concentrating on why substantive innovation has been difficult to achieve.

Evers, Williamson M., ed. *School Reform: The Critical Issues*. Stanford, Calif.: Stanford University Press, 2001. Presents a collection of articles on a wide range of critical education reform issues, including teacher improvement, student responsibility, and the pitfalls of "progressive" education.

Fields, Belden, and Walter Feinberg. *Education and Democratic Theory: Finding a Place for Community Participation in Public School Reform*. Albany: State University of New York Press, 2001. Analyzes how an educational reform group, the Project for Educational Democracy, attempted to increase awareness as well as access to decision making in the public school system to make it more democratic and inclusive of diverse racial groups.

Flesch, Rudolph. *Why Johnny Can't Read*. Reprint, New York: Harper-Collins, 1986. Asserts that reading instruction has suffered due to the abandonment of the phonics method. Originally published in 1955, the best-selling book represented a rejection of much of progressive education's curricular philosophy.

Forness, Steven R., and James M. Kaufmann. *Education Deform: Bright People Sometimes Say Stupid Things About Education*. Lanham, Md.: Scarecrow Press, 2002. Rejects the common ideological rhetoric from the Left and the Right in favor a reasoned focus on improving instruction for the entire spectrum of students.

Frase, Larry E., and William Streshly. *Top Ten Myths in Education: Fantasies Americans Love to Believe*. Lanham, Md.: Scarecrow Press, 2000. Describes how commonly held beliefs about education actually impede school improvement and suggests conservative-minded reforms that would not cost taxpayers.

Fraser, James. *Reading, Writing, and Justice: School Reform As If Democracy Matters*. Albany: State University of New York Press, 1997. Provides a critique of the economic rationale for school reform and offers a more democratic, radical, and humanistic vision of what schools are designed to accomplish.

Fuller, Bruce, ed. *Inside Charter Schools*. Cambridge, Mass.: Harvard University Press, 2001. Provides an analysis of the charter school movement through studies of six diverse charter schools.

Gardner, Howard. *The Disciplined Mind: Beyond Facts and Standardized Tests the K–12 Education Every Child Deserves*. New York: Penguin, 2000. Argues that K–12 education should strive for traditional humane education as opposed to the popular movement for standardized tests.

Gartner, Alan, and Dorothy Kerzner Lipsky. *Inclusion and School Reform: Transforming America's Classrooms*. Baltimore: Brooks Publishing, 1997. Emphasizes the need for development of inclusion of special education students with school restructuring plans.

Glasser, William. *The Quality School.* New York: HarperPerennial, 1998. Recommends abandoning the common school practice of boss management in favor of the noncoercive lead management in which students view the teacher as a team captain rather than an adversary whose power is resented.

Goldring, Ellen B., and Claire Smrekar. *School Choice in Urban America: Magnet Schools and the Pursuit of Equity.* New York: Teachers College Press, 1999. Integrates research on school choice, parental involvement, and desegregation to analyze policies, practices, and experiences of magnet schools.

Griffith, Mary. *The Home Schooling Handbook: From Preschool to High School, A Parent's Guide.* Roseville, Calif.: Prima Publishers, 1999. Describes the homeschooling experience, including strategies dealing with legal regulation and curriculum.

Gross, Martin L. *The Conspiracy of Ignorance: The Failure of American Public Schools.* New York: HarperPerennial, 2000. Describes how the typical teacher is academically inferior and trained in dubious methods and decries educational establishment's efforts to maintain control of a failing system.

Guthrie, James W., Lawrence C. Pierce, and Paul Thomas Hill. *Reinventing Public Education: How Contracting Can Transform America's Schools.* Chicago: University of Chicago Press, 1997. Touts benefits of contracting, using public funds to select private providers to operate schools and to strengthen accountability, standards, choice, and instructional quality.

Hacsi, Timothy A. *Children As Pawns: The Politics of Educational Reform.* Cambridge, Mass.: Harvard University Press, 2002. Presents stories of five important topics in education reform—Head Start, bilingual education, small class size, social promotion, and school funding—and shows the problems with the design of these popular policies and programs.

Harvey, James, and David T. Kearns. *A Legacy of Learning: Your Stake in Standards and New Kinds of Schools.* Washington, D.C.: Brookings Institute, 2000. Explores reasons behind the United States's low standing in international academic comparisons and recommends an emphasis on standards to improve the situation.

Hassel, Bryan C., and Paul E. Peterson, eds. *Learning from School Choice.* Washington, D.C.: Brookings Institute, 1998. Reviews evidence from early school choice programs and examines the implications of choice and competition in education.

Hauser, Roger Mason, and Jay Heubert, eds. *High Stakes: Testing for Tracking, Promotion, and Graduation.* Washington, D.C.: National Academy Press, 1999. Looks at how testing is used in schools to make decisions about tracking, placement, promotion, and retention, and the awarding or withholding of high school diplomas.

Henig, Jeffrey R. *Rethinking School Choice.* Princeton, N.J.: Princeton University Press, 2001. Counters the claims of voucher and other choice proposal supporters and disputes the accuracy of the market metaphor as a guide to improving education.

Henig, Jeffrey, Desiree S. Redescleaux, Marion Orr, and Richard C. Hula. *The Color of School Reform: Race, Politics, and the Challenge of Urban Education.* Princeton, N.J.: Princeton University Press, 2001. Focuses on influence of race in education reform in Atlanta, Baltimore, Detroit, and Washington, D.C., where local governmental authority has passed from white to black leaders and explains that black administrative control of big-city school systems has not yet translated into broad improvements in the quality of public education.

Hess, Frederick M. *Spinning Wheels: The Politics of Urban School Reform.* Washington, D.C.: Brookings Institute, 1998. Concludes that school reform, although politically useful to school boards' and superintendents' survival, is so pervasive in urban districts that it has become a hindrance to long-term school improvement.

Heubert, Jay Philip, ed. *Law and School Reform: Six Strategies for Promoting Educational Equity.* New Haven, Conn.: Yale University Press, 2000. Evaluates how lawyers and educators have shaped the direction of schools and how they could collaborate more effectively.

Hiebert, James, and James W. Stigler. *The Teaching Gap: Best Ideas from the World's Teachers for Improving Education.* New York: Free Press, 1999. Analyzes math instruction in Germany, Japan, and the United States and concludes that U.S. teaching methods, not the teachers themselves, are limited and improvement is needed.

Hirsch, E. D., Jr. *Cultural Literacy.* New York: Vintage, 1988. Argues that children are being deprived of the basic knowledge that would enable them to function in contemporary society and includes, in dictionary style, 5,000 essential facts to know.

———. *The Schools We Need: And Why We Don't Have Them.* New York: Anchor, 1999. Supports content-based curriculum and rigorous testing and criticizes the application of different educational theories at the expense of teaching core knowledge.

Holt, Mikel. *Not Yet "Free At Last": The Unfinished Business of the Civil Rights Movement—Our Battle for School Choice.* Oakland, Calif.: Institute for Contemporary Studies, 1999. Chronicles the recent history of Milwaukee, Wisconsin's public schools and the rise of the system's school choice program.

Howell, William H., and Paul E. Peterson. *The Education Gap: Vouchers and Public Schools.* Washington, D.C.: Brookings Institute, 2002. Analyzes research on various voucher programs and indicates that, while not a panacea for the complex problems facing U.S. schools, vouchers may help close the achievement gap between African-American and white students.

Jennings, John F. *Why National Standards and Tests? Politics and the Quest for Better Schools.* Thousand Oaks, Calif.: Sage Publications, 1998. Provides an inside view of how national education policy is crafted and describes political pressures and agendas that have impacted the development of laws.

Jennings, Nancy E. *Interpreting Policy in Real Classrooms: Case Studies of State Reform and Teacher Practice.* New York: Teachers College Press, 1996. Looks at policy implementation, exploring how and what teachers learn from state policy and how policymakers "teach" their messages.

Johnston, Michael. *In the Deep Heart's Core.* New York: Grove Atlantic Press, 2002. Recounts the experience in Greenville, Mississippi, of a member of Teach For America, the nation's largest alternative certification organization.

Jordan, K. Forbis, Arlene Metha, and L. Dean Webb. *Foundations of American Education.* Upper Saddle River, N.J.: Merrill, 2000. Provides history of U.S. education reform as well as a broad overview of legal, curricular, and fiscal issues relating to schools.

Kemerer, Frank R., and Stephen D. Sugarman, eds. *School Choice and Social Controversy: Politics, Policy, and Law.* Washington, D.C.: Brookings Institute, 2000. Describes the key issues involved in drafting and implementing school choice programs with a legal and public policy perspective.

Knowles, Kaeli T., Barbara S. Plake, and David Z. Robinson, eds. *Testing Teacher Candidates: The Role of Licensure Tests in Improving Teacher Quality.* Washington, D.C.: National Academy Press, 2001. Examines teacher licensure tests, evaluates the merits of using test results to hold states and institutions accountable, and suggests alternatives for developing beginning teacher competence.

Kohn, Alfie. *The Case Against Standardized Testing: Raising the Scores, Ruining the Schools.* Westport, Conn.: Heinemann, 2000. Claims that politicians' and businesspeople's increased emphasis on standardized tests comes at the expense of more meaningful forms of learning.

———. *The Schools Our Children Deserve: Moving Beyond Traditional Classrooms and Tougher Standards.* New York: Mariner Books, 2000. Attacks the back-to-basics movement within education reform and nostalgic notions about the quality and efficiency of schools of the past.

Kopp, Wendy. *One Day, All Children . . . : The Unlikely Triumph of Teach For America and What I Learned Along the Way.* New York: Public Affairs, 2001. Describes the creation and impact of Teach For America, which recruits, trains, and places top college graduates in districts with persistent teaching shortages, founded by the author as a 21-year-old college senior.

Kornhaber, Mindy, and Gary Orfield, eds. *Raising Standards or Raising Barriers? Inequality and High Stakes Testing in Public Education.* Washington, D.C.: Century Foundation Press, 2001. Examines economic and educational assumptions behind the prominence of high stakes tests and suggests that they may be doing more harm than good.

Kozol, Jonathan. *Savage Inequalities: Children in America's Schools.* New York: HarperPerennial, 1992. Explores the deplorable conditions of decaying buildings, overcrowded classrooms, understaffed faculty, and deteriorating neighborhoods in which inner-city children are educated.

Levin, Henry M., ed. *Privatizing Education: Can the School Marketplace Deliver Freedom of Choice, Efficiency, Equity, and Social Cohesion?* Boulder, Colo.: Westview Press, 2001. Comprises a collection of essays about efforts to move education from the public to private sector through such tactics as tuition tax credits and vouchers.

Levine, David, ed. *Rethinking Schools—an Agenda for Change: A Collection from the Leading Journal of School Reform.* New York: New Press, 1995. Offers a mix of essays from *Rethinking Schools*, a leading liberal journal of school reform, for improving educational quality and equity.

Lieberman, Myron. *The Teacher Unions: How They Sabotage Educational Reform and Why.* San Francisco: Encounter Books, 2000. Critiques the two largest teachers' unions, the National Education Association and the American Federation of Teachers, and describes how they have resisted meaningful education reform.

Lissitz, Robert W., and William D. Schafer, eds. *Assessment in Educational Reform: Both Means and Ends.* Explores, through a collection of essays, how assessments can be utilized for curriculum design and instruction.

Loveless, Tom, ed. *Conflicting Missions? Teachers Unions and Educational Reform.* Washington, D.C.: Brookings Institute, 2000. Examines the role teachers' unions play in encouraging and resisting education reform, including analysis of the unions' critics and supporters.

Lucas, Christopher, J. *Teacher Education in America: Reform Agendas for the Twenty-First Century.* New York: Palgrave MacMillan, 1997. Explores the history and condition of how teachers learn to teach by asking, "What is needed in the way of basic preparation for beginning teachers seeking initial licensure."

Making the Grade: Reinventing America's Schools. New York: Routledge, 2001. Describes the need for accountability systems that focus on what students can do with their knowledge and smaller schools where teachers and students know one another and the children feel valued.

Marschall, Melissa, Mark Schneider, and Paul Teske. *Choosing Schools: Consumer Choice and the Quality of Schools.* Princeton, N.J.: Princeton University Press, 2000. Provides evidence on choice-related topics and interprets it with theories of economics, social psychology, and public opinion.

McEwan, Elaine K. *Angry Parents, Failing Schools: What's Wrong with the Public Schools and What You Can Do About It.* Colorado Springs, Colo.: Shaw Books, 1998. Criticizes the methodology of poorly designed and executed curriculum reforms and suggests solutions for improvement.

McLaughlin, Margaret, and Martyn Rose, eds. *Special Education and School Reform in the United States and Britain.* New York: Routledge, 1999. Compares how increased attention on education reform has influenced special education instruction in the United States and Great Britain.

McNeil, Linda M. *Contradictions of School Reform: Educational Costs of Standardized Testing.* New York: Routledge, 2000. Argues that the preparation of students for standardized testing endangers teaching methods, significantly compromising the quality of education in U.S. schools.

Meier, Deborah, ed. *In Schools We Trust: Creating Communities of Learning in an Era of Testing and Standardization.* Boston: Beacon Press, 2002. Promotes the idea that schools must be smaller, more self-governed places of choice to allow kids and their families to feel part of a genuine learning community.

———. *Will Standards Save Public Education?* Boston: Beacon Press, 2000. Contests the validity of the idea that a centralized authority can dictate how and what teachers teach and suggests that it undermines the development of teachers' ability to serve as models for students.

Moe, Terry M. *Schools, Vouchers, and the American Public.* Washington, D.C.: Brookings Institute, 2001. Offers a description of the voucher movement and explains that though Americans like public school, they, particularly the socially disadvantaged, are also very open to vouchers.

Moffitt, Robert E., ed. *School Choice 2001: What's Happening in the States.* Washington, D.C.: Heritage Foundation, 2001. Explores popularity and success of school choice programs across the country.

Mondale, Sarah, and Sarah Patton, eds. *School: The Story of American Public Education.* Boston: Beacon Press, 2001. Provides the history of public education in the United States for the layperson, with an emphasis on photos and the perspectives of minorities. The book serves as the companion piece to the PBS television special of the same name.

Nehring, James. *Upstart Startup: Creating and Sustaining a Public Charter School.* New York: Teachers College Press, 2002. Takes the reader on a tour of one charter school, describing daily challenges and ultimate achievements.

Noll, James W., ed. *Taking Sides: Clashing Views on Controversial Educational Issues.* Guilford, Conn.: Dushkin Publishing Group, 2000. Introduces debate-style analysis of major controversies in education, including compulsory school attendance, charter schools' effectiveness, and whether school uniforms promote safety and improve discipline.

Ohanian, Susan. *One Size Fits Few: The Folly of Educational Standards.* New York: Heinemann, 1999. Uses narrative by a teacher to attack "standardistas," describing the dangers of attempts to "streamline, sanitize, and standardize education."

Palestini, Robert H. *Ten Steps to Educational Reform.* Lanham, Md.: Scarecrow, 2000. Explains how success in school reform can result from commitment to key components of the school's organizational structure, leadership, communication, planning, decision-making, and conflict management processes; power distribution; and attitude toward change.

Petersen, Paul E., ed. *The Future of School Choice.* Stanford, Calif.: Hoover Press, 2003. Consists of essays from leading education reform experts, describing the post–Cleveland school vouchers decision landscape.

Picus, Lawrence O., and James L. Wattenbarger, eds. *Where Does the Money Go? Resource Allocation in Elementary and Secondary Schools.* Thousand Oaks, Calif.: Corwin, 1996. Provides overview of how public education funds are spent and suggests methods for more effective implementation.

Plato. *The Republic.* Rev. ed. Trans. Desmond Lee. New York: Viking Press, 1955. Includes first written expression of value of organized education system. The work was originally written in the fourth century B.C.

Pope, Denise. *Doing School.* New Haven, Conn.: Yale University Press, 2001. Offers a view of the ways today's high school students pursue high grades and success and raises questions about the ability of schools to provide an engaging and positive culture of growth.

Pope, Denise Clark, Diane Ravitch, and Maris A. Vinovskis, eds. *Learning from the Past: What History Teaches Us About School Reform.* Baltimore: Johns Hopkins Press, 1995. Provides historical perspectives on current education reforms from authors reflecting a wide range of views and experiences in the field of education analysis.

Ravitch, Diane. *Left Back: A Century of Failed School Reforms.* New York: Simon & Schuster, 2000. Surveys the history of U.S. school reform and reveals how schools' role in job training, social planning, political reform, social sorting, personality adjustment, and social efficiency have prevented the effective education of children.

———. *National Standards in American Education: A Citizen's Guide.* Washington, D.C.: Brookings Institute, 1995. Defines what standards are and what purposes they might serve and reviews evidence about student achievement.

Ravitch, Diane, ed. *Debating the Future of American Education: Do We Need National Standards and Assessments?* Washington, D.C.: Brookings Institute, 1995. Brings together representatives of various viewpoints on the utility and equity of the increased use of tests for students, teachers, and schools.

Reed, Douglas S. *On Equal Terms: The Constitutional Politics of Educational Opportunity.* Princeton, N.J.: Princeton University Press, 2001. Focuses on evolution of "resource segregation" of U.S. schools and describes efforts to improve poorly funded schools.

Reeves, Douglas B. *Crusade in the Classroom: How George W. Bush's Education Policies Will Affect Your Child.* New York: Kaplan, 2001. Explains President Bush's policies for school reform and illustrates how early tests of these policies have played out in schools across the country.

Rothman, Robert. *Measuring Up: Standards, Assessment, and School Reform.* New York: Jossey-Bass, 1995. Recommends discarding traditional means of determining what students know and replacing them with performance-based assessments stressing metacognitive skills useful in the "real world."

Rothstein, Richard. *The Way We Were? The Myths and Realities of America's Student Achievement.* Washington, D.C.: Brookings Institute, 1998. Analyzes the statistical and anecdotal evidence of U.S. school achievement and shows that, contrary to popular beliefs, public schools are doing better than in the past, particularly in educating poor and minority students

Rousseau, Jean-Jacques. *Emile.* Reprint, New York: Everyman's Library, 1993. Describes an ideal child-centered education focused on the child's natural abilities. The book was originally published in France in 1762.

Sacks, Peter. *Standardized Minds: The High Price of America's Testing Culture and What We Can Do to Change It.* Cambridge, Mass.: Perseus, 2001. Explains how standardized tests sustain the privileged and punish the poor and includes a plan for alternative means of assessment.

Sarason, Seymour Bernard. *Questions You Should Ask About Charter Schools and Vouchers.* New York: Heinemann, 2002. Warns of the danger of moving ahead in these key and complex reform areas without closely scrutinizing the important issues that affect the ultimate success or failure of efforts to improve public education.

Schlechty, Phillip C. *Inventing Better Schools: An Action Plan for Educational Reform.* New York: Jossey-Bass, 1997. Argues that old rules, roles, and relationships of education must be changed and shows how to implement reform by developing a mission statement, setting goals, and assessing results.

Senge, Peter. *Schools That Learn: A Fifth Discipline Fieldbook for Educators, Parents, and Everyone Who Cares About Education.* New York: Doubleday, 2000. Features articles, case studies, and anecdotes from prominent educators to provide examples of successful school improvement techniques.

Shirley, Dennis. *Community Organizing for Urban School Reform.* Austin: University of Texas Press, 1997. Presents strategies for increasing parental engagement in public schools and describes different cases of urban schools and neighborhoods that improved their conditions through sustained collaborations.

Silberman, Charles. *Crisis in the Classroom.* New York: Random House, 1971. Decries the "grim, joyless" conditions in public schools and extols the advantages of open education, which encourages increased informality in schools and student freedom in course selection and instructional time.

Sizer, Ted. *Horace's Compromise.* Boston: Houghton Mifflin, 1984. Calls for significant reform of schools burdened by unresponsive leadership, rushed classes, and excessive testing that does not meaningfully assess students.

Steinberg, Laurence. *Beyond the Classroom: Why School Reform Has Failed and What Parents Need to Do.* Carmichael, Calif.: Touchstone Books, 1997. Describes negative effect of current attitudes regarding schooling among students, parents, and popular culture and makes recommendations for change.

Temes, Peter S. *Against School Reform (and in Praise of Great Teaching).* Chicago: Ivan R. Dee, Inc., 2002. Argues in favor of the need to provide greater support for individual teachers rather than the more commonly proposed solutions for education reform.

United States Department of Education. *A Nation At Risk: The Imperative for Education Reform.* Washington, D.C.: Government Printing Office, 1983. Influential report commissioned by the Reagan administration's Department of Education. The report warns of the weaknesses of the U.S. education system, stating, "If an unfriendly foreign power had attempted to impose on America the mediocre educational performance that exists today, we might well have viewed it as an act of war."

Vander Ark, Thomas, Tony Wagner, and Joseph P. Viteritti. *Choosing Equality: School Choice, the Constitution, and Civil Society.* Washington, D.C.: Brookings Institute, 2001. Argues that critics of school choice have been proven wrong and suggests a policy designed to benefit the poor rather than a pure market approach to education reform.

Webster, Noah. *The American Spelling Book: Containing the Rudiments of the English Language for the Use of Schools in the United States.* Reprint, Bedford, Mass.: Applewood Books, 1999. Emphasizes distinctively American spelling, grammar, and content. Originally published in 1783, it became the most influential textbook of the 19th century, eventually selling more than 75 million copies.

Weil, Danny K. *Charter Schools: A Reference Handbook.* Santa Barbara, Calif.: ABC-CLIO, 2000. Provides overview of evolution, controversy, and status of charter school movement.

Witte, John F., Jr. *The Market Approach to Education: An Analysis of America's First Voucher Program.* Princeton, N.J.: Princeton University Press, 2001. Analyzes the Milwaukee, Wisconsin, school choice experiment and explains that although it seems to be working, it may not promote equal education when applied on a broader scale.

Wong, Kenneth K. *Funding Public Schools: Politics and Policies.* Lawrence: University Press of Kansas, 1999. Explains how lack of political will has led to legislative deadlock on school finance reform and how failure to enact new approaches endangers schools in greatest need.

PERIODICALS

Alexander, Kelly King. "*Parents* Report: Homeschooling—Is It Right for You?" *Parents*, vol. 75, no. 4, April 1, 2000, p. 114. Summarizes laws and population, portrays day-in-the-life homeschooling, and addresses issues of socialization.

Allen, Mike. "For Lynne Cheney, the Children's Hour: Ex-NEA Leader Plays Teacher in Toned-Down Role." *Washington Post*, September 18, 2002, p. A27. Explains how the Vice President Dick Cheney's wife and former leading conservative voice for education reform has lowered her profile on controversial issues, while becoming a best-selling author of a children's book.

"Alternative Certification: Risky Business." *Virginia Journal of Education*, vol. 87, no. 8, May 1994, p. 6. Warns of the growing influence of allowing teachers into the classroom who have not received traditional teacher training.

Apple, Michael W. "The Cultural Politics of Home Schooling." *Peabody Journal of Education*, vol. 75, nos. 1 and 2, 2000, p. 256. Examines the reasons behind the often contentious issue of parents formally educating their children at home.

Arai, A. Bruce. "Home Schooling and the Redefinition of Citizenship." *Education Policy Analysis*, vol. 7, no. 27, 1999. Available online. URL: http://epaa.asu.edu/epaa/v7n27.html. Reviews research on homeschooling's effects and concludes that the practice does not harm the development of good citizens and may actually encourage greater diversity and understanding of citizenships.

Archer, Jeff. "Changing the Rules of the Game." *Education Week*, vol. 19, no. 40, June 14, 2000, p. 24. Focuses on an elementary school in impoverished Pacoima, California, to illustrate how the idea of linking teachers' pay to performance has been gaining momentum nationally.

———. "Foundation Stirs Debate with Report Questioning Research on Licensure." *Education Week*, vol. 21, no. 7, October 17, 2001, p. 17. Examines reaction to a report by the Abell Foundation saying that there is little evidence that students benefit when teacher candidates are required to complete coursework in education.

Arey, Kelly. "When Standardization Replaces Innovation." *Education Week*, vol. 21, May 8, 2002, p. 32. Decries efforts in many urban schools that require teachers to follow instructional and classroom management techniques prescribed by outside authorities.

Arguelles, Lourdes, and Susan L. Flynn. "The Story of a Charter School Closure." *Paths of Learning: Options for Families and Communities,* Summer 2001, p. 44. Tells the story of a charter school closing from the perspectives of students, parents, teachers, and community members who feel that the sponsoring district revoked the charter for political reasons, despite broad local support.

Arsen, David, David Plank, and Gary Sykes. "Charter Schools and Private Profits." *School Administrator,* vol. 57, no. 5, May 2000, p. 12. Points out how educational management organizations that run charter schools have found it difficult to create profits, and questions whether the pursuit of profit is good for students.

Ballou, Dale, and Michael Podgursky. "The Case Against Teacher Certification." *Public Interest,* Summer 1998, p. 17. Analyzes the report of the National Commission on Teaching and America's Future stating that public schools employ large numbers of unqualified teachers, mainly because of inadequate and poorly enforced standards for teacher training and licensing.

Banchero, Stephanie, and Ana Beatriz Cholo. "Only 7% Seek to Transfer to a Better School." *Chicago Tribune,* August 20, 2002, p. A1. Sheds light on why parents are not transferring students despite federal law allowing transfers for students in underperforming schools.

Banchero, Stephanie, and Michael Martinez. "Federal School Reform Stumbles." *Chicago Tribune,* August 28, 2002, p. A1. Explains that the initial implementation of the No Child Left Behind Act has been marked by widespread confusion, infighting among local authorities, and circumventing of the law's requirements.

Banchero, Stephanie, and Diane Rado. "Chicago Restricts Transfer Options." *Chicago Tribune,* July 30, 2002, p. B1. Portrays the difficulties that big cities such as Chicago are facing in complying with new federal education law, mainly because of enrollment pressures and high rates of student failure.

Banks, Ann. "Is Zero Tolerance a Good Idea for School Discipline and Safety?" *NEA Today,* vol. 20, no. 5, February 2002, p. 11. Presents a point-counterpoint-style examination of the effectiveness of zero-tolerance policies in schools.

Barone, Michael. "In Plain English Bilingual Education Flunks Out of Schools in California." *U.S. News & World Report,* May 29, 2000, p. 37. Lauds the return to a system of learning English experienced by previous groups of immigrants following the passage and implementation of California's Proposition 227, which limited Spanish-language instruction for native speakers to one year.

Barrett, Wayne. "Ticket to Nowhere." *Village Voice*, July 9, 2002, vol. 47, no. 27, p. 23. Criticizes the school funding formula used in New York State as insufficient for the poor and middle class.

Beem, Kate. "Nontraditional Homeschoolers Cherish Nonconformity." *Kansas City Star*, April 16, 2000, p. A1. Profiles two students' positive experiences with homeschooling.

Belluck, Pam. "State of the Union—Education Programs: In Chicago, the Story Behind the Rising Test Scores." *New York Times*, January 21, 1999, p. 20. Profiles the improvement in the Chicago public schools, following a major phase of education reform, discussed in President Bill Clinton's State of the Union speech.

Berends, Mark, Sheila Natraj Kirby, and Susan Bodilly. "Looking Back over a Decade of Whole School Reform: The Experience of New American Schools." *Phi Delta Kappan*, vol. 84, no. 2, October 2002, p. 168. Warns that policymakers may be overreaching by seeking reforms that are not well integrated and analyzes the experience of the New American Schools imitative.

Berry, Barnett. "No Shortcuts for Preparing Good Teachers." *Educational Leadership*, vol. 58, no. 8, May 2001, p. 32. Criticizes alternative teacher certification programs that fail to produce qualified educators and shortchange students.

Bierlein, Louann E., Bruno V. Manno, Chester E. Finn, Jr., and Gregg Vanourek. "Charter Schools: Accomplishments and Dilemmas." *Teachers College Record*, vol. 99, no. 3, 1998, p. 37. Concludes that charter schools have accomplished a great deal in the past decade, particularly by spurring innovation, serving minority and special needs students, attracting top teachers, providing a safe environment, and emphasizing high standards.

Bigelow, Bill. "Why Standardized Tests Threaten Multiculturalism." *Educational Leadership*, vol. 56, no. 7, 1999, p. 37. Stresses the notion that government-appointed social studies curricula are not representing the diversity of and understanding for U.S. culture.

Blair, Julie. "Teacher-Trainers Fear a Backfire from New ESEA." *Education Week*, vol. 21, March 6, 2002, pp. 1, 38–39. Explains concerns that the federal requirement that all K–12 teachers who serve poor children be "highly qualified" may actually lower standards for educators by dumbing down measures such as licensure tests and preservice exams that are supposed to bar easy entry into the field.

Bliss, Traci, and Sharon Brennan. "Increasing Minority Representation in the Teaching Profession Through Alternative Certification: A Case Study." *The Teacher Educator*, vol. 34, no. 1, Summer 1998, p. 1. Investigates the role that nontraditional paths to learning have in diversifying the racial and ethnic makeup of the professional educator population.

Bohn, Anita Perna. "Multicultural Education and the Standards Movement: A Report from the Field." *Phi Delta Kappan*, vol. 82, no. 2, October 2000, p. 156. Claims that the push toward a standardized curriculum stifles students' exploration and recognition of cultural diversity.

Bolick, Clint. "The ACLU's Hypocrisy on School Vouchers." *Wall Street Journal*, August 2, 1999, p. A19. Claims that the American Civil Liberties Union has abandoned its principles by steadfastly opposing Florida's A+ education reform program allowing student use of vouchers to attend private schools.

———. "Charter Reformer." *National Review*, vol. 50, no. 6, April 6, 1998, p. 42. Describes the educational reform leadership of Arizona superintendent of schools Lisa Graham-Keegan.

———. "Warning: School Choice Misinformation Abounds." *Human Events*, vol. 57, no. 44, November 26, 2001, p. 10. Defends school choice from commonly held misconceptions among media and U.S. citizens.

Bomba, Anne K., Charles K. West, and Diane K. Tidwell. "Attitudes of Parents About School Uniforms." *Journal of Family and Consumer Sciences: From Research to Practice*, vol. 91, no. 2, 1999, p. 92. Looks at the varying views of parents regarding the wisdom, fairness, and effectiveness of school uniform policies designed to improve safety.

Boss, Shira J. "Virtual Charters: Public Schooling at Home." *Christian Science Monitor*, January 8, 2002, p. 14. Explains both sides of the argument over "cyber charters," public schools with classes held via computer and teleconference by real-time teachers, and examines their legality.

Bracey, Gerald W. "What Happened to America's Public Schools? Not What You Think." *American Heritage*, November 1997, p. 39. Claims that many educational reformers since World War II suffer from "nostalgia and amnesia," contradicting the notion that public education was better in the past than at present.

Breslau, Karen. "Edison's Report Card." *Newsweek*, July 2, 2001, vol. 138, no. 1, p. 48. Details the for-profit school management company's controversial experience in the San Francisco public school system.

Brown, Thomas J., David L. Brunsma, and Kerry A. Rockquemore. "Effects of Student Uniforms on Attendance, Behavior Problems, Substance Use, and Academic Achievement." *Journal of Educational Research*, vol. 92, no. 1, September–October 1998, p. 53. Tests the claims made by school uniform policy advocates and finds that these policies have no direct effect on substance use, behavioral problems, and attendance and do not have a negative effect on academic achievement.

Browning, Melissa. "A Critical Analysis of Charter Schools." *Equity & Excellence in Education*, vol. 33, no. 2, September 2000, p. 16. Reviews the intended and unintended results of the charter school movement, explaining that increased autonomy can heighten inequality, and choice can exclude some members of society.

Buck, G. H., E. A. Polloway, and S. M. Robb. "Alternative Certification Programs: A National Survey." *Teacher Education and Special Education*, vol. 18, no. 1, 1995, p. 39. Finds that 62 percent of states partially rely on alternative certification programs and projects that by 2000, 85 percent of states would provide these programs.

Burroughs, Robert. "Composing Standards and Composing Teachers: The Problem of National Board Certification." *Journal of Teacher Education*, vol. 52, no. 3, 2001, p. 223. Considers whether the National Board for Professional Teaching Standards Certification is more an evaluation of a teacher's writing about teaching than an evaluation of teaching itself.

Busch, Carolyn, Allan Odden, and Linda Hertert. "School Financing Inequities Among the States: The Problem from a National Perspective." *Journal of Education Finance*, vol. 19, no. 3, Winter 1994, p. 231. Explains that despite a significant increase in resources available for public school systems, the education dollar is distributed unfairly and inefficiently, and offers suggestions for solutions.

"California Legislature to Consider K–12 Overhaul." *What Works in Teaching and Learning*, vol. 34, no. 19, September 18, 2002, p. 3. Focuses on the proposed changes in the educational system in California, whose school reform measures are often followed in the rest of the United States.

Carnoy, Martin. "School Choice? Or Is It Privatization?" *Educational Researcher*, vol. 29, no. 7, October 2000, p. 15. Argues that school choice programs need to be closely scrutinized to determine how schools involved in such programs can best serve social goals.

Carper, James C. "Pluralism to Establishment to Dissent: The Religious and Educational Context of Home Schooling." *Peabody Journal of Education*, vol. 75, nos. 1 & 2, 2000, p. 8. Provides social and historical background to increased parental choice in education, including homeschooling.

Caruana, Vicki. "Partnering with Homeschoolers." *Educational Leadership*, vol. 57, no. 1, September 1999, p. 58. Explores ways part-time homeschoolers and their families can forge meaningful relationships with professional educators.

Caruso, Peter. "Individuality vs. Conformity: The Issue Behind School Uniforms." *NASSP Bulletin*, vol. 80, no. 581, September 1996, p. 83. Offers a variety of perspectives on the topic of mandatory uniform policies in schools.

"A Charter for Innovation." *Christian Science Monitor*, July 23, 2002, p. 8. Op-ed piece describing varied views of charter school effectiveness but proposing their role in seeking positive change in public education reform.

Cloud, John, and Jodie Morse. "Home Sweet School." *Time*, August 27, 2001, p. 47. Details the growth of homeschooling and notes how well-publicized academic success has improved its image nationwide.

Coeyman, Marjorie. "Just When You Thought You Knew the Rules." *Christian Science Monitor*, July 9, 2002, p. 11. Explores ways the No Child Left Behind Act has turned the status quo "upside down."

———. "Summer School—Despite Rising Role—Faces Major Cuts." *Christian Science Monitor*, May 22, 2002, p. 1. Explains how the recent economic downturn has diminished options for a highly touted education reform.

Cohen, Adam. "A First Report Card on Vouchers." *Time*, April 26, 1999, p. 36. Examines the mixed results of school voucher programs on student achievement and their controversial role in the education reform debate.

Conley, David T. "The 'Goldilocks' Phenomenon." *Education Week*, vol. 21, no. 29. April 3, 2002, pp. 40, 43. Examines how states determine whether assessment standards are too high, too low, or "just right" and suggests ways to fix the inconsistencies.

Cookson, Peter W., and Jeanne M. Powers. "The Politics of School Choice Research: Fact, Fiction, and Statistics." *Educational Policy*, vol. 13, no. 1, 1999, p. 104. Focuses on market-based approaches in education such as vouchers and charter schools included in the Milwaukee, Wisconsin, parental choice program.

Coons, John E. "The Pro-Voucher Left and the Pro-Equity Right." *Annals of the American Academy of Political and Social Science*, vol. 572, November 2000, p. 98. Discusses the sometimes surprising ideological shifts on the school choice issue.

Cordova, Kathryn M. "Buenos Días, Ahem, Good Morning!" *Hispanic*, vol. 14, no. 5, May 2001, p. 34. Describes the dismantling of bilingual programs throughout the country and decries the effect this has on serving Latino students.

Coulter, Ann. "Home Schooling Gets Inadvertent Boost from the United States Supreme Court." *Human Events*, vol. 56, no. 25, July 7, 2000, p. 1. Chronicles the legal momentum for parents who choose to educate their children at home.

Crawford, James R. "Teacher Autonomy and Accountability in Charter Schools." *Education and Urban Society*, vol. 33, no. 2, 2001, p. 186. Compares charter schools in Michigan and Colorado and finds that teachers in charter schools may have less autonomy than their traditional school counterparts.

Crisham, Catherine L. "The Writing Is on the Wall of Separation: Why the Supreme Court Should and Will Uphold Full-Choice School Voucher Programs." *Georgetown Law Journal*, vol. 89, no. 1, 2000, p. 225. Analyzes recent Supreme Court rationale and projects how the Court will interpret voucher-related cases.

Crowson, Robert L. "The Home Schooling Movement: A Few Concluding Observations." *Peabody Journal of Education*, vol. 75, nos. 1 and 2, 2000, p. 294. States that homeschooling merits increased research to fairly assess its impact on education reform.

Curwin, Richard L., and Allen N. Mendler. "Zero Tolerance for Zero Tolerance." *Phi Delta Kappan*, vol. 81, no. 1, October 1999, p. 119. Asserts that schools should reject any policy that treats all students the same and proposes a different approach to ensuring a safe educational environment.

Darling-Hammond, Linda. "Alternatives to Grade Retention." *School Administrator*, vol. 55, no. 7, August 1998, p. 18. Explains strategies that administrators may use instead of retention or social promotion, including enhanced teacher training and redesign of school structure, to promote intensive learning.

Davis, Matthew D. "The Christian Right and School Choice: Reshaping the Educational Landscape." *Educational Forum*, vol. 60, no. 1, 1995, p. 14. Assesses the significant influence cultural conservatives have had on education reform, with particular emphasis on school choice.

Doerr, E. "Give Us Your Money." *Phi Delta Kappan*. vol. 80, no. 10, June 1999, p. 778. Claims that vouchers, including the use of private schools to relieve public school overcrowding, would entangle religion and the state and create an "administrative nightmare."

Elmore, Richard F., Bruce Fuller, Charles F. Glenn, and Gary Orfield. "Who Chooses? Who Loses? Culture, Institutions, and the Unequal Effects of School Choice." *Journal of Church and State*, vol. 40, no. 3, 1998, p. 706. Reports empirical evidence on a wide range of choice programs nationwide.

"An ESEA Primer." *Education Week*, vol. 21, January 9, 2002, pp. 28–29. Provides a thorough explanation of the No Child Left Behind Act.

Essex, Nathan L. "Zero Tolerance Approach to School Violence: Is It Going Too Far?" *American Secondary Education*, vol. 29, no. 2, Winter 2000, p. 37. Recommends that administrators involve teachers, parents, community leaders, and student representatives to formulate policies that will strengthen school safety and help students who need special counseling.

Evans, Dennis L. "School Uniforms: An 'Unfashionable' Dissent." *Phi Delta Kappan*, vol. 78, no. 2, October 1996, p. 139. Counters arguments favoring the growing popularity of school uniform policies.

Ferguson, J. M. "Vouchers—An Illusion of Choice: Results to Date Show Voucher Programs Aren't Working." *American School Board Journal*, vol. 189, 2002, p. 42. Criticizes the philosophy behind the implementation of voucher programs as well as their effectiveness.

Finn, Chester E., Jr. "Can Parents Be Trusted?" *Commentary*, vol. 108, no. 2, 1999, p. 49. Worries that despite the logical basis for strengthening parental voice in their children's education, poor parenting remains a major crisis in the lives of America's youth.

———. "Fixing Schools Without a Voucher Fight." *New York Times*, January 13, 2001, p. A13. Claims that the federal government should allow states to set their own rules and limits on the use of federal dollars in education spending.

———. "Removing the Barriers for Teacher Candidates." *Educational Leadership*, vol. 58, no. 8, May 2001, p. 29. Explains how traditional routes to teacher certification may deter potentially strong teachers from entering the classroom and describes how alternative certification programs may help open the door.

———. "What if All Schools Were Schools of Choice?" *Weekly Standard*, June 19, 2000, vol. 5, no. 38, p. 26. Suggests that the growing influence of choice in education is improving the lives of thousands of students and can have a greater impact with wider application.

Finn, Chester E., Jr., Bruno V. Manno, and Gregg Vanourek. "The Future of Charter Schools: How Big, How Bright?" *Teaching and Change*, vol. 7, no. 3, Spring 2000, p. 222. Explores the systematic effects charter schools are having on public education and presents eight critical challenges the charter school movement faces in the future.

Fisher, Marc. "Charter Schools: To Each Its Own." *Current*, October 2001, p. 3. Tours five charter schools in Washington, D.C., and evaluates their impact and potential future role in strengthening the public education system.

Fiske, Edward B., and Helen F. Ladd. "When Schools Compete: A Cautionary Tale." *Teachers College Record*, vol. 103, no. 1, February 2001, p. 77. Provides quantitative and qualitative analysis of reform efforts in New Zealand, whose school system is similar to that of a U.S. state.

Fitz, John, Chris Taylor, and Stephen Gorard, "School Choice Impacts: What Do We Know?" *Educational Researcher*, vol. 30, no. 7, 2001, p. 18. Depicts a positive portrayal of school choice programs, noting their positive impact on standards and socioeconomic stratification.

Fletcher, Michael A. "Big Gift to Schools Brings Small Gains: Study Says $1.1 Billion Donation Could Not Overcome Serious Problems." Details the findings of a report released by the Annenberg Challenge, which has sought to improve the academic performance in beleaguered schools through more than $1 billion in grants.

———. "Panel Supports Special Ed Vouchers." *Washington Post*, July 6, 2002, p. A4. Describes the federal push to allow special education funds to pay for the cost of private services or private schools attended by the disabled.

"Florida Judge Throws Out School Vouchers." *Chicago Tribune*, August 6, 2002, p. 9. Reports state court ruling throwing out wide-ranging school voucher program, saying it violates a constitutional ban on giving tax dollars to religious institutions.

"For-Profit Schools." *Business Week*, February 7, 2000, p. 64. Profiles movement nationwide to increase accountability through the use of market-based reforms in public schools.

Fraser, James W. "Time to Cut the Link Between Teacher Preparation and Certification?" *Education Week*, vol. 20, January 31, 2001, p. 56. Op-ed piece by an education professor proposing acceptance of an increased role for state and local governments in deciding who is qualified and hired to teach.

Fuller, Bruce, and Howard Gardner. "Inside Charter Schools: The Paradox of Radical Decentralization." *New York Review of Books*, vol. 47, no. 16, 2000, p. 44. Travels into six philosophically, demographically, and geographically different charter schools and analyzes their challenges.

Gallup, Alec M., and Lowell C. Rose. "The 31st Annual Phi Delta Kappa/Gallup Poll of the Public's Attitudes Toward the Public Schools." *Phi Delta Kappan*, vol. 81, no. 1, September 1999, p. 41. Presents a wide-ranging evaluation of perceptions of public schools and points out that 80 percent of respondents give their local school a grade of A, B, or C, a slight increase over the previous year's poll.

Gehring, John. "Voucher Battles Head to State Capitals." *Education Week*, vol. 21, July 10, 2002, pp. 1, 24–25. Explains how lawmakers in many states are seeking to ride momentum of the Supreme Court's decision in the Cleveland voucher case to advance school choice.

Gewertz, Catherine. "A Great Day, or Dark One, for Schools?" *Education Week*, vol. 21, July 10, 2002, pp. 19, 21. Profiles how families and educators affected by the Supreme Court decision in the Cleveland voucher case have reacted.

———. "More Chicago Pupils Flunk Grade." *Education Week*, October 9, 2002, p. 1. Points out trends relating to the Chicago public schools' policy designed to end the social promotion of students.

———. "N.Y.C. Mayor Gains Control over Schools." *Education Week*, vol. 21, June 19, 2002, p. 1. Examines a New York State law giving near total control of schools to New York City's mayor, as previously done in Chicago, Cleveland, Detroit, and Boston.

———. "Philadelphia Lines Up Outside Groups to Run Schools." *Education Week*, vol. 21, August 7, 2002, p. 1. Portrays significant activity in Philadelphia school reform, including the hiring of former Chicago public schools CEO Paul Vallas and the possible movement toward privatization.

Gibbon, Peter H. "A Hero of Education." *Education Week*, vol. 21, May 29, 2002, p. 33. Features excerpted essay profiling the vision and accomplishments of early U.S. education pioneer Horace Mann.

Gilroy, Marilyn. "Bilingual Education on the Edge." *Education Digest*, vol. 67, no. 5, January 2002, p. 50. Explores the political ramifications of bilingual education programs, which have been lauded by supporters as great successes or by critics as dismal failures.

Glickstein, Howard A. "Inequalities in Educational Financing." *Teachers College Record*, vol. 96, no. 4, Summer 1995, p. 722. Criticizes the unfair system that determines what districts spend per pupil and warns of the damaging effects its continued use may bring.

Goben, Jan. "It Takes a Neighborhood: A Case Study in Turning a School Around." *San Francisco Chronicle*, August 11, 2002, p. E4. Describes one Bay Area community's effort to enact school reform.

Godwin, R. Kenneth. "School Choice Trade-Offs." *Education Week*, vol. 21, May 15, 2002, p. 52. Analyzes how school choice programs force education policymakers to confront core values of resource allocation and local control.

Godwin, R. Kenneth, Frank R. Kemerer, Laura Perna, and Valerie J. Martinez. "The Consequences of School Choice: Who Leaves and Who Stays in the Inner City." *Social Science Quarterly*, vol. 76, no. 3, 1995, p. 485. Examines the demographics of school choice programs and the impact of these programs on urban areas.

Goetz, William W. "Ravitch and Reform: Should Left Back Be Left Back?" *Teachers College Record*, vol. 104, no. 6, September 2002, p. 1204. Examines the trend against social promotion through the perspective of noted education reformer Diane Ravitch.

Goldberg, Bruce. "A Liberal Argument for School Choice." *American Enterprise*, vol. 7, no. 5, 1996, p. 26. Claims school choice could help counter public schools' greatest problem—the denial of individuality.

Goldhaber, Dan D. "School Choice: An Examination of the Empirical Evidence on Achievement, Parental Decision Making, and Equity." *Educational Researcher*, vol. 28, no. 9, December 1999, p. 16. Focuses on quantitative assessments of the impact of school choice on educational outcomes, effectiveness, and fairness.

Goode, Stephen. "Forked Tongue: Bilingual Instruction Is Losing Favor Among Educators." *Insight*, vol. 12, no. 14, April 15, 1996, p. 17. Reports on the diminished popularity of bilingual education programs in public schools.

Goodnough, Abby. "Policy Eases the Way Out of Bad Schools." *New York Times*, December 9, 2002, p. B1. Describes how New York City will grant students in the system's more than 300 failing schools preferential transfer treatment in compliance with mandates from the No Child Left Behind Act.

Gordon, Joanne. "Who Doesn't Want to Be a Millionaire?" *Forbes*, October 2, 2000, p. 58. Describes philanthropist Lovett Peters's unaccepted offer to help the 22 lowest performing schools convert into charter schools with a pledge to give $1 million to each school that did not outperform its district peers in five years.

Greve, Michael S. "The End of Education Reform." *Weekly Standard*, vol. 6, no. 34, May 21, 2001, p. 16. Argues that without strong provisions for parental choice, hopes for genuine accountability and public school improvement are dim.

Griffin, Noelle C., and Priscilla Wohlstetter. "Building a Plane While Flying It: Early Lessons from Developing Charter Schools." *Teachers College Record*, vol. 103, no. 2, April 2001, p. 336. Investigates 17 charter schools, with a focus on the key instructional and organizational practices that they established in the start-up phase and the many logistical difficulties encountered.

Guthrie, Stan. "Conservatives Vow to Revive Vouchers." *Christianity Today*, vol. 45, no. 10, August 6, 2001, p. 20. Describes efforts by conservatives in Congress to allow parents to use taxpayer money to attend religious and private schools.

Gutmann, Amy. "What Does 'School Choice' Mean?" *Dissent*, vol. 47, no. 3, Summer 2000, p. 19. Summarizes and analyzes key aspects of the school choice debate and concludes that there is no evidence that vouchers will produce good schools for the "vast majority of children who need them most."

Hanushek, Eric A. "Moving Beyond Spending Fetishes." *Educational Leadership*, vol. 53, no. 3, November 1995, p. 60. Argues that neither funding increases nor smaller classes nor graduate teacher training has positively affected public school performance and claims that charter schools and private school vouchers would help align rewards with performance.

Harrington-Lueker, Donna. "Free-Market School Reform." *School Administrator*, vol. 54, no. 2, February 1997, p. 16. Raises concerns about the fairness, funding, and learning environment of schools run by free-market innovations in a working-class Massachusetts district.

———. "Retention vs. Social Promotion." *School Administrator*, vol. 55, no. 7, August 1998, p. 6. Reviews key aspects of the debate over how best to help students who do not meet academic requirements for passage to the next grade and explores the pros and cons of various approaches tried by different schools and districts.

Hartocollis, Anemona. "Study Links Rises in School Financing and Test Scores." *New York Times*, November 21, 2000, p. B4. Makes the connection between the increased amount in district spending per pupil and the growth of academic achievement.

———. "Two Schools Two Strategies, One Goal: Keeping Top Students." *New York Times*, December 1, 1999, p. B15. Describes the brain drain of ambitious and bright students with choosy parents in New York City.

Hayasaki, Erika. "Class-Size Reduction Initiatives Faltering." *Los Angeles Times*, May 18, 2002, p. A1. Explains that school districts and states across the country are abandoning the once-popular reform of class-size reduction due to severe budget cuts and mixed findings of the reform's effectiveness.

Hayward, Steven. "The 'Neighborhood Effect' of School Choice." *Policy Review*, January–February 1999, p. 47. Explains how school choice could help strengthen cities by helping attract families who flee to the suburbs because of better schools.

Heise, Michael. "The Courts vs. Educational Standards." *Public Interest*, Summer 1995, p. 55. Describes legal challenges to increasing movement toward implementation of academic standards in schools.

Helfand, Duke. "Schools Challenge Mandatory Testing." *Los Angeles Times*, May 29, 2002, p. B1. Reports on Los Angeles and San Francisco school districts' efforts to change or abandon the controversial Stanford 9 test and California's new high school exit exam.

Hendrie, Caroline. "For Small Schools, an Identity Crisis." *Education Week*, vol. 17, no. 34, May 6, 1998, p. 1. Explains how urban small-school proponents generally favor charter schools while others feel that these schools represent an attempt to undermine the efforts of genuine public education reform.

Henig, Jeffrey R., and Gary Scott. "Public Schools and Public Funds—Rethinking School Choice: Limits of the Market Metaphor." *Review of Politics*, vol. 57, no. 3, 1995, p. 551. Identifies and refutes several common arguments for privatizing public education systems.

Hernandez, Alex, and Mathew Mahoney. "Is the Private Sector Qualified to Reform Schools." *Education Week*, vol. 22, no. 3, September 18, 2002, p. 34. Claims that the private sector has struggled to manage school systems in the same way professional educators have.

Hess, Frederick M. "Resistance in the Trenches: What Shapes Teachers' Attitudes Toward School Choice?" *Educational Policy*, vol. 14, no. 2, May 2000, p. 195. Presents analysis of teachers' views on school choice, finding significant opposition on the issue, particularly among more experienced teachers whose background is in education.

———. "Whaddya Mean You Want to Close My School? The Politics of Regulatory Accountability in Charter Schooling." *Education and Urban Society*, vol. 33, no. 2, February 2001, p. 141. Observes that less that 1 percent of charter schools have ever been closed or not had their charters renewed due to poor performance, suggesting that charter school accountability is mainly political rhetoric.

Hess, Mary Anne. "America's Public Schools Under Attack." *NEA Today*, vol. 20, no. 4, p. 38. Uses war metaphors to describe the intensity of critics who seek the dismantling of public schools.

Hicks, Chester L. "Eight Years of Charter Schools." *Spectrum*, vol. 73, part 2, 2000, p. 4. Evaluates the history of charter schools and projects future issues relating to accountability, start-up funding, and external bureaucratic barriers.

Hill, Paul T. "Home Schooling and the Future of Public Education." *Peabody Journal of Education*, vol. 75, nos. 1 and 2, 2000, p. 20. Reports on the pros and cons of homeschooling, noting that more students are homeschooled than are enrolled in the entire New York City public school system.

Hoff, David J. "School Choice Programs Growing More Rapidly Outside the U.S." *Education Week*, vol. 20, no. 41, June 20, 2001, p. 5. Notes the trend of school choice methods, such as charter schools and vouchers in foreign countries including Great Britain, Belgium, the Netherlands, and Spain.

Holmes, Barbara J. "Understanding the Pros and Cons of Alternative Routes to Teacher Certification." *Teaching and Change*, vol. 8, no. 4, 2001, p. 317. Summarizes the main arguments in the teacher certification debate.

Hornbeck, Mark. "Charter Schools Lack Oversight." *Detroit News*, June 14, 2002, p. G1. Reports Michigan's auditor general's charge that the state's education department has failed to monitor the state's charter schools responsibly.

Jackson, Derrick Z. "The Big Lie: No Child Left Behind." *Boston Globe*, August 2, 2002, p. A19. Op-ed piece that criticizes the philosophy, approach, and implementation of the No Child Left Behind Act.

———. "Wall Street and Education Don't Mix." *Boston Globe*, June 14, 2002, p. A27. Op-ed piece that argues against the wisdom and effectiveness of private ventures in the classroom, such as Chris Whittle's Channel One.

Jacobs, Joanne. "Threatened by Success: One Charter School's Fight Against the Education Establishment." *Reason*, vol. 33, part 9, 2002, p. 38. Depicts opposition from teachers' unions and many school administrators to largely successful management of a San Francisco elementary school by Edison Schools.

Jeffords, Jim. "Back to School." *New York Times*, December 13, 2001, p. 39. Op-ed article by the senator whose departure from the Republican Party gave Senate majority to Democrats decries President George W. Bush's failure to adequately support education reform plans and warns that this lack of fiscal support may lead the bill to cause more harm than good.

Johnson, LouAnne. "The Queen of Education." *Education Week*, vol. 22, no. 3, May 8, 2002, p. 35. Op-ed piece by the former teacher made famous by her portrayal in the movie *Dangerous Minds* that outlines her desires to shrink classroom enrollment and curtail the emphasis on testing.

Johnston, Robert C. "Texas Study Links Teacher Certification, Student Success." *Education Week*, vol. 14, no. 2, May 12, 1999, p. 19. Reports findings of a University of Texas–Arlington study showing a direct relationship between student academic achievement and teacher certification in their field and claiming that needy students are more likely to have teachers not certified in their field.

Jonsson, Patrik. "When the Tests Fail." *Christian Science Monitor,* August 20, 2002, p. 11. Explains the difficulty states have had establishing effective and reliable assessment programs to hold schools and districts accountable for academic success.

Kahlenberg, Richard D. "All Together Now: Creating Middle-Class Schools Through Public School Choice." *Harvard Educational Review,* vol. 71, no. 4, 2001, p. 756. Argues that economically integrated schools will do more to promote achievement and equity than private school vouchers, standards, or other leading education reform proposals.

Kahlenberg, Richard D., and Lowell P. Weicker. "The New Education Divide." *Christian Science Monitor,* October 9, 2002, p. 9. Argues that efforts must intensify to break down socioeconomic segregation in schools, citing studies demonstrating concentrated poverty's relationship to poor student academic performance.

Kantrowitz, Barbara, and Pat Wingert. "Does Home Schooling Pass?" *Newsweek,* vol. 132, no. 14, 1998, p. 64. Examines characteristics of home-schooled students and finds that with networks of social support, many are very successful.

Keller, Bess. "In Staffing Policies, Charter Schools Seen as 'Innovative.'" *Education Week,* vol. 21, no. 4, September 26, 2001, p. 5. Reports on a study by the Thomas B. Fordham Foundation stating that charter schools tend to resemble private schools in teacher personnel matters, including higher rates of performance bonuses awarded and uncertified teachers hired.

———. "Paige Uses Report As a Rallying Cry to Fix Teacher Ed." *Education Week,* vol. 21, June 19, 2002, p. 25. Chronicles Secretary of Education Rod Paige's call to reform teacher certification, which he describes as "broken," and notes his recommendations.

Kemerer, Frank R. "The Constitutionality of School Vouchers." *West's Education Law Quarterly,* vol. 4, no. 4, October 1995, p. 646. Analyzes constitutional law as it relates to various school voucher programs across the United States.

Kemerer, Frank R., Thomas Kay, and Valerie Martinez. "Who Chooses and Why: A Look at Five School Choice Plans." *Phi Delta Kappan,* vol. 75, no. 9, May 1994, p. 678. Examines the reasoning and diversity of families who enroll their children in school choice programs.

Kennedy, Sheila Suess. "Privatizing Education: The Politics of Vouchers." *Phi Delta Kappan,* vol. 82, no. 6, February 2001, p. 450. Questions whether vouchers improve anything other than parental attitudes about education and expresses worry about their practical, constitutional, and fiscal effects.

Klagholz, Leo. "State Policy and Effective Alternative Teacher Certification." *Education Digest*, vol. 67, no. 1, September 2001, p. 33. Explores ways states such as New Jersey have been able to implement high standards for teachers without causing a teaching shortage by creating an alternative certification program.

Klein, M. Francis. "Whose Standards? What Curriculum?" *Kappa Delta Pi*, vol. 35, no. 2, Winter 1999, p. 60. Breaks down fundamental questions of how to select methods of education and evaluating students and how these decisions are made.

Kleiner, Carolyn. "Home Schooling Comes of Age." *U.S. News & World Report*, October 16, 2000, p. 52. Describes the growing popularity and influence of the homeschooling movement.

Kolbert, Elizabeth. "Unchartered Territory." *New Yorker*, vol. 76, no. 30, October 9, 2000, p. 34. Profiles an inner-city elementary school run by Advantage Schools, which uses the direct instruction method requiring teachers to follow a script during class lessons.

Kronholz, June. "For Florida Schools Size Is a Big Deal." *Wall Street Journal*, October 10, 2002, p. A4. Examines how proposed amendments to limit class size are causing political problems for Governor Jeb Bush, who opposes the measures.

Lankford, Hamilton, and James Wyckoff. "Who Would Be Left Behind by Enhanced Private School Choice?" *Journal of Urban Economics*, vol. 50, no. 2, 2001, p. 288. Looks at who will leave public schools and who will be left behind, an issue known as "skimming."

Lapham, Lewis H. "School on a Hill." *Harper's*, vol. 303, no. 1,816, September 2001, p. 49. Presents conversations between the magazine's editor and four leading education experts about the past, present, and future of U.S. public schools.

Lemann, Nicholus. "Ready, Read!" *Atlantic*, November 1998, p. 92. Argues that the takeover of public schools by outside authorities who prescribe a standardized curriculum works, despite diminishing the autonomy of teachers and local schools.

Levin, Henry M. "Privatizing Education: Can the Marketplace Deliver Choice, Efficiency, Equity, and Social Cohesion?" *Educational Administration Abstracts*, vol. 36, no. 4, 2001, p. 411. Uses a collection of essays by leading education scholars to look at the initiative to move education from the public sector to the private sector.

Lewin, Tamar. "For Mayoral Control of Schools, Chicago Has a Working Blueprint." *New York Times*, June 15, 2002, p. B1. Describes how Chicago reformed its public schools and how that model may be emulated by New York City mayor Michael Bloomberg in the nation's largest school system.

———. "Leaders from Other Professions Reshape America's Schools, from Top to Bottom." *New York Times*, June 8, 2000, p. 18. Describes how many urban districts are turning to law, business, government, and the military for new leadership and outside perspective.

———. "Schools Taking Tougher Stance with Standards." *New York Times*, September 6, 1999, p. A1. Examines how schools across the United States are establishing specific academic standards for students and how this intensified emphasis on assessment tests affects the process, perception, and quality of education.

"A Long Road to the Court." *Education Week*, vol. 21, July 10, 2002, pp. 18–21. Offers extensive and detailed chronology of school voucher movement.

Lord, Mary. "The New School Choice." *U.S. News & World Report*, August 5, 2002, p. 38. Illustrates one family's experience with the failing school provisions of recent federal education law.

Lubienski, Chris. "Whither the Common Good? A Critique of Home Schooling." *Peabody Journal of Education*, vol. 75, nos. 1 & 2, 2000, p. 207. Portrays negative aspects of homeschooling, including its money-draining effect on public schools.

Lytle, James H. "Whole School Reform from the Inside." *Phi Delta Kappan*, vol. 84, no. 2, October 2002, p. 164. Discusses how urban superintendents with experience collaborating with other school system leaders have worked to improve schools and minority student achievement.

Mac Iver, Martha Abele. "Seeking Justice in Educational Opportunity: An Analysis of the Evidence on School Vouchers and Children Placed at Risk." *Journal of Education for Students Placed at Risk*, vol. 5, no. 4, 2000, p. 397. Provides analysis of vouchers' role in improving the education of at-risk students.

Magliaro, Susan, and William A. Owings. "Grade Retention: A History of Failure." *Educational Leadership*, vol. 56, no. 1, September 1998, p. 86. Disputes claims that retention benefits students and warns of its continued practice in the face of research showing its damaging effects.

Malveaux, Julianne. "Guide to the School-Choice Debate: Charters, Vouchers, For-Profit: The Fundamentals Explained." *Essence*, vol. 31, no. 5, September 1, 2000, p. 158. Breaks down key components of the school choice issues with emphasis on how school choice affects the African-American community.

Manno, Bruno V. "The Case Against Charter Schools." *School Administrator*, vol. 58, no. 5, May 2001, p. 28. Debunks the 10 most common complaints about the charter school movement, including charges that charters rob funds from traditional public schools and that they are too risky and unproven.

"Many Children Left Behind." *San Francisco Chronicle*, September 18, 2002, p. A22. Op-ed piece that explains the rift between President George W. Bush and California Democratic representative George Miller, who blames the president for failing to adequately support federal education reform that Miller helped push through Congress.

Marantz Cohen, Rosetta. "The Key to School Reform: Becoming Teacher-Centered." *Current*, September 2002, p. 3. Calls for school reforms to focus on boosting the training and work conditions of teachers.

Matthews, Jay. "Success for Some." *Washington Post*, July 21, 2002, p. W30. Examines a controversial method for teaching reading in underachieving schools that focuses on a highly structured and monitored form of instruction.

McCarthy, Martha M. "What Is the Verdict on School Vouchers?" *Phi Delta Kappan*, vol. 81, no. 5, January 2000, p. 371. Summarizes key school voucher litigation in Cleveland, Ohio; Milwaukee, Wisconsin; Vermont; and Maine.

McCombs, Barbara L. "What Makes a Comprehensive School Reform Model Learner Centered?" *Urban Education*, vol. 37, no. 4, September 2002, p. 476. Focuses on improving schools by prioritizing effective instructional approaches for students.

McDonald, Sister Dale. "A Chronology of Parental Choice in Education." *Momentum*, vol. 32, no. 2, April–May 2001, p. 10. Provides historical overview of parental choice with an emphasis on its relation to Catholic education.

McEwan, Patrick J. "The Potential Impact of Large-Scale Voucher Programs." *Review of Educational Research*, vol. 70, no. 2, Summer 2000, p. 103. Posits that there is insufficient evidence for either implementing or opposing a large-scale voucher plan.

McPherson, Stephanie Sammartino. "*Lau v. Nichols:* Bilingual Education in Public Schools." *School Library Journal*, February 2001, vol. 47, no. 2, p. 136. Explains the history of education for non-English speakers in the United States and details the landmark Supreme Court case that helped establish bilingual education programs.

Medlin, Richard G. "Home Schooling and the Question of Socialization." *Peabody Journal of Education*, vol. 75, nos. 1 and 2, 2000, p. 107. Depicts how homeschoolers participate in social activities and generally have good self-esteem when reaching adulthood.

Meeks, Loretta F. "Racial Desegregation: Magnet Schools, Vouchers, Privatization, and Home Schooling." *Education and Urban Society*, vol. 33, no. 1, November 2000, p. 88. Explains that diminished court-ordered desegregation has resulted in the emergence of school choice programs to help poor families gain access to better schools.

Milbank, Dana. "Schoolyard Tussle." *New Republic*, December 14, 1998, p. 22. Notes Massachusetts senator John Kerry's call to end current use of teacher tenure, suggesting that other Democrats traditionally supportive of teachers' unions are sensing a deep degree of dissatisfaction among parents with the condition of public schools.

Mintrom, Michael. "The Market Approach to Education: An Analysis of America's First Voucher Program." *American Political Science Review*, vol. 95, no. 1, March 2001, p. 227. Provides framework for understanding Milwaukee, Wisconsin's school choice program, arguing that although it seems to be working in Milwaukee, such programs, if applied more broadly, may harm the poor.

Molnar, Alex. "Charter Schools: The Smiling Face of Disinvestment." *Educational Leadership*, vol. 54, no. 2, 1996, p. 9. Asserts that charter schools attack the democratic ideal represented by traditional public schools through a market mentality that "threatens to turn every relationship into a commercial transaction."

Morse, Jodie. "Do Charter Schools Pass the Test?" *Time*, June 4, 2001, p. 60. Analyzes the mixed results charter schools have had on education reform in Arizona and nationwide.

———. "A Victory for Vouchers." *Time*, vol. 160, July 8, 2002, p. 32. Reviews the Supreme Court decision in the Cleveland school voucher case and previews other potential legal skirmishes over school choice.

Muir, Edward. "Smaller Schools: How Much More Than a Fad?" *American Educator*, vol. 24, no. 4, Winter 2000–2001, p. 40. Claims that the movement toward smaller schools is not just another temporary education trend but suggests that many questions remain about the effects of school size on learning.

Murray, Richard K. "The Impact of School Uniforms on School Climate." *NASSP Bulletin*, vol. 81, no. 593, December 1997, p. 106. Depicts how a uniform policy has led to a significantly higher perception of the school climate at a middle school in South Carolina.

Natriello, Gary. "Failing Grades for Retention." *School Administrator*, vol. 55, no. 7, August 1998, p. 14. Highlights research indicating that holding students back causes mainly negative effects and urges an expansion of the social promotion debate in order to better serve students.

"Nine Shared Strengths of Reform-Minded Districts." *What Works in Teaching and Learning*, vol. 34, no. 19, September 18, 2002, p. 6. Comprises a report by the Council of Great City School, identifying characteristics exhibited by four districts that have helped spur successful changes in student achievement, instructional quality, and system accountability.

O'Connor, Lona. "More and More Parents Opt for Home-Schooling, Census Study Finds." *South Florida Sun Sentinel,* July 15, 2002, p. 1A. Relates information from a U.S. Census Bureau study noting homeschooled population of more than 670,000 compared to about 500,000 enrolled in charter schools.

Olson, Carl O. "Is a Ban on Social Promotion Necessary?" *School Administrator,* vol. 56, no. 11, December 1999, p. 48. Describes increasingly popular sentiment against social promotion as "draconian" and explains reasons why such a ban would be ill advised.

Olson, Lynn. "Testing Rules Would Grant States Leeway." *Education Week,* March 6, 2002, vol. 21, pp. 1, 36–7. Describes new federal regulations for standardized assessments that have been generally welcomed by state officials while criticized by others as creating a patchwork system.

Opfer, V. Darleen. "Charter Schools and the Panoptic Effect of Accountability." *Education and Urban Society,* vol. 33, no. 2, 2001, p. 201. Analyzes Georgia's charter school policy and points out that the centralizing effect of accountability laws can prevent the autonomy promised by charter school advocates.

Oplinger, Doug, and Dennis J. Willar. "School Overhaul Ordered." *Akron Beacon Journal,* December 12, 2002, p. A1. Explains the Ohio Supreme Court ruling that requires the state to reduce its reliance on property tax funding.

Osborne, David. "Healthy Competition." *New Republic,* October 4, 1999, p. 31. Uses positive reform results from charter school legislation in Michigan, Arizona, Massachusetts, and Minnesota to explain why the greatest beneficiaries of charter schools may be the students who remain in regular public schools.

Paglin, Catherine. "Why Charter Schools Stumble—and Sometimes Fall." *Northwest Education,* vol. 6, no. 3, Spring 2001, p. 20. Describes common financial, legal, technical, and personal obstacles experienced by charter school founders that often prevent the successful implementation of charter schools.

Parker, Wendy. "The Color of Choice: Race and Charter Schools." *Tulane Law Review,* vol. 75, no. 3, 2001, p. 563. Critiques the growing charter school movement from the perspective of the Equal Protection Clause, claiming that schools geared toward one racial or ethnic group are unconstitutional.

Paulson, Amanda. "A Plan to Trust Schools—Not Just Tests." *Christian Science Monitor,* September 17, 2002, p. 14. Features an interview with prominent education reform advocate Deborah Meier, who states that testing lowers standards by emphasizing breadth over depth and makes schools accountable for the wrong things.

———. "True Believer." *Christian Science Monitor,* September 10, 2002, p. 15. Profiles the background, educational philosophy, and current impact of Secretary of Education Rod Paige.

Perlstein, Daniel. "Failing at Kindness: Why Fear of Violence Endangers Children." *Educational Leadership,* vol. 57, no. 6, 2000, p. 76. Explains the futility of attempts to promote tolerance for students through policies of zero tolerance.

Pestritto, Ronald J. "Home School Backlash." *Orange County Register,* September 2, 2002. Op-ed piece defending homeschooling from attacks by state bureaucracies and teachers' unions.

Peterson, Paul. "Top Ten Questions Asked about School Choice." *Brookings Papers on Education Policy,* 1999, p. 371. Discusses the most commonly raised questions regarding school choice, including what it is, who supports it, and who takes advantage of opportunity to choose schools.

Pipho, Chris. "A New Reform Model for Teachers and Teaching." *Phi Delta Kappan,* vol. 81, no. 6, February 2000, p. 421. Suggests allowing teachers to have more influence in the creation of teacher certification programs.

Pooley, Eric. "Who Gets the 'A' in Education?" *Time,* March 27, 2000, p. 38. Analyzes the stated positions on education policy of Vice President Al Gore and Governor George W. Bush before the 2000 presidential election.

Ramanathan, Arun K., and Nancy J. Zollers. "For-Profit Charter Schools and Students with Disabilities: The Sordid Side of the Business of Schooling." *Phi Delta Kappan,* vol. 80, no. 4, 1998, p. 297. Rips three for-profit education management companies for failing to provide required services, using inappropriate disciplinary procedures, and segregating disabled students.

Rangazas, Peter. "Competition and Private School Vouchers." *Education Economics,* vol. 5, no. 3, December 1997, p. 245. Uses economic models of interpretation to determine whether private school vouchers would increase educational quality in public and private schools.

Rasheed, Aesha. "Mayoral Takeovers of Schools Show Promise: Expert Recommends Multifaceted Plan." *New Orleans Times-Picayune,* October 8, 2002, p. 1. Details meeting between Vanderbilt University professor and education reform expert Kenneth Wong and Louisiana's Local Education Governance and Administration Task Force, which is evaluating various approaches to school improvement.

Ratnesar, Romesh. "The Bite on Teachers." *Time,* July 20, 1998, p. 22. Details how attacks on teachers' unions by conservative education critics have intensified the political struggle for education reform.

Rees, Nina Shokraii. "Public School Benefits of Private School Vouchers." *Policy Review,* January–February 1999, p. 16. Claims that school choice programs are gaining momentum and that they improve the overall quality of all schools.

Reid, Karla Scoon. "Black Alliance Weighs in with Pro-Voucher Campaign." *Education Week*, May 30, 2001, vol. 20, no. 38, p. 8. Describes efforts of the Black Alliance for Educational Options, organized by the former Milwaukee, Wisconsin, schools superintendent.

———. "Minority Parents Quietly Embrace School Choice." *Education Week*, vol. 21, no. 14, December 5, 2001, p. 1. Explains emergence of minority parents as visible and vocal leaders in cities with voucher programs.

"Revise Teacher Certification." *Detroit News*, July 16, 2002, p. A6. Op-ed piece that calls for significant changes in the way teachers become certified, including a loosening of the emphasis on pedagogy popular in schools of education.

Rimer, Sara. "More Chaotic Start, More Orderly Students." *New York Times*, September 27, 2002, p. 22. Presents the ups and downs of Edison, Inc.'s management of some Philadelphia schools.

Robelen, Erik W. "ESEA to Boost Federal Role in Education." *Education Week*, January 9, 2002, vol. 21, pp. 1, 28–29, 31. Previews the reauthorization of the Elementary and Secondary Education Act by President George W. Bush, emphasizing the increased prominence of the federal government, particularly in school accountability and assessment.

———. "Few Choosing Public School Choice for This Fall." *Education Week*, vol. 21, August 7, 2002, p. 1. Examines reasons why, despite new federal regulations allowing transfers from underperforming schools, very few students have switched schools and explains that some districts do not have available slots.

———. "Paige, Bush Upbeat on Making ESEA Work." *Education Week*, September 11, 2002, vol. 22, pp. 23, 25. Describes federal officials' optimistic outlook regarding how the new federal education law is playing out in states and school districts.

———. "Ruling Gives Second Wind to Capitol Hill Voucher Advocates." *Education Week*, July 10, 2002, vol. 21, p. 27. Depicts how the Cleveland voucher case has spurred legislative activity within the U.S. Congress.

———. "Senate Deal Would Allow Vouchers for Tutors." *Education Week*, vol. 20, no. 30, April 11, 2001, p. 29. Reports agreement between key senators and the White House that would allow students in persistently failing schools to use federal dollars for private tutoring but not for private schools.

Romanowski, Michael H. "Common Arguments About the Strengths and Limitations of Home Schooling." *Clearing House*, vol. 75, no. 2, November–December 2001, p. 79. Details various aspects of the homeschooling debate, including socialization and public school quality.

Annotated Bibliography

————. "Undoing the 'Us vs. Them' of Public and Home Schooling." *Education Digest*, vol. 66, no. 9, May 2001, p. 41. Discusses the lack of understanding among public school educators regarding parental motivation to homeschool children and presents strategies to strengthen dialogue between these groups.

Rosen, Gary. "Are School Vouchers Un-American?—The Arguments Against Educational Choice Are Serious but Wrong." *Commentary*, vol. 109, no. 2, 2000, p. 26. Criticizes the staunch opposition among liberals to school choice initiatives, claiming that this opposition amounts to a "stonewalling in favor of a clearly unacceptable status quo."

Rothstein, Richard. "Raising School Standards and Cutting Budget: Huh?" *New York Times*, July 10, 2002, p. B8. Points out conflict between pursuing higher academic standards and cutting of programs due to likely drops in fiscal support for education.

————. "Where Is Lake Wobegone, Anyway? The Controversy Surrounding Social Promotion." *Phi Delta Kappan*, vol. 80, no. 3, November 1998, p. 195. Details the emerging conflict over the issue of allowing students to continue to the next grade based on age, not academic mastery.

Rouse, Cecilia Elena. "Market Approaches to Education: Vouchers and School Choice." *Economic of Education Review*, vol. 19, no. 4, 2000, p. 458. Presents generally positive summary of market-related education reforms.

Ruenzel, David. "Tortuous Routes." *Education Next*, Spring 2002, p. 42. Criticizes roadblocks preventing nontraditional teaching candidates, usually recent college graduates and career changers who have not attended standard teacher certification programs, from teaching in the classroom.

Ryan, Jim. "School Choice and the Suburbs." *Journal of Law & Politics*, vol. 14, no. 3, Summer 1998, p. 459. Argues that the most significant barrier to expansion of school choice programs are suburban parents who fear urban students having unlimited access to suburban schools.

Sack, Joetta. "State Leaders Gauge Impact of New ESEA, Voucher Ruling." *Education Week*, vol. 21, August 7, 2002, p. 43. Reports states' efforts to understand and comply with recent changes in federal education law.

Sandham, Jessica L. "Challenges to Charter Laws Mount." *Education Week*, vol. 20, no. 33, May 2, 2001, p. 1. Notes serious legal opposition to existing charter school laws in states such as Pennsylvania and Texas that have traditionally been friendly to publicly financed but administratively independent schools.

Sansbury, Jen. "School Reform Guidelines Come Late." *Atlanta Journal-Constitution*, August 3, 2002, p. H1. Explains how the No Child Left Behind regulations were released too late for school systems to comply.

Schnaiberg, Lynn. "Home Schooling Queries Spike After Shootings." *Education Week*, vol. 18, no. 39, June 9, 1999, p. 3. Cites concerns about the correlation between the highly publicized Columbine High School massacre and the marked increase in requests for homeschooling information by parents across the country.

"School Choice Battles Embroil Many States." *CQ Researcher,* vol. 7, no. 27, July 18, 1997, p. 629. Details the common characteristics and unique qualities of the many education reform debates throughout the United States.

"School Standards Paradox." *Los Angeles Times,* September 15, 2002, p. M4. Op-ed piece that decries how states such as Connecticut and Ohio have lowered the definition of proficiency in order to reduce the chances that their schools will be punished for poor performance under federal measures.

Schorr, Jonathan. "You Still Need a Blackboard—What's Right and Wrong with the Charter Schools." *Washington Monthly,* vol. 32, no. 6, 2000, p. 15. Supports the use of charter schools but urges increased scrutiny in granting of charters to prevent poorly planned, low-quality education for students.

Sianjina, Rayton R. "Parental Choice, School Vouchers, and Separation of Church and State: Legal Implications." *Educational Forum,* vol. 63, no. 2, Winter 1999, p. 108. Reviews claims of school voucher supporters and addresses constitutionality issues.

Simpson, Michael D. "Dress Codes Are Back in Style." *NEA Today,* vol. 19, no. 7, p. 18. Reports on three court rulings that rejected student free speech claims and reaffirmed broad authority of school officials to tell students how to dress.

Skiba, Russell J. "School Discipline at a Crossroads: From Zero Tolerance to Early Response." *Exceptional Children,* vol. 66, no. 3, Spring 2000, p. 335. States that despite the dramatic rise in the use of zero-tolerance policies, there has been little evidence demonstrating that these procedures have increased school safety or improved student behavior.

Soler, Stephanie. "Teacher Quality Is Job One: Why States Need to Revamp Teacher Certification." *Spectrum,* vol. 72, no. 2, Spring 1999, p. 23. Emphasizes that ensuring teacher quality is as important to academic achievements as high standards, adequate resources, and accountability.

Staples, Brent. "School Vouchers: A Small Tool for a Very Big Problem." *New York Times,* August 5, 2002, p. A14. Op-ed piece describing weaknesses in arguments of school voucher advocates.

Starr, Jennifer. "School Violence and Its Effect on the Constitutionality of Public School Uniform Policies." *Journal of Law and Education,* vol. 29, no. 1, January 2000, p. 113. Discusses an Arizona court of appeals decision that mandatory school uniforms do not violate students' First Amendment rights.

Sterngold, James. "Taking a New Look at Uniforms and Their Impact on Schools." *New York Times,* June 28, 2000, p. B11. Surveys the recent history of school uniform policies across the United States, including Long

Beach, California's program that many claim has resulted in a rise in academic achievement and drops in absenteeism and discipline problems.

Stevenson, Kenneth R. "Privatization of Public Education: Panacea or Pandora's Box?" *School Business Affairs*, vol. 65, no. 11, November 1999, p. 14. Explains that, although the privatizing of charter schools is becoming big business, its cost effectiveness is unproven.

Stodghill, Ron. "Mayors Rule the Schools." *Time*, April 12, 1999, p. 74. Describes the increasing influence big city mayors have in enacting education reform and its broader implications.

Stricherz, Mark. "Nonprofit Group Forms to Challenge 'Monopoly.'" *Education Week*, vol. 20, no. 30, April 11, 2001, p. 4. Describes efforts of philanthropist and financier Theodore Forstman, as well as a bipartisan board of prominent leaders including Martin Luther King II and Senator John McCain, to form Parents in Charge, an organization designed to help strengthen parental voice in choosing schools for their children.

Sugarman, Stephen D. "Approving Charter Schools: The Gate-Keeper Function." *Administrative Law Review*, vol. 53, no. 3, Summer 2001, p. 869. Examines the charter-granting administrative powers of local school districts and state boards of education and recommends new arrangements to improve the quality of charter schools.

Sullivan, Patricia. "The PTA's National Standards." *Educational Leadership*, vol. 55, no. 8, 1998, p. 43. Evaluates the national organization's guidelines for parent and family involvement in schools, including homework help and tips for serving on school councils.

Tebo, Margaret Graham. "School Discipline: Zero Tolerance, Zero Sense." *ABA Journal*, April 2000, p. 40. Offers anecdotal evidence to lambaste the philosophy and implementation of zero-tolerance policies.

Thampy, George Abraham. "Home Schooling Spells Success." *Wall Street Journal*, June 7, 2000, p. A26. Op-ed piece written by the 12-year-old homeschooled winner of the National Spelling Bee, lauding the quality of his educational experience.

Thomas, M. Donald. "No Child Left Behind: Facts and Fallacies." *Phi Delta Kappan*, vol. 83, no. 10, June 2002, p. 781. Details the commonly held beliefs and misconceptions of recent federal education law.

Tierney, John. "A Liberal Case for Vouchers (No Kidding)." *New York Times*, September 8, 2000, p. B1. Op-ed piece offering former Clinton administration secretary of labor Robert Reich's support of voucher programs as evidence of the shifting thought within the Democratic Party on school choice.

Toch, Thomas. "Education Bazaar." *U.S. News & World Report*, vol. 124, no. 16, April 27, 1998, p. 34. Profiles a charter school in Arizona that offers franchises to the operator for a fee of $1,000 per student.

Toppo, Greg. "Study: Charter School Students Score Lower." *Washington Post*, September 3, 2002, p. A7. Cites information for a study by the Brookings Institute that indicates weaker reading and math scores by charter school students compared to students in regular public schools, noting how many charter schools are designed to attract underachieving students.

Traub, James. "The Test Mess." *New York Times Magazine*, April 7, 2002, p. 46. Expresses the opposition among many educators, parents, and students to the prominence of state-administered tests and how these tests are used to judge students, schools, and teachers.

———. "What No School Can Do." *New York Times Magazine*, January 16, 2000, p. 52. States that much of the discussion of education reform is predicated on the flawed view that schools, by themselves, can cure poverty and claims that efforts to improve inner-city schools have done little to raise achievement of poor children.

Trotter, Andrew. "Bennett's Online Education Venture Opens for Business." *Education Week*, vol. 21, no. 7, p. 8. Reports on K12, Inc., a for-profit company started by former Reagan administration secretary of education William Bennett and designed to deliver "classical" education to U.S. children.

Tumulty, Karen, and Douglass Waller. "The President Who Used to Care About Education." *Time*, April 16, 2001, p. 18. Explains the view that President George W. Bush has abandoned educational initiatives expressed during his 2000 campaign and how this inattention has weakened conservative efforts for federal education reform.

Urbanski, Adam. "School Reform, TURN, and Teacher Compensation." *Phi Delta Kappan*, vol. 81, no. 5, January 2000, p. 367. Discusses how important aspects of school reform require new forms of labor/management collaboration and argues that such partnerships have already brought about successful innovation.

Vaishnav, Anand. "Bilingual Edition Advocates Marshal Forces: Statehouse Rally Sparks War of Words." *Boston Globe*, October 1, 2002, p. B2. Recounts demonstration by bilingual education supporters against a Massachusetts ballot initiative, led by California businessman Ron Unz, that would replace bilingual programs with English immersion.

———. "MCAS Divides Voters, Poll Finds English Immersion Has Strong Support." *Boston Globe*, September 2, 2002, p. B1. Reports steady approval among Massachusetts citizens for English immersion strategies for teaching English as opposed to bilingual programs.

Viadero, Debra. "Increased Choice Found to Have Modest Impact on School Improvement." *Education Week*, vol. 21, no. 14, December 5, 2001, p. 11. Cites findings of competition on education by Columbia University's Teachers College National Center for the Study of Privatization of Education, showing a slight improvement in education achievement.

Viteritti, Joseph P. "Abolish the Board of Education." *New York Times*, January 6, 2002, section 4, p. 15. Op-ed article by education professor states that New York City mayor Michael Bloomberg should seek to wrest control of the public schools, as other mayors in major cities have in recent years.

Volokh, Alexander. "School Choice Could Help Alleviate Violence." *Wall Street Journal*, April 29, 1999, p. 1. States that schools will be safer when they are allowed the freedom and accountability to set up systems that work for them.

Walsh, Mark. "Advocates' Post-Ruling Choice: Bubbly" *Education Week*, vol. 21, July 10, 2002, p. 25. Examines the reaction and strategies of provoucher advocates following the Supreme Court's decision in the Cleveland voucher case.

———. "Justices Settle Case, Nettle Policy Debate." *Education Week*, vol. 21, July 10, 2002, pp. 1, 18–21. Analyzes the U.S. Supreme Court's landmark ruling upholding the Cleveland voucher program and its implications on the debate over how best to improve public education.

———. "RAND Study Balances the Debate on School Choice." *Education Week*, vol. 21, no. 15, December 12, 2001, p. 1. Reviews major scholarly research of private school vouchers and charter schools, concluding that there are no clear answers about whether they are an effective alternative to traditional public school systems.

Weiher, Gregory R. "Does Choice Lead to Racially Distinctive Schools? Charter Schools and Household Preferences." *Journal of Policy Analysis and Management*, vol. 21, no. 1, Winter 2002, p. 79. Analyzes survey of families who chose charter schools and finds that whites, Latinos, and African Americans typically transfer into charter schools where their groups comprise 11–14 percent more of the student body than the traditional public schools they are leaving.

White, Charles, and Charles F. Williams. "School Voucher Plans Raise Key Church-State Issues: Looking at the Law." *Social Education*, vol. 64, no. 1, January–February 2000, p. 56. Examines key constitutional issues separating advocates on both sides of school choice debate.

White, Kerry A. "Do School Uniforms Fit?" *School Administrator*, vol. 57, no. 2, February 2000, p. 36. Evaluates research on school uniform polices and concludes that tighter dress codes may be just as effective and less litigious.

Whitford, David. "Big Idea Capitalism." *Esquire*, vol. 138, August 2002, p. 50. Examines the difficulties Edison Schools and CEO Chris Whittle have experienced in Philadelphia.

Wildavsky, Ben. "A Blow to Bilingual Education English Immersion May Raise Test Scores." *U.S. News & World Report*, September 4, 2000, p. 20.

Cites evidence from studies in California demonstrating a possible link between growth in academic achievement and intensive English instruction to non-English-speaking students.

Wilgoren, Jodi. "Chief Executive of Chicago Schools Resigns." *New York Times*, June 7, 2001, p. 26. Reports the resignation of Paul Vallas, who led the turnaround of Chicago's troubled school system and became national role model for urban school reform.

———. "The New Administration: The Education Issue." *New York Times*, January 23, 2001, p. A1. Summarizes important aspects of President George W. Bush's policies for education reform, including accountability measures such as standardized tests, school report cards, and pay incentives for teachers.

———. "School Vouchers: A Rose by Other Name?" *New York Times*, December 20, 2000, p. A1. Explains how many school choice advocates have avoided the word *'vouchers'* as they seek to advance the movement following recent defeats in court.

———. "Wendy Kopp, Leader of Teach For America." *New York Times—Education Supplement*, November 12, 2000, p. 23. Explores influential impact of Teach For America in impoverished schools and on the discussion of teacher certification.

Wilkins, Julia. "School Uniforms: The Answer to Violence in American Schools or a Cheap Educational Reform?" *Humanist*, vol. 59, no. 2, March 1, 1999, p. 19. Claims that despite the Clinton administration's endorsement of school uniform policies, such plans create more problems than they solve.

Winans, Dave. "School Funding Adequacy—What It Costs to Do the Job Right." *NEA Today*, vol. 21, no. 1, September 2002, p. 18. Describes the concept of adequacy, in which components of quality education required by law, standards, or court decisions, are costed out and funded by the state on an ongoing basis with adjustments for inflation, enrollment changes, and evolving student needs.

Winters, Rebecca. "Trouble for School Inc." *Time*, May 27, 2002, p. 53. Describes the recent problems experienced by Edison Schools, including dissolution of contracts and accusations of accounting irregularities.

———. "Vouchers: More Heat Than Light." *Time*, vol. 156, no. 15, October 9, 2000, p. 76. Explains opposing viewpoints on the voucher issue within the context of the 2000 presidential election.

Wraga, William G. "The Educational and Political Implications of Curriculum Alignment and Standards-Based Reform." *Journal of Curriculum and Supervision*, vol. 15, no. 1, 1999, p. 4. Reveals that both curriculum alignment and standards-based reform are heavy on political expediency but light on educational efficacy.

Zehr, Mary Ann. "Bush Plan Could Alter Bilingual Education." *Education Week*, vol. 20, no. 23, February 21, 2001, p. 17. Details President George W. Bush's proposed education plan seeking the elimination of a federal government stipulation that gives preference to bilingual education programs over English-only programs.

———. "Catholics Laud Voucher Decision, See Potential for Growth." *Education Week*, July 10, 2002, vol. 21, p. 26. Chronicles how religiously affiliated schools view the prospects of increased private school choice.

———. "Ethnic-Based Schools Popular." *Education Week*, vol. 21, no. 2, September 12, 2001, p. 38. Reports on prominence of minority groups establishing charter schools, noting that these schools cannot exclude students based on the basis of race or national origin.

———. "Poll: Immigrants Value Speaking English." *Education Week*, January 22, 2003, p. 3. Reports findings of survey by Public Agenda that indicates that immigrants are no more likely than the general public to support bilingual education in public schools.

Zellner, Wendy. "Going to Bat for Vouchers: Wal-Mart Heir John Walton Leads a Crusade for Taxpayer-Funded School Reform." *Business Week (Industrial/Technology Edition)*, February 7, 2000, p. 76. Describes the billionaire's program to fund 40,000 private scholarships that allow poor children to attend private schools and his work supporting publicly supported vouchers.

Zernike, Kate. "Crackdown on Threats in School Fails a Test." *New York Times*, May 17, 2001, p. A1. Describes the application of a zero-tolerance policy in suburban Manalapan, New Jersey, where more than 50 elementary students were suspended in less than two months for what were deemed verbal threats and notes the increasing frustration of parents to this policy.

———. "Decisions That Have Shaped U.S. Education." *Educational Leadership*, vol. 59, no. 4, December 2001–January 2002, p. 6. Analyzes the most critical legal decisions in education over the past six decades, including decisions affecting freedom of expression, school safety, and equality.

———. "A Uniform Policy." *Phi Delta Kappan*, vol. 79, no. 7, March 1998, p. 550. Reviews a Phoenix court decision upholding a school's decision to transfer a student to a nonuniform policy school for not complying with the school's uniform policy, pointing out the court's justification for its decision.

Zitterkopf, R. A. "Home Schooling: Just Another Silver Bullet." *School Administrator*, vol. 57, part 11, 2000, p. 55. Criticizes advocates who claim homeschooling is a genuine reform, describing it as a simpleminded step backward in providing quality education and equity.

INTERNET DOCUMENTS

American Federation of Teachers, AFL-CIO. "AFT Study Reveals Charter Schools Not Meeting Expectations." aft.org. Available online. URL: http://www.aft.org/press/2002/071702.html. Posted July 17, 2002. Press release that summarizes the findings of a report criticizing the effectiveness of charter schools.

Benfer, Amy. "A Reprieve for Public Schools." Salon.com. Available online. URL: http://dir.salon.com/mwt/feature/2000/11/10/kozol/index.html. Posted November 10, 2000. Essay that features the thoughts of author and education reform proponent Jonathan Kozol following the 2000 elections.

"Blum Center Pamphlets." Blum Center Home Page. Available online. URL: http://www.marquette.edu/blum/pamph.html. Updated January 26, 1999. This site lists links to pamphlets written by Quentin Quade, an early leader in the school choice movement. The Blum Center shut its doors in August 1999.

Capitol Resource Institute. "Reprint of Superintendent of Public Instruction Delaine Eastin's Letter to California Legislators." Capitol Resource Institute. Available online. URL: http://capitolresource.org/deletter.htm. Posted August 27, 2002. Letter asserts that homeschooling in California is illegal because there is no explicit law in the state governing it.

Center for Education Reform. "Charter Law Scorecard Ranks States: 5th Annual Analysis Finds New Trends, Weakened Laws." Center for Education Reform Website. Available online. URL: http://www.edreform.com/press/2001/cslaws.htm. Posted November 9, 2001. This press release outlines criteria for annual analysis of charter school laws and laments the lack of legislative momentum in the movement.

———. "Charter Leaders Dismiss AFT Report: Data Deliberately Skewed for AFT Gain." Center for Education Reform Website. Available online. URL: http://www.edreform.com/press/2002/aft_charter_report.htm. Posted July 16, 2002. This press release rips the credibility of an AFT report on charter school failure.

———. "Poll Finds 63% of Americans Support School Choice: Other Surveys Find Growing Support." Center for Education Reform Website. Available online. URL: http://www.edreform.com/press/2002/choicepoll.htm. Posted August 20, 2002. This press release cites poll data that notes high rates of support for school choice programs, particularly among African Americans, and criticizes methods used in a Phi Delta Kappa poll that reported very different opinions on the issue.

———. "Statement by Center for Education Reform President Jeanne Allen on Supreme Court Ruling Supporting School Choice for Cleveland Children." Center for Education Reform Website. Available online.

URL: http://www.edreform.com/press/2002/ohiovictory.htm. Posted June 27, 2002. This press release presents the organization's official endorsement of the Supreme Court's decision in the Cleveland voucher program case.

"CNN.com—Web Search with Look Smart—School Reform." CNN.com/ Search with Look Smart. Available online. URL: http://cnn.looksmart. com/eus1/eus317836/eus317912/eus53720/eus72125/eus72093/r?1& izch&. Downloaded January 1, 2003. A directory of links to web sites on charter schools, class-size reduction, curriculum and instruction, school vouchers, and other education reform issues.

Committee for Education Funding. "American Public Links Education Funding to a Strong and Secure Nation." Committee for Education Funding Website. Available online. URL: http://www.cef.org/News/ templates/press.asp?articleid=5&zoneid=1. Posted March 19, 2002. This press release reports that 85 percent of Americans believe it is important that federal funding for education receive a substantial increase even if it means a large federal budget deficit.

Dykema, Ravi. "How Schools Fail Kids and How They Could Be Better: An Interview with Ted Sizer." NEXUS, Colorado's Holistic Journal. Available online. URL: http://www.nexuspub.com/articles/2002/may2002/ interview1.htm. Posted May/June 2002. This features the thoughts of the prominent education reform advocate and founder of the Coalition of Essential Schools.

Educational Testing Service. Education Poll: "Increased Funding and Accountability Essential to Reform." Educational Testing Service. Available online. URL: http://www.ets.org/news/01052401.html. Posted May 24, 2001. This press release explains how a broad national public opinion poll indicates a majority of Americans are demanding both increased federal funding and greater accountability for schools.

"The Education Electorate." *Education Week.* Available online. URL: http:// www.edweek.org/sreports/special_reports_article.cfm?slug=electorate. htm. Downloaded July 20, 2002. Article highlights results of Public Education Network's annual opinion poll on the public's attitude toward education and finds that Americans continue to place education and school funding issues among their top priorities.

"The Education Gadfly." Thomas B. Fordham Foundation. Available online. URL: http://www.edexcellence.net/gadfly/v02/gadfly26.html. Page features broad collection of reports, opinion pieces, and links on contemporary issues in education reform.

Feldman, Sandra. "Statement by Sandra Feldman, President, American Federation of Teachers, on the Supreme Court's Ruling on School Vouchers." aft.org. Available online. URL: http://www.aft.org/press/2002/062702.

html. Posted June 27, 2002. This states AFT's vigorous opposition to the Supreme Court ruling in the Cleveland voucher program case.

Fisher, Ann L. "Exploring Homeschooling Diversity: A Friendly Little Chat." National Home Education Network. Available online. URL: http://www.nhen.org/media/default.asp?id=361. Downloaded January 22, 2003. This statement dismisses the notion that homeschooling is dominated by the Christian Right and details the wide variety of families who have adopted homeschooling.

Freedman, Samuel G. "Giuliani Flunks School-Voucher Test." Salon.com Available online. URL: http://www.salon.com/news/feature/1999/05/12/vouchers/index.html. Posted May 12, 1999. The article criticizes the New York City mayor for deriding the city's public schools as "terrible" and suggesting that the whole system should be "blown up."

"*Frontline:* Testing Our Schools." PBS. Available online. URL: http://www.pbs.org/wgbh/pages/frontline/shows/schools/. Posted March 28, 2002. This page includes a rich variety of links on topics addressed in the television program as well as a downloadable transcript of the episode.

Gallup, Alec M., and Lowell C. Rose. "The 34th Annual Phi Delta Kappa/Gallup Poll of the Public's Attitudes Toward the Public Schools." Phi Delta Kappa International. Available online. URL: http://www.pdkintl.org/kappan/k0209pol.htm. Posted August 20, 2002. The posting features a complete set of links relating to Phi Delta Kappa's annual evaluation.

General Accounting Office. "School Vouchers: Characteristics of Privately Funded Programs," General Accounting Office. Available online. URL: http://www.gao.gov/new.items/d02752.pdf. Downloaded on January 21, 2003. Article analyzes 78 privately funded voucher programs and praises their role in helping support academic improvement of students and school satisfaction of parents.

Education Week. "Hot Topics." Education Week. Available online. http://www.edweek.org/context/topics/. Page contains background essays on key education issues in America and includes links to relevant stories from the *Education Week* archives.

———. "School of Lies." Salon.com. Available online. URL: http://dir.salon.com/politics/feature/2001/05/07/education/index.html. Posted May 7, 2001. Author laments lack of creativity and innovation in recent congressional plans for education reform.

———. "A Weak Rx for Schools." Salon.com. Available online. URL: http://dir.salon.com/politics/feature/2001/07/12/education/index.html. Posted July 12, 2001. Article labels President George W. Bush's education proposals as "unimaginative" and "watered-down" approaches to reform.

Internet Education Exchange. "News and Data." Internet Education Exchange. Available online. URL: http://www.iedx.org/news/data.asp#ws/276.

Downloaded January 21, 2003. Page provides a variety of information and links to further research on vouchers, charter schools, and the 2002 election's education-related outcomes.

Jennings, Jack. "Knocking on Your Door: With the No Child Left Behind Act, the Federal Government Is Taking a Stronger Role in Your Schools." Center on Education Police. Available online. URL: http://www.ctredpol. org/fededprograms/knockingonyourdooraug2002.pdf. Downloaded January 22, 2003. Piece compliments the goals of recent federal education legislation but questions whether states and local school districts possess the capacity to carry out its goals.

Kaufman, King. "Tuition-Free, Back-to-Basics, Inner-City Private Schools." Salon.com. Available online. URL: http://dir.salon.com/mwt/ feature/2001/10/29/academies/index.html. Posted October 29, 2001. Describes two uniquely financed schools in poor areas of St. Louis, Missouri, that were organized by a former marine and local churches.

Kaus, Mickey. "Why the Voucher Issue Really Could Hurt the Dems." Slate.com. Available online. URL: http://slate.msn.com/?id=2067375. Posted July 1, 2002. Article analyzes the political ramifications of the Supreme Court's decision in the Cleveland school voucher case.

LeFevre, Andrew T., and Rea S. Hederman, Jr. "Report Card on American Education: A State-by-State Analysis, 1976–2001." American Legislative Exchange Council. Available online. URL: http://www.alec.org/newsfiles/ pdf/Education_Report_Card.pdf. Downloaded January 21, 2003. Report explains that there is "no immediate evident correlation" between per-pupil spending and pupil performance by examining two generations of school funding and standardized test results.

Lindsey, Daryl. "Vouchers and the Law." Salon.com. Available online. URL: http://dir.salon.com/news/feature/2000/03/27/vouchers/index.html. Posted March 27, 2000. Explores various legal experts' views of the constitutionality of school voucher programs.

Lines, Patricia L. "Homeschooling Comes of Age." Discovery Institute. Available online. URL: http://www.discovery.org/viewDB/index.php3?program= Misc&command=view&id=277. Posted July 1, 2000. Reprinted article, originally published in *Public Interest*, describes the homeschooling movement as "one of the most significant social trends of the past half century."

Lithwick, Dahlia. "The Supremes Pledge Allegiance to God: Praise the Lord and Pass the Vouchers to the Churches!" Slate.com. Available online. URL: http://slate.msn.com/?id=2067471. Posted June 27, 2002. Piece criticizes the Supreme Court's decision in the Cleveland school voucher case because of its provisions allowing public money use for support of religious institutions.

Maran, Meredith. "Deadly Ambivalence." Salon.com. Available online. URL: http://dir.salon.com/news/feature/2001/03/06/misfit/index.html. Posted March 6, 2001. Author recommends that schools take a far more active role in preventing bullying in order to prevent the kinds of school shootings seen at Columbine, in Colorado, and Santee, in California.

Morgan, Fiona. "Banning the Bullies." Salon.com. Available online. URL: http://dir.salon.com/news/feature/2001/03/15/bullying/index.html. Posted March 15, 2001. Article details how state legislatures are considering laws to diminish harassment and violence in schools but warns that the proposed solutions may not be sufficient to solve this complex problem.

National Education Association. "Federal Legislation Update." National Education Association. Available online. URL: http://www.nea.org/lac/fedupdat.html. Downloaded January 1, 2003. This list of legislation features current and thorough descriptions of key changes and developments in education regulations and trends.

New American Schools. "Evaluating Success: KIPP Education Program Evaluation." New American Schools. Available online. URL: http://www.naschools/org/ContentViewer.asp?highlightID=203&catID=439. Downloaded January 21, 2003. Piece lauds the achievements of three of the 15 Knowledge Is Power Program (KIPP) schools that emphasize parental involvement, high student achievement, and extended school days, weeks, and years.

New York Times. "Bloomberg Calls for Standard Curriculum in City Schools." New York Times.com. Available online. URL: http://www.nytimes.com/2003/01/15/nyregion/15WEB_SCHO.html. Posted January 15, 2003. Article describes New York City mayor Michael Bloomberg's school reform plan, which includes strategies for a standard curriculum, reduction in class size, and efforts to attract greater parental involvement.

Noah, Timothy. "Federalize the Schools! In Praise of Clinton's State of the Union Power Grab. Slate.com. Available online. URL: http://slate.msn.com/?id=14309. Posted January 22, 1999. Piece favors the proposal for an increased federal role in public education featured in President Bill Clinton's 1999 State of the Union Address.

Partnership for Learning. "Making Standards Work." Partnership for Learning. Available online. URL: http://www.partnership4learning.org/PDF/MSW2.pdf. Downloaded January 22, 2003. Report details what strategies and practices have been most successful at helping students meet academic goals at schools, making the most rapid gains in reading and math.

Pell, Eva. "The Charter School Magnate." Salon.com. Available online. URL: http://dir.salon.com/news/feature/2000/05/24/brennan/index.html. Posted May 24, 2000. Profile spotlights entrepreneur David Brennan's effort to increase the use of privately run schools in Ohio.

Public Agenda Online. "Quick Takes." Public Agenda. Available online. URL: http://www.publicagenda.org/issues/angles.cfm?issue_type=education. Downloaded October 20, 2002. Page highlights the noteworthy findings of public opinion of education and includes links to graphs.

"Public Education: Hope for the Future." Soros Foundation. Available online. URL: http://www.soros.org/events/education/index.htm. Posted October 8, 2002. Features includes written and audio transcripts from an Open Society Institute forum discussing key issues in school reform.

Public Education Network. "Accountability for All: What Voters Want from Education Candidates." Public Education Network/Education Week National Survey of Public Opinion, 2002. Available online. URL: http://www.publiceducation.org/download/2002PollReport.pdf. Downloaded January 21, 2003. Findings underscore education's power as a political issue and express voter concern and commitment for public schools.

RAND. "What Do We Know About Vouchers and Charter Schools? Separating the Rhetoric from the Reality." RAND. Available online. URL: http://rand.org/publications/RB/RB8018/2001. Downloaded January 21, 2003. Research brief analyzes evidence on key school choice measures and determines that initial outcomes show promise.

Rebora, Anthony. "The Military Response." *Education Week*. Available online. URL: http://www.edweek.org/jobs/jobstory.efm?slug=11ttt_tr.h01. Downloaded July 20, 2002. Article explains the increased prominence of the federal Troops to Teachers program and its implications on teacher certification.

"Reducing Class Size: What Do We Know?" U.S. Department of Education. Available online. URL: http://www.ed.gov/pubs/ReducingClass/. Downloaded July 12, 2002. Report summarizes research on the influence of class size on student achievement.

Sandler, Michael R. "The Emerging Educational Industry—The First Decade." Association of Education Practitioners and Providers. Available online. URL: http://www.aepp.org/news/emedu4-02.pdf. White paper calls for greater involvement of the business community in education and more for-profit education endeavors.

"School." PBS. Available online. URL: http://www.pbs.org/kcet/publicschool/. Downloaded July 12, 2002. Page includes relevant links to a variety of topics covered in the network's broadcast history of U.S. public K–12 education.

Siegel, Loren. "Point of View: school uniforms." American Civil Liberties Union (ACLU). Available online. URL: http://www.aclu.org/congress/uniform.html. Posted March 1, 1996. Piece questions the fairness and effectiveness of school uniforms policies designed to improve discipline.

Stecher, Brian M., and George W. Bohrnstedt. "Class Size Reduction in California: Findings from 1999–00 and 2000–01." CSR Research Consortium. Available online. URL: http://classize.org/summary/99-01/index. htm. Downloaded January 21, 2003. Summary includes results of California's Class Size Reduction (CSR) program, concluding that there is not a strong association between student achievement and class-size reduction.

"Studies of Education Reform." U.S. Department of Education. Available online. URL: http://www.ed.gov/pubs/SER/index.html. Downloaded July 20, 2002. Series of 13 studies that focus on such areas in education as assessment of student performance, curriculum reform, parent and community involvement in education, school-based management, systemic reform, and professionalism of educators.

Tapper, Jake. "The Kennedy Compromise. Salon.com. Available online. URL: http://dir.salon.com/politics/feature/2001/05/21/education/index.html. Posted May 21, 2001. Article explains that despite expression of frustration by conservatives, Democrats made the biggest concessions in the construction of recent education legislation.

"The State of Charter Schools Fourth-Year Report." U.S. Department of Education. Available online. URL: http://www.ed.gov/pubs/charter4thyear/. Downloaded July 12, 2002. Report details the rapid growth of the national charter school and explains that charter schools typically have a more diverse student population, lower student to teacher ratios, and better access to computers compared to the average for all public schools.

Traub, James. "The Curriculum Crusades." Salon.com. Available online. URL: http://dir.salon.com/news/feature/2000/05/31/curriculum/index. html. Posted May 31, 2000. Article questions the continued use of progressive teaching methods, arguing that they do not work as well as a traditional focus on basic skills.

U.S. Department of Education. "A New Era: Revitalizing Special Education for Children and Their Families." U.S. Department of Education Website. Available online. URL: http://www.ed.gov/inits/commissionboards/whspecial education/. Posted July 1, 2002. Report recommends that parents removing their disabled child from a failing public school should be allowed to use state funds earmarked for these students to send them to any school they select.

———. "The Secretary's Annual Report on Teacher Quality: Meeting the Highly Qualified Teachers Challenge." U.S. Department of Education Website. Available online. URL: http://www.ed.gov/offices/OPE/News/teacherprep/index.html. Posted August 16, 2002. Report presents key findings and opinions reflecting the Bush administration's approach to improving teaching according to strategies and requirements of the No Child Left Behind Act.

———. "A Study of Charter School Accountability." U.S. Department of Education Website. Available online. URL: http://www.ed.gov/pubs/chartacct/. Downloaded July 12, 2002. Report includes an extensive, nationwide study of charter school accountability and studies how school districts, universities, or state agencies are learning to oversee charter schools.

———. "Taking Responsibility for Ending Social Promotion: A Guide for Educators and State and Local Leaders." U.S. Department of Education Website. Available online. URL: http://www.ed.gov/pubs/socialpromotion/. Posted July 1, 1999. Outlines strategies to counter the practice of passing students through school who haven't satisfied academic requirements for their grade.

———. "Venturesome Capital: State Charter School Financing Systems." U.S. Department of Education Website. Available online. URL: http://www.ed.gov/pubs/chartfin/. Downloaded July 20, 2002. Article examines the laws, regulations, and state practices governing charter school finance during the 1998–99 school year in 23 states and two cities and assesses comparability of charter school funding compared to other public schools with similar students and education programs.

Waldrip, Donald. "A Brief History and Philosophy of Magnet Schools." Magnet Schools of America. Available online. URL: http://www.magnet.edu/history.html. Downloaded July 12, 2002. Summary presents a concise and positive review of the magnet school movement.

Walsh, Joan. "Surprise: Bush Could Be the 'Education President.'" Salon.com. Available online. URL: http://www.salon.com/news/feature/1999/09/17/education/index.html. Posted September 17, 1999. Article suggests that Texas governor George W. Bush may represent the best hope among the 2000 presidential candidates for poor families with students in underperforming schools.

———. "The Truth About Texas School Reform." Salon.com. Available online. URL: http://www.salon.com/news/feature/1999/11/01/elpaso/index.html. Posted November 1, 1999. Article examines the widely praised education reforms supported by Texas governor George W. Bush by focusing on changes in one El Paso elementary school.

WGBH/Eye on Education. Available online. URL: http://www.eyeoneducation.tv/index.html. Downloaded January 1, 2003. A web site collaboration between the Department of Education of Massachusetts and the Boston public schools that provides Boston public school parents with grade-by-grade resources to help them better advocate for their children in school.

"Yahoo! News: Education Curriculum and Policy." Yahoo! Available online. URL: http://news.yahoo.com/fc?tmpl=fc&cid=34&in=us&cat=education_

curriculum_and_policy. Downloaded January 21, 2003. Newsroom comprises links to a variety of sources, including the *New York Times, Time,* and *Education Week,* and includes featured daily articles on a wide range of reform issues.

York, Anthony. "Money Also Matters." Salon.com. Available online. URL: http://www.salon.com/mwt/feature/2002/02/20/class_size/index.html. Posted February 20, 2002. Report explains why, despite its popularity, a California initiative limiting class size is in jeopardy because of lack of funding.

OTHER MEDIA

A Day in the Life (2002). PBS/WGBH/Boston: VHS, 2002. Documentary video presents personal moments of students, their teachers and their families at a struggling Boston high school to illustrate the impact of education reform.

Engaging Americans in Public Education (1998). PBS/WGBH/Boston: VHS, 1998. Two-hour video that profiles three public-engagement initiatives seeking to build relationships between the public and its schools and also includes a town-hall-style discussion of these initiatives.

Evans, Robert. *Professional Community and the Problems of Change* (1998). Annenberg Institute at Brown University: VHS, 1998. Video features the prominent organizational psychologist's address to National School Reform Faculty, focusing on the strengthening of teacher and administrator standards.

Hope, Fairness, and Power: Building Strong Schools in Urban America (1998). PBS/WGBH/Boston: VHS, 1998. Documentary follows students, teachers, and administrators at two urban high schools working to improve the quality of education through reform strategies.

Lehrer, Tom. *That Was the Year That Was* (1965). Warner Brothers/Reprise Records: CD, 1990. Recording includes collection of satirical songs covering important events of 1964 and features the progressive education–themed song "New Math."

Merrow, John. *Frontline: Testing Our Schools* (2002). PBS/WGBH/Boston: VHS, 2002. Public television program examines how President George W. Bush's proposals for federal involvement in public education may change schools and analyzes how states decide what is important for students to know, what standardized tests really measure, and how the quest for higher scores is changing teaching and learning in the United States.

Nightline: One Last Chance (2002). ABC News: VHS, 2002. Network television program profiles public charter boarding school in Washington,

D.C., that seeks to help students from some of the most impoverished areas of the city.

School (2001). Stone Lantern Films/PBS/KCET: VHS, 2001. Originally aired as a PBS series airing in four episodes, video covers the development of public education in the United States from the late 1770s to the 21st century, focusing on the system's origins, its role in Americanizing immigrants and as a catalyst for and site of social change, and recent challenges and trends.

Students at the Center: A National Teleconference on School Reform (1998). U.S. Department of Education Office of Educational Research and Improvement: VHS, 1998. Video features teachers, principals, and research experts engaged in comprehensive school reform around the country sharing their ideas about what has worked for them.

CHAPTER 8

ORGANIZATIONS AND AGENCIES

The following entries include current and active public, private, and academic groups involved in the debate about education reform. The list features organizations dedicated to examining and/or advocating positions on school choice, homeschooling, school financing, standards, teacher certification and quality, and legal issues.

ACCESS (Advocacy Center for Children's Educational Success with Standards)
URL: http://www. accessednetwork.org
E-mail: access@cfequity.org
Phone: (212) 867-8455
Fax: (212) 867-8460
6 East 43rd Street
New York, NY 10017
National network of advocates, attorneys, researchers, educators, and parents that seeks to strengthen the links between school finance litigation, public engagement, and the standards-based reform movement.

Achieve, Inc.
URL: http://www.achieve.org
Phone: (202) 624-1460
400 North Capitol Street, NW
Suite 351
Washington, DC 20001

Founded by a nonpartisan group of governors and CEOs. Achieve focuses on advocacy of academic standards and school accountability measures.

Alliance for the Separation of School & State
URL: http://www.sepschool.org
Phone: (559) 292-1776
Fax: (559) 292-7582
4578 North First Street
No. 310
Fresno, CA 93726
Seeks to influence educational policy debate by attracting public leaders and private citizens to sign a proclamation stating, "I proclaim publicly that I favor ending government involvement in education."

American Civil Liberties Union (ACLU)
URL: http://www.aclu.org

Phone: (212) 549-2500
Fax: (212) 549-2616
125 Broad Street
18th Floor
New York, NY 10004-2400
Prominent national organization seeking to preserve and defend individual rights. The ACLU is active in support of students' rights issues.

**American Federation of
Teachers (AFT)**
URL: http://www.aft.org
E-mail: online@aft.org
Phone: (202) 879-4400
555 New Jersey Avenue, NW
Washington, DC 20001
Trade union with more than 1 million members, active in wide range of labor and educational issues.

**Americans United for Separation
of Church and State**
URL: http://www.au.org
Phone: (202) 466-3234
Fax: (202) 466-2587
518 C Street, NE
Washington, DC 20002
Organization that promotes litigation, advocacy, and education to protect the constitutional principle of church-state separation, including the opposition to school prayer and the use of tax-supported vouchers for use in parochial schools.

**Annenberg Institute for School
Reform**
URL: http://www.
annenberginstitute.org
E-mail: AISRInfo@brown.edu

Phone: (401) 863-7990
Fax: (401) 863-1290
Brown University
Box 1985
Providence, RI 02912
Develops and shares information that seeks to improve the condition and outcomes of schooling in the United States, especially in urban communities and in schools serving disadvantaged children.

**Association of Education
Practitioners and Providers**
URL: http://www.aepp.org
Phone: (800) 252-3280
Fax: (920) 206-1475
P.O. Box 348
Watertown, WI 53094-0348
Professional network of education businesses promoting education reform through entrepreneurship.

**Carnegie Foundation for the
Advancement of Teaching**
URL: http://www.
carnegiefoundation.org
E-mail: clyburn@
carnegiefoundation.org
Phone: (650) 566-5100
Fax: (650) 326-0278
555 Middlefield Road
Menlo Park, CA 94025
National center for research and policy studies about teaching since 1905.

Center for Education Reform
URL: http://www.edreform.com
E-mail: cer@edreform.com
Phone: (800) 521-2118

Fax: (202) 822-5077
1001 Connecticut Avenue, NW
Washington, DC 20036
Thorough network of information resources and reform advocacy that provides updated reporting of key developments in education reform and includes many links to local groups.

Center for Equal Opportunity (CEO)
URL: http://www.ceousa.org
E-mail: comment@ceousa.org
Phone: (703) 421-5443
Fax: (703) 421-6401
14 Pidgeon Hill Drive
Suite 500
Sterling, VA 20165
Led by conservative activist Linda Chavez, the CEO is in opposition to bilingual education and in support of school choice initiatives.

Center for Leadership in School Reform
URL: http://www.clsr.org
E-mail: info@clsr.org
Phone: (502) 895-1942
Fax: (502) 895-7901
950 Breckenridge Lane
Suite 200
Louisville, KY 40207
Seeks to provide support to school reform efforts through consultation and training to district leadership.

Center on Education Policy
URL: http://www.ctredpol.org
E-mail: ctredpol@ctredpol.org
Phone: (202) 822-8065
Fax: (202) 822-6008

1001 Connecticut Avenue, NW
Suite 522
Washington, DC 20036
Produces publications and convenes meetings to help citizens "make sense of conflicting opinions and perceptions about public education." The center is sponsored by Phi Delta Kappa and several private foundations.

Charter Friends National Network
URL: http://www.charterfriends.org
E-mail: jon@charterfriends.org
Phone: (651) 644-6115
Fax: (651) 644-0433
1295 Bandana Boulevard
Suite 165
St. Paul, MN 55108
Supports charter schools through research, publications, and multistate initiatives on key issues including accountability, financing, and policy development.

Coalition of Essential Schools
URL: http://www.essentialschools.org
E-mail: tstrohmeier@essentialschools.org
Phone: (510) 433-1451
Fax: (510) 433-1455
1814 Franklin Street
Suite 700
Oakland, CA 94612
Network committed to increasing student achievement by improving school design, leadership, classroom practice, and community connections.

Committee for Education Funding
URL: http://www.cef.org
Phone: (202) 383-0083
Fax: (202) 383-0097
122 C Street, NW
Suite 280
Washington, DC 20001
Coalition of more than 100 education organizations seeking adequate federal financial support for schools.

Core Knowledge Foundation
URL: http://www.
coreknowledge.org
E-mail: coreknow@
coreknowledge.org
Phone: (800) 238-3233
801 East High Street
Charlottesville, VA 22902
Organization founded by professor and best-selling author E. D. Hirsch, promoting a specific, shared curriculum for schools.

Council for Basic Education
URL: http://www.c-b-e.org
E-mail: info@c-b-e.org
Phone: (202) 347-4171
Fax: (202) 347-5047
1319 F Street, NW
Suite 900
Washington, DC 20004-1152
Founded in 1956, the council advocates for the development of high academic standards in K–12 education through the use of programs designed to strengthen content in curriculum, excellence in teaching, and student performance.

Cross City Campaign for Urban School Reform
URL: http://www.crosscity.org
Phone: (312) 322-4880
Fax: (312) 322-4885
407 South Dearborn Street
Suite 1500
Chicago, IL 60605
National network of education reform leaders from nine cities that advocates policies moving authority, resources, and accountability to the school level.

Education Commission of the States
URL: http://www.ecs.org
E-mail: ecs@ecs.org
Phone: (303) 299-3600
Fax: (303) 296-8332
700 Broadway
Suite 1200
Denver, CO 80203-3460
An interstate compact created in 1965 on the recommendation of James Conant to improve public knowledge about current and emerging issues, trends, and innovations in state education policy.

Education Law Association
URL: http://www.educationlaw.
org
E-mail: ela@udayton.edu
Phone: (937) 229-3589
Fax: (937) 229-3845
300 College Park
Dayton, OH 45369
Community of educational and legal scholars and practitioners that supports scholarly research of education law through publications,

conferences, seminars, and professional forums.

Education Leaders Council
URL: http://www.
  educationleaders.org
E-mail: info@educationleaders.
  org
Phone: (202) 261-2600
Fax: (202) 26-2638
225 19th Street, NW
Suite 400
Washington, DC 20036
Advocate of standards and local control of schools that believes, "education initiatives are strongest when they are generated from within individual American communities and weakest when imposed upon communities by the national government."

Education Policy Institute (EPI)
URL: http://www.
  educationpolicy.org
E-mail: info@educationpolicy.
  org
Phone: (202) 244-7535
Fax: (202) 244-7584
4401-A Connecticut Avenue,
  NW
Washington, DC 20008
Chaired by public education critic Myron Lieberman, EPI strives to increase parental choice in education and a competitive education industry through research and policy analysis.

**George Lucas Educational
  Foundation**
URL: http://www.glef.org
E-mail: feedback@glef.org
Phone: (415) 507-0399
Fax: (415) 507-0499
P.O. Box 3494
San Rafael, CA 94912
Established by filmmaker George Lucas, the foundation profiles hundreds of successful teaching and learning examples to stimulate education reform.

**KIPP (Knowledge Is Power
  Program)**
URL: http://www.kipp.org
E-mail: info@kipp.org
Phone: (415) 399-1556
Fax: (415) 348-0588
345 Spear Street
San Francisco, CA 94105
National nonprofit organization that trains school leaders to open and run schools in underserved areas that emphasize high expectations, an extended school day and school year, and parental and student commitment.

**Leadership for Quality
  Education**
URL: http://www.lqe.org
E-mail: info@lqe.org
Phone: (312) 853-1200
Fax: (312) 853-1209
21 South Clark Street
Suite 3120
Chicago, IL 60603-2006
Chicago-based, business-backed organization at forefront of significant and widely emulated reforms including local school councils and school and student accountability.

Learning Communities Network, Inc.
URL: http://www.lcn.org
E-mail: info@lcn.org
Phone: (216) 575-7535
Fax: (216) 575-7523
1422 Euclid Avenue
Suite 1668
Cleveland, OH 44115-2001
Builds support networks of policy-makers, educators, and citizens to promote equitable improvements in schools.

Magnet Schools of America
URL: http://www.magnet.edu
E-mail: director@magnet.edu
Phone: (202) 824-0672
Fax: (202) 638-7895
733 15th Street, NW
Suite 330
Washington, DC 20005
Promotes legislation to foster development and improvement of magnet schools.

National Association for Bilingual Education
URL: http://www.nabe.org
Phone: (202) 898-1829
Fax: (202) 789-2866
1030 15th Street, NW
Suite 470
Washington, DC 20003
The only national organization exclusively concerned with the education of language minority students in U.S. schools, it promotes educational equity through bilingual education.

National Association of Charter School Authorizers
URL: http://www.charterauthorizers.org
E-mail: info@charterauthorizers.org
Phone: (202) 363-8434
Fax: (703) 683-9703
3901 Connecticut Avenue, NW
Suite 308
Washington, DC 20008-6404
Network of groups charged with licensing and oversight of charter schools, seeking to strengthen capacity and success of charter schools.

National Board for Professional Teaching Standards
URL: http://www.nbpts.org
Phone: (703) 465-2700
1525 Wilson Boulevard
Suite 500
Arlington, VA 22209
Independent nonpartisan organization created in response to *A Nation at Risk*. Promotes standards for what teachers should know and a voluntary system of assessment and certification for teachers who meet those standards.

National Center for Education Statistics
URL: http://www.nces.ed.gov
Phone: (202) 502-7400
Assessment Division
8th Floor
1990 K Street, NW
Washington, DC 20806
Primary federal source for collection and analysis of data related to

education in the United States and other nations.

National Center for Home Education–Home School Legal Defense Association
URL: http://www.hslda.org
E-mail: info@hslda.org
Phone: (540) 538-5600
Fax: (540) 338-2733
P.O. Box 3000
Purcellville, VA 20134
Advocates homeschooling in court-rooms, before government officials, and in the public arena.

National Center for Research on Evaluation, Standards, and Student Testing
URL: http://www.cse.ucla.edu
E-mail: mary@cse.ucla.edu
Phone: (310) 206-1532
Fax: (310) 825-3883
301 GSE & IS Building
Mailbox 951522
300 Charles E. Young Drive North
Los Angeles, CA 90095-1522
Partnership of universities addressing issues relating to the design and use of assessment systems that serve multiple purposes.

National Center for the Study of Privatization in Education
URL: http://www.ncspe.org
E-mail: ncspe@columbia.edu
Phone: (212) 678-1258
Fax: (212) 678-3474
Teachers College
Columbia University
Box 181

230 Thompson Hall
525 West 120th Street
New York, NY 10027-6696
Source of analysis on national and international privatization in education issues ranging from preschool to higher education, focusing on research, evaluation, and the dissemination of information.

National Center on Education and the Economy
URL: http://www.ncee.org
One Thomas Circle, NW
Suite 700
Washington, DC 20005
Emphasizes standards-based reform through policies, technical assistance, and professional development.

National Clearinghouse for Comprehensive School Reform
URL: http://www.goodschools. gwu.edu
E-mail: askNCCSR@ goodschools.gwu.edu
Phone: (877) 766-4277
2121 K Street, NW
Suite 250
Washington, DC 20037-1801
Collects and disseminates information that seeks to help schools raise the academic achievement of students.

National Commission on Teaching and America's Future
URL: http://www.nctaf.org
Phone: (212) 678-4153
Fax: (212) 678-4039
525 West 12th Street

Box 117
New York, NY 10027
Cross-section of public officials, business and community leaders, and educators focusing on methods to improve the quality of teaching.

National Council on Teacher Quality (NCTQ)
URL: http://www.nctq.org
E-mail: TQBulletin@nctq.org
Phone: (202) 261-2621
1225 19th Street, NW
Suite 400
Washington, DC 20036
New organization encouraging innovation and experimentation with teacher quality practices. The NCTQ serves as an information clearinghouse and assists states and districts in teacher quality strategies.

National Education Association (NEA)
URL: http://www.nea.org
E-mail: owww-feedback@list.
  nea.org
Phone: (202) 833-4000
1201 16th Street, NW
Washington, DC 20036
Oldest and largest U.S. organization committed to advancing the cause of public education with a membership of more than 2.5 million.

National Education Goals Panel
URL: http://www.negp.gov
E-mail: NEGP@ed.gov
Phone: (202) 724-0015
Fax: (202) 632-0959
1255 22nd Street, NW

Suite 502
Washington, DC 20037
Independent executive branch agency that monitors national and state progress toward national education goals.

National Forum to Accelerate Middle Grades Reform
URL: http://www.mgforum.org
E-mail: mgforum@edc.org
Phone: (617) 969-7100
Education Development Center
55 Chapel Street
Newton, MA 02458-1060
Alliance of educators, researchers, and foundations promoting academic performance and development of young adolescents.

National Home Education Network
URL: http://www.nhen.org
E-mail: info@nhen.org
Fax: (413) 581-1463
P.O. Box 7844
Long Beach, CA 90807
Encourages grassroots work of homeschooling groups through information, networking, and public petitions.

National PTA
URL: http://www.pta.org
E-mail: info@pta.org
Phone: (800) 307-4782
Fax: (312) 670-6783
330 North Wabash Avenue
Suite 2100
Chicago, IL 60611
Supports effective schools through participation of families and educa-

tors, with more than 6.5 million members in 26,000 local units in all 50 states.

New American Schools
URL: http://www.naschools.org
Phone: (703) 908-9500
Fax: (703) 908-0622
1560 Wilson Boulevard
Suite 601
Arlington, VA 22209
Nonprofit organization founded by leading CEOs that supports educational entrepreneurs with technical assistance and financing for programs.

**North Central Regional
  Educational Laboratory**
URL: http://www.ncrel.org
E-mail: info@ncrel.org
Phone: (800) 356-2735
1120 East Diehl Road
Suite 200
Naperville, IL 60563
Provides research-based expertise, resources, assistance, and professional development for teachers, administrators, and policymakers.

Parents in Charge
URL: http://www.
  parentsincharge.org
Phone: (973) 735-0522
744 Broad Street
16th Floor
Newark, NJ 07102
Coalition that seeks to ensure that all students, regardless of household income, are provided an opportunity to receive a quality education determined by parental choice. The organization's board of advisers includes prominent members of Congress and many former cabinet secretaries.

Project Zero
URL: http://www.pz.harvard.edu
Phone: (617) 496-7097
Fax: (617) 495-9709
**Harvard Graduate School of
  Education**
124 Mount Auburn Street
Fifth Floor
Cambridge, MA 02138
An educational research group that focuses on the role of the arts in learning, thinking, and creativity, particularly in schools serving disadvantaged populations.

Public Education Network
URL: http://www.
  publiceducation.org
E-mail: pen@publiceducation.
  org
Phone: (202) 628-7460
Fax: (202) 628-1893
601 13th Street, NW
Suite 900 North
Washington, DC 20005
National association of nonprofit community-based organizations advancing school reform in low-income areas across the country. The network focuses on improving funding, assessment, and professional development.

Rebuild America's Schools
URL: http://www.
  modernschools.org

E-mail: information@
modernschools.org
Phone: (202) 462-5911
Fax: (202) 588-8094
144ø N Street, NW
Suite 1016
Washington, DC 20005
Works for federal support of local
communities' efforts to build, reno-
vate, and modernize school facilities.

Recruiting New Teachers, Inc.
URL: http://www.rnt.org
E-mail: rnt@rnt.org
Phone: (617) 489-6000
385 Concord Avenue
Suite 1B
Belmont, MA 02478
National nonprofit organization
that seeks to raise esteem for teaching, expand the pool of prospective
teachers, and improve the nation's
teacher recruitment and development policies and practices.

Small Schools Network
URL: http://www.
smallschoolsworkshop.org
Phone: (312) 413-8066
Fax: (312) 413-5847
1640 West Roosevelt Road
6th Floor
Chicago, IL 60608
Group of educators, organizers, and
researchers collaborating with teachers, principals, and parents to create
small, innovative public schools.

Standards for Success
URL: http://www.s4s.org
E-mail: contact@s4s.org
Phone: (877) 766-2279

Fax: (541) 346-6154
5276 University of Oregon
Eugene, OR 97403-5276
Seeks to establish effective alignment between desires of university
admissions departments and K–12
standards and assessments.

Standards Work
URL: http://www.goalline.org
E-mail: connect@goalline.org
Phone: (202) 835-2000
Fax: (202) 659-4494
1001 Connecticut Avenue, NW
Suite 901
Washington, DC 20036
Nonprofit educational consultancy
promoting grade-by-grade stan-
dards and results-based evaluation
systems in communities and schools.

Teach For America (TFA)
URL: http://www.
teachforamerica.org
Phone: (800) 832-1230
Fax: (202) 279-2081
315 West 36th Street
New York, NY 10018
National corps of recent college
graduates who commit two years to
teach in low-income communities.

Thomas B. Fordham Foundation
URL: http://www.edescellence.
net
E-mail: backtalk@edexcellence.
net
Phone: (202) 223-5452
Fax: (202) 223-9226
1627 K Street, NW
Suite 600
Washington, DC 20006

Research and grant-awarding body that emphasizes issues of standards, accountability, charter schools, school choice, and teacher quality.

U.S. Department of Education
URL: http://www.ed.gov

Phone: (800) 872-5327
400 Maryland Avenue, SW
Washington, DC 20202-0498
Federal department established in 1980 whose mission includes the co-ordination and management of grant programs, research, and assessment.

PART III

APPENDICES

APPENDIX A

EXCERPTS FROM *CARDINAL PRINCIPLES OF SECONDARY EDUCATION*, 1918

The following extract is taken from the influential 1918 report published by the National Education Association's Commission on the Reorganization of Secondary Education, Department of the Interior, Bureau of Education, which was instrumental in propelling the progressive education movement and shaping comprehensive high school instructional practice throughout much of the 20th century.

I. THE NEED FOR REORGANIZATION

Secondary education should be determined by the needs of the society to be served, the character of the individuals to be educated, and the knowledge of educational theory and practice available. These factors are by no means static. Society is always in process of development; the character of the secondary-school population undergoes modification; and the sciences on which educational theory and practice depend constantly furnish new information. Secondary education, however, like any other established agency of society, is conservative and tends to resist modification. Failure to make adjustments when the need arises leads to the necessity for extensive reorganization at irregular intervals. The evidence is strong that such a comprehensive reorganization of secondary education is imperative at the present time.

1. *Changes in society.*—Within the past few decades changes have taken place in American life profoundly affecting the activities of the individual. As a citizen, he must to a greater extent and in a more direct way cope with

problems of community life, State and National Governments, and international relationships. As a worker, he must adjust himself to a more complex economic order. As a relatively independent personality, he has more leisure. The problems arising from these three dominant phases of life are closely interrelated and call for a degree of intelligence and efficiency on the part of every citizen that cannot be secured through elementary education alone, or even through secondary education unless the scope of that education is broadened.

The responsibility of the secondary school is still further increased because many social agencies other than the school afford less stimulus for education than heretofore. In many vocations there have come such significant changes as the substitution of the factory system for the domestic system of industry; the use of machinery in place of manual labor; the high specialization of processes with a corresponding subdivision of labor; and the breakdown of the apprentice system. In connection with home and family life have frequently come lessened responsibility on the part of the children; the withdrawal of the father and sometimes the mother from home occupations to the factory or store; and increased urbanization, resulting in less unified family life. Similarly, many important changes have taken place in community life, in the church, in the State, and in other institutions. These changes in American life call for extensive modifications in secondary education.

2. *Changes in the secondary-school population.*—In the past 25 years there have been marked changes in the secondary-school population of the United States. The number of pupils has increased, according to Federal returns, from one for every 210 of the total population in 1889–90, to one for every 121 in 1899–1900, to one for every 89 in 1909–10, and to one for every 73 of the estimated total population in 1914–15. The character of the secondary-school population has been modified by the entrance of large numbers of pupils of widely varying capacities, aptitudes, social heredity, and destinies in life. Further, the broadening of the scope of secondary education has brought to the school many pupils who do not complete the full course but leave at various stages of advancement. The needs of these pupils cannot be neglected, nor can we expect in the near future that all pupils will be able to complete the secondary school as fulltime students.

At present only about one-third of the pupils who enter the first year of the elementary school reach the four-year high school, and only about one in nine is graduated. Of those who enter the seventh school year, only one-half to two-thirds reach the first year of the four-year high school. Of those who enter the four-year high school about one-third leave before the beginning of the second year, about one-half are gone before the beginning of the third year, and fewer than one-third are graduated. These facts can no longer be safely ignored.

3. *Changes in educational theory.*—The sciences on which educational theory depends have within recent years made significant contributions. In particular, educational psychology emphasizes the following factors:

(a) *Individual differences in capacities and aptitudes among secondary-school pupils.*—Already recognized to some extent, this factor merits fuller attention.

(b) *The reexamination and reinterpretation of subject values and the teaching methods with reference to "general discipline."*—While the final verdict of modern psychology has not as yet been rendered, it is clear that former conceptions of "general values" must be thoroughly revised.

(c) *Importance of applying knowledge.*—Subject values and teaching methods must be tested in terms of the laws of learning and the application of knowledge to the activities of life, rather than primarily in terms of the demands of any subject as a logically organized science.

(d) *Continuity in the development of children.*—It has long been held that psychological changes at certain stages are so pronounced as to overshadow the continuity of development. On this basis secondary education has been sharply separated from elementary education. Modern psychology, however, goes to show that the development of the individual is in most respects a continuous process and that, therefore, any sudden or abrupt break between the elementary and the secondary school or between any two successive stages of education is undesirable.

The foregoing changes in society, in the character of the secondary school population, and in educational theory, together with many other considerations, call for extensive modifications of secondary education. Such modifications have already begun in part. The present need is for the formulation of a comprehensive program of reorganization, and its adoption, with suitable adjustments, in all the secondary schools of the Nation. Hence it is appropriate for a representative body like the National Education Association to outline such a program. This is the task entrusted by that association to the Commission on the Reorganization of Secondary Education.

II. THE GOAL OF EDUCATION IN A DEMOCRACY

Education in the United States should be guided by a clear conception of the meaning of democracy. It is the ideal of democracy that the individual and society may find fulfillment each in the other. Democracy sanctions neither the exploitation of the individual by society, nor the disregard of the interests of society by the individual. More explicitly—the purpose of democracy is so to organize society that each member may develop his personality primarily through activities designed for the well-being of his fellow members and of society as a whole.

This ideal demands that human activities be placed upon a high level of efficiency; that to this efficiency be added an appreciation of the significance of these activities and loyalty to the best ideals involved; and that the individual choose that vocation and those forms of social service in which his personality may develop and become most effective. For the achievement of these ends democracy must place chief reliance upon education.

Consequently, education in a democracy, both within and without the school, should develop in each individual the knowledge, interests, ideals, habits, and powers whereby he will find his place and use that place to shape both himself and society toward ever nobler ends.

III. THE MAIN OBJECTIVES OF EDUCATION

In order to determine the main objectives that should guide education in a democracy, it is necessary to analyze the activities of the individual. Normally he is a member of a family, of a vocational group, and of various civic groups, and by virtue of these relationships he is called upon to engage in activities that enrich the family life, to render important vocational services to his fellows, and to promote the common welfare. It follows, therefore, that worthy home membership, vocation, and citizenship demand attention as three of the leading objectives.

Aside from the immediate discharge of these specific duties, every individual should have a margin of time for the cultivation of personal and social interests. This leisure, if worthily used, will recreate his powers and enlarge and enrich life, thereby making him better able to meet his responsibilities. The unworthy use of leisure impairs health, disrupts home life, lessens vocational efficiency, and destroys civic-mindedness. The tendency in industrial life, aided by legislation, is to decrease the working hours of large groups of people. While shortened hours tend to lessen the harmful reactions that arise from prolonged strain, they increase, if possible, the importance of preparation for leisure. In view of these considerations, education for the worthy use of leisure is of increasing importance as an objective.

To discharge the duties of life and to benefit from leisure, one must have good health. The health of the individual is essential also to the vitality of the race and to the defense of the Nation. Health education is, therefore, fundamental.

There are various processes, such as reading, writing, arithmetical computations, and oral and written expression, that are needed as tools in the affairs of life. Consequently, command of these fundamental processes, while not an end in itself, is nevertheless an indispensable objective.

And, finally, the realization of the objectives already named is dependent upon ethical character, that is, upon conduct founded upon right principles, clearly perceived and loyally adhered to. Good citizenship, vocational excellence, and the worthy use of leisure go hand in hand with ethical character; they are at once the fruits of sterling character and the channels through which such character is developed and made manifest. On the one hand, character is meaningless apart from the will to discharge the duties of life, and, on the other hand, there is no guaranty that these duties will be rightly discharged unless principles are substituted for impulses, however well-intentioned such impulses may be. Consequently, ethical character is at once involved in all the other objectives and at the same time requires specific consideration in any program of national education.

This commission, therefore, regards the following as the main objectives of education: 1. Health. 2. Command of fundamental processes. 3. Worthy home membership. 4. Vocation. 5. Citizenship. 6. Worthy use of leisure. 7. Ethical character.

The naming of the above objectives is not intended to imply that the process of education can be divided into separated fields. This cannot be, since the pupil is indivisible. Nor is the analysis all-inclusive. Nevertheless, we believe that distinguishing and naming these objectives will aid in directing efforts; and we hold that they should constitute the principal aims in education.

IV. THE ROLE OF SECONDARY EDUCATION IN ACHIEVING THESE OBJECTIVES

The objectives outlined above apply to education as a whole—elementary, secondary, and higher. It is the purpose of this section to consider specifically the role of secondary education in achieving each of these objectives.

For reasons stated in Section X, this commission favors such reorganization that secondary education may be defined as applying to all pupils of approximately 12 to 18 years of age.

1. *Health.*—Health needs cannot be neglected during the period of secondary education without serious danger to the individual and the race. The secondary school should therefore provide health instruction, inculcate health habits, organize an effective program of physical activities, regard health needs in planning work and play, and cooperate with home and community in safeguarding and promoting health interests.

To carry out such a program it is necessary to arouse the public to recognize that the health needs of young people are of vital importance to society, to secure teachers competent to ascertain and meet the needs of individual pupils and able to inculcate in the entire student body a love for clean sport; to furnish adequate equipment, for physical activities, and to make the school building, its rooms and surroundings, conform to the best standards of hygiene and sanitation.

2. *Command of fundamental processes.*—Much of the energy of the elementary school is properly devoted to teaching certain fundamental processes, such as reading, writing, arithmetical computations, and the elements of oral and written expression. The facility that a child of 12 or 14 may acquire in the use of these tools is not sufficient for the needs of modern life. This is particularly true of the mother tongue. Proficiency in many of these processes may be increased more effectively by their application to new material than by the formal reviews commonly employed in grades seven and eight. Throughout the secondary school, instruction and practice must go hand in hand, but as indicated in the report of the committee on English, only so much theory should be taught at any one time as will show results in practice.

3. *Worthy home membership.*—Worthy home membership as an objective calls for the development of those qualities that make the individual a worthy member of a family, both contributing to and deriving benefit from that membership. This objective applies to both boys and girls. The social studies should deal with the home as a fundamental social institution and clarify its relation to the wider interests outside. Literature should interpret and idealize the human elements that go to make the home. Music and art should result in more beautiful homes and in greater joy therein. The co-educational school with a faculty of men and women should, in its organization and its activities, exemplify wholesome relations between boys and girls and men and women. Home membership as an objective should not be thought of solely with reference to future duties. These are the better guaranteed if the school helps the pupils to take the right attitude toward pre-

sent home responsibilities and interprets to them the contribution of the home to their development.

In the education of every high-school girl, the household arts should have a prominent place because of their importance to the girl herself and to others whose welfare will be directly in her keeping. The attention now devoted to this phase of education is inadequate, and especially so for girls preparing for occupations not related to the household arts and for girls planning for higher institutions. The majority of girls who enter wage-earning occupations directly from the high school remain in them for only a few years, after which home making becomes their lifelong occupation. For them the high-school period offers the only assured opportunity to prepare for that lifelong occupation, and it is during this period that they are most likely to form their ideals of life's duties and responsibilities. For girls planning to enter higher institutions—our traditional ideals of preparation for higher institutions are particularly incongruous with the actual needs and future responsibilities of girls. It would seem that such high-school work as is carefully designed to develop capacity for, and interest in, the proper management and conduct of a home should be regarded as of importance at least equal to that of any other work. We do not understand how society can properly continue to sanction for girls high-school curriculums that disregard this fundamental need, even though such curriculums are planned in response to the demands made by some of the colleges for women.

In the education of boys, some opportunity should be found to give them a basis for the intelligent appreciation of the value of the well-appointed home and of the labor and skill required to maintain such a home, to the end that they may cooperate more effectively. For instance, they should understand the essentials of food values, of sanitation, and of household budgets.

4. *Vocation.*—Vocational education should equip the individual to secure a livelihood for himself and those dependent on him, to serve society well through his vocation, to maintain the right relationships toward his fellow workers and society, and, as far as possible, to find in that vocation his own best development. This ideal demands that the pupil explore his own capacities and aptitudes, and make a survey of the world's work, to the end that he may select his vocation wisely. Hence, an effective program of vocational guidance in the secondary school is essential.

Vocational education should aim to develop an appreciation of the significance of the vocation to the community and a clear conception of right relations between the members of the chosen vocation, between different vocational groups, between employer and employee, and between producer and consumer. These aspects of vocational education, heretofore neglected, demand emphatic attention.

Education Reform

The extent to which the secondary school should offer training for a specific vocation depends upon the vocation, the facilities that the school can acquire, and the opportunity that the pupil may have to obtain such training later. To obtain satisfactory results those proficient in that vocation should be employed as instructors and the actual conditions of the vocation should be utilized either within the high school or in cooperation with the home, farm, shop, or office. Much of the pupil's time will be required to produce such efficiency.

5. *Civic education* should develop in the individual those qualities whereby he will act well his part as a member of neighborhood, town or city, State, and Nation, and give him a basis for understanding international problems.

For such citizenship the following are essential: A many-sided interest in the welfare of the communities to which one belongs; loyalty to ideals of civic righteousness; practical knowledge of social agencies and institutions; good judgment as to means and methods that will promote one social end without defeating others . . .

Among the means for developing attitudes and habits important in a democracy are the assignment of projects and problems to groups of pupils for cooperative solution and the socialized recitation whereby the class as a whole develops a sense of collective responsibility. Both of these devices give training in collective thinking. Moreover, the democratic organization and administration of the school itself as well as the cooperative relations of pupil and teacher, pupil and pupil, and teacher and teacher, are indispensable. While all subjects should contribute to good citizenship, the social studies—geography, history, civics, and economics—should have this as their dominant aim. Too frequently, however, does mere information, conventional in value and remote in its bearing, make up the content of the social studies. History should so treat the growth of institutions that their present value may be appreciated. Geography should show the interdependence of men while it shows their common dependence on nature. Civics should concern itself less with constitutional questions and remote governmental functions, and should direct attention to social agencies close at hand and to the informal activities of daily life that regard and seek the common good. Such agencies as child-welfare organizations and consumers' leagues afford specific opportunities for the expression of civic qualities by the older pupils.

The work in English should kindle social ideals and give insight into social conditions and into personal character as related to these conditions. Hence the emphasis by the committee on English on the importance of a knowledge of social activities, social movements, and social needs on the part of the teacher of English.

214

The comprehension of the ideals of American democracy and loyalty to them should be a prominent aim of civic education. The pupil should feel that he will be responsible, in cooperation with others, for keeping the Nation true to the best inherited conceptions of democracy, and he should also realize that democracy itself is an ideal to be wrought out by his own and succeeding generations.

Civic education should consider other nations also. As a people we should try to understand their aspirations and ideals that we may deal more sympathetically and intelligently with the immigrant coming to our shores, and have a basis for a wiser and more sympathetic approach to international problems. Our pupils should learn that each nation, at least potentially, has something of worth to contribute to civilization and that humanity would be incomplete without that contribution. This means a study of specific nations, their achievements and possibilities, not ignoring their limitations. Such a study of dissimilar contributions in the light of the ideal of human brotherhood should help to establish a genuine internationalism, free from sentimentality, founded on fact, and actually operative in the affairs of nations.

6. *Worthy use of leisure.*—Education should equip the individual to secure from his leisure the recreation of body, mind, and spirit, and the enrichment and enlargement of his personality.

This objective calls for the ability to utilize the common means of enjoyment, such as music, art, literature, drama, and social intercourse, together with the fostering in each individual of one or more special vocational interests.

Heretofore the high school has given little conscious attention to this objective. It has so exclusively sought intellectual discipline that it has seldom treated literature, art, and music so as to evoke right emotional response and produce positive enjoyment. Its presentation of science should aim, in part, to arouse a genuine appreciation of nature.

The school has failed also to organize and direct the social activities of young people as it should. One of the surest ways in which to prepare pupils worthily to utilize leisure in adult life is by guiding and directing their use of leisure in youth. The school should, therefore, see that adequate recreation is provided both within the school and by other proper agencies in the community. The school, however, has a unique opportunity in this field because it includes in its membership representatives from all classes of society and consequently is able through social relationships to establish bonds of friendship and common understanding that can not be furnished by other agencies. Moreover, the school can so organize recreational activities that they will contribute simultaneously to other ends of education, as in the case of the school pageant or festival.

7. *Ethical character.*—In a democratic society ethical character becomes paramount among the objectives of the secondary school. Among the means for developing ethical character may be mentioned the wise selection of content and methods of instruction in all subjects of study, the social contacts of pupils with one another and with their teachers, the opportunities afforded by the organization and administration of the school for the development on the part of pupils of the sense of personal responsibility and initiative and, above all, the spirit of service and the principles of true democracy which should permeate the entire school—principal, teachers, and pupils.

Specific consideration is given to the moral values to be obtained from the organization of the school and the subjects of study in the report of this commission entitled "Moral Values in Secondary Education." That report considers also the conditions under which it may be advisable to supplement the other activities of the school by offering a distinct course in moral instruction . . .

XX. CONCLUSION

. . . It is the firm belief of this commission that secondary education in the United States must aim at nothing less than complete and worthy living for all youth, and that therefore the objectives described herein must find place in the education of every boy and girl.

Finally, in the process of translating into daily practice the cardinal principles herein set forth, the secondary school teachers of the United States must themselves strive to explore the inner meaning of the great democratic movement now struggling for supremacy. The doctrine that each individual has a right to the opportunity to develop the best that is in him is reinforced by the belief in the potential, and perchance unique, worth of the individual. The task of education, as of life, is therefore to call forth that potential worth.

While seeking to evoke the distinctive excellencies of individuals and groups of individuals, the secondary school must be equally zealous to develop those common ideas, common ideals, and common modes of thought, feeling, and action, whereby America, through a rich, unified, common life, may render her truest service to a world seeking for democracy among men and nations.

APPENDIX B

PRESIDENT LYNDON B. JOHNSON'S REMARKS UPON SIGNING THE ELEMENTARY AND SECONDARY EDUCATION BILL (HR 2362), APRIL 11, 1965

President Lyndon B. Johnson made these remarks in Johnson City, Texas.

Ladies and gentlemen:
I want to welcome to this little school of my childhood many of my former school mates and many who went to school with me at Cotulla and Houston and San Marcos, as well as some of my dear friends from the educational institutions of this area.

My Attorney General tells me that it is legal and constitutional to sign this act on Sunday, even on Palm Sunday. My minister assured me that the Lord's day will not be violated by making into law a measure which will bring mental and moral benefits to millions of our young people.

So I have chosen this time and this place for two reasons.

First, I do not wish to delay by a single day the program to strengthen this Nation's elementary and secondary schools. I devoutly hope that my sense of urgency will be communicated to Secretary Celebrezze, Commissioner Keppel, and the other educational officers throughout the country who will be responsible for carrying out this program.

Second, I felt a very strong desire to go back to the beginnings of my own education—to be reminded and to remind others of that magic time when the world of learning began to open before our eyes.

Education Reform

In this one-room schoolhouse Miss Katie Deadrich taught eight grades at one and the same time. Come over here, Miss Katie, and sit by me, will you? Let them see you. I started school when I was 4 years old, and they tell me, Miss Kate [sic], that I recited my first lessons while sitting on your lap.

From our very beginnings as a nation, we have felt a fierce commitment to the ideal of education for everyone. It fixed itself into our democratic creed.

Over a century and a quarter ago, the President of the Republic of Texas, Mirabeau B. Lamar, proclaimed education as "the guardian genius of democracy . . . the only dictator that free men acknowledge and the only security that free men desire."

But President Lamar made the mistaken prophecy that education would be an issue "in which no jarring interests are involved and no acrimonious political feelings excited." For too long, political acrimony held up our progress. For too long, children suffered while jarring interests caused stalemate in the efforts to improve our schools. Since 1946 Congress tried repeatedly, and failed repeatedly, to enact measures for elementary and secondary education.

Now, within the past 3 weeks, the House of Representatives, by a vote of 263 to 153, and the Senate, by a vote of 73 to 18, have passed the most sweeping educational bill ever to come before Congress. It represents a major new commitment of the Federal Government to quality and equality in the schooling that we offer our young people. I predict that all of those of both parties of Congress who supported the enactment of this legislation will be remembered in history as men and women who began a new day of greatness in American society.

We are delighted that Senator McCarthy could be speaking at the University of Texas yesterday, and he came up and had lunch with me today, and is returning to Washington with me at 7:30 in the morning. Senator McCarthy is an old friend of mine from Minnesota. Stand up, Senator, and let them see you. He has been working for this educational bill ever since the first day he came to the House of Representatives, and ever since he has been in the Senate.

I am delighted to have another good friend of mine who spent the weekend in his home district—McAlester, Oklahoma—and who came down here to spend the evening with me, and is returning in the morning, the distinguished majority leader of the House, without whose efforts we would never have passed this bill—Carl Albert of Oklahoma.

By passing this bill, we bridge the gap between helplessness and hope for more than 5 million educationally deprived children.

We put into the hands of our youth more than 30 million new books, and into many of our schools their first libraries.

We reduce the terrible time lag in bringing new teaching techniques into the Nation's classrooms.

We strengthen State and local agencies which bear the burden and the challenge of better education.

And we rekindle the revolution—the revolution of the spirit against the tyranny of ignorance.

As a son of a tenant farmer, I know that education is the only valid passport from poverty.

As a former teacher—and, I hope, a future one—I have great expectations of what this law will mean for all of our young people.

As President of the United States, I believe deeply no law I have signed or will ever sign means more to the future of America.

To each and everyone who contributed to this day, the Nation is indebted.

On Tuesday afternoon we will ask the Members of the House and Senate who were instrumental in guiding this legislation through the Congress to meet with us at a reception in the White House.

So it is not the culmination but only the commencement of this journey. Let me urge, as Thomas Jefferson urged his fellow countrymen one time to, and I quote, "Preach, my dear sir, a crusade against ignorance; establish and improve the law for educating the common people . . . "

We have established the law. Let us not delay in putting it to work.

APPENDIX C

EXCERPTS FROM *A NATION AT RISK*, NATIONAL COMMISSION ON EXCELLENCE IN EDUCATION, APRIL 1983

INTRODUCTION

Secretary of Education T. H. Bell created the National Commission on Excellence in Education on August 26, 1981, directing it to examine the quality of education in the United States and to make a report to the Nation and to him within 18 months of its first meeting. In accordance with the secretary's instructions, this report contains practical recommendations for educational improvement and fulfills the commission's responsibilities under the terms of its charter.

A NATION AT RISK

All, regardless of race or class or economic status, are entitled to a fair chance and to the tools for developing their individual powers of mind and spirit to the utmost. This promise means that all children by virtue of their own efforts, competently guided, can hope to attain the mature and informed judgement needed to secure gainful employment, and to manage their own lives, thereby serving not only their own interests but also the progress of society itself.

Our Nation is at risk. Our once unchallenged preeminence in commerce, industry, science, and technological innovation is being overtaken by competitors throughout the world. This report is concerned with only one of the many causes and dimensions of the problem, but it is the one that undergirds American prosperity, security, and civility. We report to the American people that while we can take justifiable pride in what our schools and colleges have historically accomplished and contributed to the United States and the well-being of its people, the educational foundations of our society are presently being eroded by a rising tide of mediocrity that threatens our very future as a Nation and a people. What was unimaginable a generation ago has begun to occur—others are matching and surpassing our educational attainments.

If an unfriendly foreign power had attempted to impose on America the mediocre educational performance that exists today, we might well have viewed it as an act of war. As it stands, we have allowed this to happen to ourselves. We have even squandered the gains in student achievement made in the wake of the Sputnik challenge. Moreover, we have dismantled essential support systems which helped make those gains possible. We have, in effect, been committing an act of unthinking, unilateral educational disarmament.

Our society and its educational institutions seem to have lost sight of the basic purposes of schooling, and of the high expectations and disciplined effort needed to attain them. This report, the result of 18 months of study, seeks to generate reform of our educational system in fundamental ways and to renew the Nation's commitment to schools and colleges of high quality throughout the length and breadth of our land.

That we have compromised this commitment is, upon reflection, hardly surprising, given the multitude of often conflicting demands we have placed on our Nation's schools and colleges. They are routinely called on to provide solutions to personal, social, and political problems that the home and other institutions either will not or cannot resolve. We must understand that these demands on our schools and colleges often exact an educational cost as well as a financial one.

On the occasion of the Commission's first meeting, President Reagan noted the central importance of education in American life when he said: "Certainly there are few areas of American life as important to our society, to our people, and to our families as our schools and colleges." This report, therefore, is as much an open letter to the American people as it is a report to the Secretary of Education. We are confident that the American people, properly informed, will do what is right for their children and for the generations to come.

THE RISK

History is not kind to idlers. The time is long past when American's [sic] destiny was assured simply by an abundance of natural resources and inexhaustible human enthusiasm, and by our relative isolation from the malignant problems of older civilizations. The world is indeed one global village. We live among determined, well-educated, and strongly motivated competitors. We compete with them for international standing and markets, not only with products but also with the ideas of our laboratories and neighborhood workshops. America's position in the world may once have been reasonably secure with only a few exceptionally well-trained men and women. It is no longer.

The risk is not only that the Japanese make automobiles more efficiently than Americans and have government subsidies for development and export. It is not just that the South Koreans recently built the world's most efficient steel mill, or that American machine tools, once the pride of the world, are being displaced by German products. It is also that these developments signify a redistribution of trained capability throughout the globe. Knowledge, learning, information, and skilled intelligence are the new raw materials of international commerce and are today spreading throughout the world as vigorously as miracle drugs, synthetic fertilizers, and blue jeans did earlier. If only to keep and improve on the slim competitive edge we still retain in world markets, we must dedicate ourselves to the reform of our educational system for the benefit of all—old and young alike, affluent and poor, majority and minority. Learning is the indispensable investment required for success in the "information age" we are entering.

Our concern, however, goes well beyond matters such as industry and commerce. It also includes the intellectual, moral, and spiritual strengths of our people which knit together the very fabric of our society. The people of the United States need to know that individuals in our society who do not possess the levels of skill, literacy, and training essential to this new era will be effectively disenfranchised, not simply from the material rewards that accompany competent performance, but also from the chance to participate fully in our national life. A high level of shared education is essential to a free, democratic society and to the fostering of a common culture, especially in a country that prides itself on pluralism and individual freedom.

For our country to function, citizens must be able to reach some common understandings on complex issues, often on short notice and on the basis of conflicting or incomplete evidence. Education helps form these common understandings, a point Thomas Jefferson made long ago in his justly famous dictum:

I know no safe depository of the ultimate powers of the society but the people themselves; and if we think them not enlightened enough to exercise their control with a wholesome discretion, the remedy is not to take it from them but to inform their discretion.

Appendix C

Part of what is at risk is the promise first made on this continent: All, regardless of race or class or economic status, are entitled to a fair chance and to the tools for developing their individual powers of mind and spirit to the utmost. This promise means that all children by virtue of their own efforts, competently guided, can hope to attain the mature and informed judgment needed to secure gainful employment, and to manage their own lives, thereby serving not only their own interests but also the progress of society itself.

INDICATORS OF THE RISK

The educational dimensions of the risk before us have been amply documented in testimony received by the Commission. For example:

- International comparisons of student achievement, completed a decade ago, reveal that on 19 academic tests American students were never first or second and, in comparison with other industrialized nations, were last seven times.
- Some 23 million American adults are functionally illiterate by the simplest tests of everyday reading, writing, and comprehension.
- About 13 percent of all 17-year-olds in the United States can be considered functionally illiterate. Functional illiteracy among minority youth may run as high as 40 percent.
- Average achievement of high school students on most standardized tests is now lower than 26 years ago when Sputnik was launched.
- Over half the population of gifted students do not match their tested ability with comparable achievement in school.
- The College Board's Scholastic Aptitude Tests (SAT) demonstrate a virtually unbroken decline from 1963 to 1980. Average verbal scores fell over 50 points and average mathematics scores dropped nearly 40 points.
- College Board achievement tests also reveal consistent declines in recent years in such subjects as physics and English.
- Both the number and proportion of students demonstrating superior achievement on the SATs (i.e., those with scores of 650 or higher) have also dramatically declined.
- Many 17-year-olds do not possess the "higher order" intellectual skills we should expect of them. Nearly 40 percent cannot draw inferences from written material; only one-fifth can write a persuasive essay; and only one-third can solve a mathematics problem requiring several steps.
- There was a steady decline in science achievement scores of U.S. 17-year-olds as measured by national assessments of science in 1969, 1973, and 1977.

- Between 1975 and 1980, remedial mathematics courses in public 4-year colleges increased by 72 percent and now constitute one-quarter of all mathematics courses taught in those institutions.

- Average tested achievement of students graduating from college is also lower.

- Business and military leaders complain that they are required to spend millions of dollars on costly remedial education and training programs in such basic skills as reading, writing, spelling, and computation. The Department of the Navy, for example, reported to the Commission that one-quarter of its recent recruits cannot read at the ninth grade level, the minimum needed simply to understand written safety instructions. Without remedial work they cannot even begin, much less complete, the sophisticated training essential in much of the modern military.

These deficiencies come at a time when the demand for highly skilled workers in new fields is accelerating rapidly. For example:

- Computers and computer-controlled equipment are penetrating every aspect of our lives—homes, factories, and offices.

- One estimate indicates that by the turn of the century millions of jobs will involve laser technology and robotics.

- Technology is radically transforming a host of other occupations. They include health care, medical science, energy production, food processing, construction, and the building, repair, and maintenance of sophisticated scientific, educational, military, and industrial equipment.

Analysts examining these indicators of student performance and the demands for new skills have made some chilling observations. Educational researcher Paul Hurd concluded at the end of a thorough national survey of student achievement that within the context of the modern scientific revolution, "We are raising a new generation of Americans that is scientifically and technologically illiterate." In a similar vein, John Slaughter, a former Director of the National Science Foundation, warned of "a growing chasm between a small scientific and technological elite and a citizenry ill-informed, indeed uninformed, on issues with a science component."

But the problem does not stop there, nor do all observers see it the same way. Some worry that schools may emphasize such rudiments as reading and computation at the expense of other essential skills such as comprehension, analysis, solving problems, and drawing conclusions. Still others are concerned that an over-emphasis on technical and occupational skills will leave little time for studying the arts and humanities that so enrich daily life, help maintain civility, and develop a sense of community. Knowledge of the humanities, they maintain, must be harnessed to science and technology if the latter are to remain creative and humane, just as the humanities need to be informed by science and technology if they are to remain relevant to the human condition. Another analyst, Paul Copperman, has drawn a sobering conclusion. Until now, he has noted:

> *Each generation of Americans has outstripped its parents in education, in literacy, and in economic attainment. For the first time in the history of our country, the educational skills of one generation will not surpass, will not equal, will not even approach, those of their parents.*

It is important, of course, to recognize that *the average citizen* today is better educated and more knowledgeable than the average citizen of a generation ago—more literate, and exposed to more mathematics, literature, and science. The positive impact of this fact on the well-being of our country and the lives of our people cannot be overstated. Nevertheless, *the average graduate* of our schools and colleges today is not as well-educated as the average graduate of 25 or 35 years ago, when a much smaller proportion of our population completed high school and college. The negative impact of this fact likewise cannot be overstated.

FINDINGS

We conclude that declines in educational performance are in large part the result of disturbing inadequacies in the way the educational process itself is often conducted. The findings that follow, culled from a much more extensive list, reflect four important aspects of the educational process: content, expectations, time, and teaching.

FINDINGS REGARDING CONTENT

By content we mean the very "stuff" of education, the curriculum. Because of our concern about the curriculum, the Commission examined patterns of courses high school students took in 1964–69 compared with course patterns in 1976–81. On the basis of these analyses we conclude:

- Secondary school curricula have been homogenized, diluted, and diffused to the point that they no longer have a central purpose. In effect, we have a cafeteria style curriculum in which the appetizers and desserts can easily be mistaken for the main courses. Students have migrated from vocational and college preparatory programs to "general track" courses in large numbers. The proportion of students taking a general program of study has increased from 12 percent in 1964 to 42 percent in 1979.

- This curricular smorgasbord, combined with extensive student choice, explains a great deal about where we find ourselves today. We offer intermediate algebra, but only 31 percent of our recent high school graduates complete it; we offer French I, but only 13 percent complete it; and we offer geography, but only 16 percent complete it. Calculus is available in schools enrolling about 60 percent of all students, but only 6 percent of all students complete it.

- Twenty-five percent of the credits earned by general track high school students are in physical and health education, work experience outside the school, remedial English and mathematics, and personal service and development courses, such as training for adulthood and marriage.

FINDINGS REGARDING EXPECTATIONS

We define expectations in terms of the level of knowledge, abilities, and skills school and college graduates should possess. They also refer to the time, hard work, behavior, self-discipline, and motivation that are essential for high student achievement. Such expectations are expressed to students in several different ways:

- by grades, which reflect the degree to which students demonstrate their mastery of subject matter;

- through high school and college graduation requirements, which tell students which subjects are most important;

- by the presence or absence of rigorous examinations requiring students to demonstrate their mastery of content and skill before receiving a diploma or a degree;

- by college admissions requirements, which reinforce high school standards; and

- by the difficulty of the subject matter students confront in their texts and assigned readings.

Our analyses in each of these areas indicate notable deficiencies:

- The amount of homework for high school seniors has decreased (two-thirds report less than 1 hour a night) and grades have risen as average student achievement has been declining.

- In many other industrialized nations, courses in mathematics (other than arithmetic or general mathematics), biology, chemistry, physics, and geography start in grade 6 and are required of *all* students. The time spent on these subjects, based on class hours, is about three times that spent by even the most science-oriented U.S. students, i.e., those who select 4 years of science and mathematics in secondary school.

- A 1980 State-by-State survey of high school diploma requirements reveals that only eight States require high schools to offer foreign language instruction, but none requires students to take the courses. Thirty-five States require only 1 year of mathematics, and 36 require only 1 year of science for a diploma.

- In 13 States, 50 percent or more of the units required for high school graduation may be electives chosen by the student. Given this freedom to choose the substance of half or more of their education, many students opt for less demanding personal service courses, such as bachelor living.

- "Minimum competency" examinations (now required in 37 States) fall short of what is needed, as the "minimum" tends to become the "maximum," thus lowering educational standards for all.

- One-fifth of all 4-year public colleges in the United States must accept every high school graduate within the State regardless of the program followed or grades, thereby serving notice to high school students that they can expect to attend college even if they do not follow a demanding course of study in high school or perform well.

- About 23 percent of our more selective colleges and universities reported that their general level of selectivity declined during the 1970s, and 29 percent reported reducing the number of specific high school courses required for admission (usually by dropping foreign language requirements, which are now specified as a condition for admission by only one-fifth of our institutions of higher education).

- Too few experienced teachers and scholars are involved in writing textbooks. During the past decade or so a large number of texts have been "written down" by their publishers to ever-lower reading levels in response to perceived market demands.

- A recent study by Education Products Information Exchange revealed that a majority of students were able to master 80 percent of the material in some of their subject-matter texts before they had even opened the books. Many books do not challenge the students to whom they are assigned.

- Expenditures for textbooks and other instructional materials have declined by 50 percent over the past 17 years. While some recommend a level of spending on texts of between 5 and 10 percent of the operating costs of schools, the budgets for basal texts and related materials have been dropping during the past decade and a half to only 0.7 percent today.

FINDINGS REGARDING TIME

Evidence presented to the Commission demonstrates three disturbing facts about the use that American schools and students make of time: (1) compared to other nations, American students spend much less time on school work; (2) time spent in the classroom and on homework is often used ineffectively; and (3) schools are not doing enough to help students develop either the study skills required to use time well or the willingness to spend more time on school work.

- In England and other industrialized countries, it is not unusual for academic high school students to spend 8 hours a day at school, 220 days per year. In the United States, by contrast, the typical school day lasts 6 hours and the school year is 180 days.
- In many schools, the time spent learning how to cook and drive counts as much toward a high school diploma as the time spent studying mathematics, English, chemistry, U.S. history, or biology.
- A study of the school week in the United States found that some schools provided students only 17 hours of academic instruction during the week, and the average school provided about 22.
- A California study of individual classrooms found that because of poor management of classroom time, some elementary students received only one-fifth of the instruction others received in reading comprehension.
- In most schools, the teaching of study skills is haphazard and unplanned. Consequently, many students complete high school and enter college without disciplined and systematic study habits.

FINDINGS REGARDING TEACHING

The Commission found that not enough of the academically able students are being attracted to teaching; that teacher preparation programs need substantial improvement; that the professional working life of teachers is on the whole unacceptable; and that a serious shortage of teachers exists in key fields.

- Too many teachers are being drawn from the bottom quarter of graduating high school and college students.
- The teacher preparation curriculum is weighted heavily with courses in "educational methods" at the expense of courses in subjects to be taught. A sur-

vey of 1,350 institutions training teachers indicated that 41 percent of the time of elementary school teacher candidates is spent in education courses, which reduces the amount of time available for subject matter courses.

- The average salary after 12 years of teaching is only $17,000 per year, and many teachers are required to supplement their income with part-time and summer employment. In addition, individual teachers have little influence in such critical professional decisions as, for example, textbook selection.

- Despite widespread publicity about an overpopulation of teachers, severe shortages of certain kinds of teachers exist: in the fields of mathematics, science, and foreign languages; and among specialists in education for gifted and talented, language minority, and handicapped students.

- The shortage of teachers in mathematics and science is particularly severe. A 1981 survey of 45 States revealed shortages of mathematics teachers in 43 States, critical shortages of earth sciences teachers in 33 States, and of physics teachers everywhere.

Half of the newly employed mathematics, science, and English teachers are not qualified to teach these subjects; fewer than one-third of U.S. high schools offer Physics taught by qualified teachers.

RECOMMENDATIONS

In light of the urgent need for improvement, both immediate and long term, this Commission has agreed on a set of recommendations that the American people can begin to act on now, that can be implemented over the next several years, and that promise lasting reform. The topics are familiar; there is little mystery about what we believe must be done. Many schools, districts, and States are already giving serious and constructive attention to these matters, even though their plans may differ from our recommendations in some details.

We wish to note that we refer to public, private, and parochial schools and colleges alike. All are valuable national resources. Examples of actions similar to those recommended below can be found in each of them.

We must emphasize that the variety of student aspirations, abilities, and preparation requires that appropriate content be available to satisfy diverse needs. Attention must be directed to both the nature of the content available and to the needs of particular learners. The most gifted students, for example, may need a curriculum enriched and accelerated beyond even the needs of other students of high ability. Similarly, educationally disadvantaged students may require special curriculum materials, smaller classes, or individual tutoring to help them master the material presented. Nevertheless, there remains a common expectation: We must demand the best effort and performance from all students, whether they are gifted or less able, affluent or disadvantaged, whether destined for college, the farm, or industry.

Our recommendations are based on the beliefs that everyone can learn, that everyone is born with an urge to learn which can be nurtured, that a solid high school education is within the reach of virtually all, and that life-long learning will equip people with the skills required for new careers and for citizenship.

RECOMMENDATION A: CONTENT

We recommend *that State and local high school graduation requirements be strengthened and that, at a minimum, all students seeking a diploma be required to lay the foundations in the Five New Basics by taking the following curriculum during their 4 years of high school: (a) 4 years of English; (b) 3 years of mathematics; (c) 3 years of science; (d) 3 years of social studies; and (e) one-half year of computer science. For the college-bound, 2 years of foreign language in high school are strongly recommended in addition to those taken earlier.*

RECOMMENDATION B: STANDARDS AND EXPECTATIONS

We recommend *that schools, colleges, and universities adopt more rigorous and measurable standards, and higher expectations, for academic performance and student conduct, and that 4-year colleges and universities raise their requirements for admission. This will help students do their best educationally with challenging materials in an environment that supports learning and authentic accomplishment.*

Implementing Recommendations

1. Grades should be indicators of academic achievement so they can be relied on as evidence of a student's readiness for further study.
2. Four-year colleges and universities should raise their admissions requirements and advise all potential applicants of the standards for admission in terms of specific courses required, performance in these areas, and levels of achievement on standardized achievement tests in each of the five Basics and, where applicable, foreign languages.
3. Standardized tests of achievement (not to be confused with aptitude tests) should be administered at major transition points from one level of schooling to another and particularly from high school to college or work. The purposes of these tests would be to: (a) certify the student's credentials; (b) identify the need for remedial intervention; and (c) identify the opportunity for advanced or accelerated work. The tests should be administered as part of a nationwide (but not Federal)

system of State and local standardized tests. This system should include other diagnostic procedures that assist teachers and students to evaluate student progress.

4. Textbooks and other tools of learning and teaching should be upgraded and updated to assure more rigorous content. We call upon university scientists, scholars, and members of professional societies, in collaboration with master teachers, to help in this task, as they did in the post-Sputnik era. They should assist willing publishers in developing the products or publish their own alternatives where there are persistent inadequacies.

5. In considering textbooks for adoption, States and school districts should: (a) evaluate texts and other materials on their ability to present rigorous and challenging material clearly; and (b) require publishers to furnish evaluation data on the material's effectiveness.

6. Because no textbook in any subject can be geared to the needs of all students, funds should be made available to support text development in "thin-market" areas, such as those for disadvantaged students, the learning disabled, and the gifted and talented.

7. To assure quality, all publishers should furnish evidence of the quality and appropriateness of textbooks, based on results from field trials and credible evaluation. In view of the enormous numbers and varieties of texts available, more widespread consumer information services for purchasers are badly needed.

8. New instructional materials should reflect the most current applications of technology in appropriate curriculum areas, the best scholarship in each discipline, and research in learning and teaching.

RECOMMENDATION C: TIME

We recommend *that significantly more time be devoted to learning the New Basics. This will require more effective use of the existing school day, a longer school day, or a lengthened school year.*

Implementing Recommendations

1. Students in high schools should be assigned far more homework than is now the case.

2. Instruction in effective study and work skills, which are essential if school and independent time is to be used efficiently, should be introduced in the early grades and continued throughout the student's schooling.

3. School districts and State legislatures should strongly consider 7-hour school days, as well as a 200- to 220-day school year.

4. The time available for learning should be expanded through better classroom management and organization of the school day. If necessary, additional time should be found to meet the special needs of slow learners, the gifted, and others who need more instructional diversity than can be accommodated during a conventional school day or school year.
5. The burden on teachers for maintaining discipline should be reduced through the development of firm and fair codes of student conduct that are enforced consistently, and by considering alternative classrooms, programs, and schools to meet the needs of continually disruptive students.
6. Attendance policies with clear incentives and sanctions should be used to reduce the amount of time lost through student absenteeism and tardiness.
7. Administrative burdens on the teacher and related intrusions into the school day should be reduced to add time for teaching and learning.
8. Placement and grouping of students, as well as promotion and graduation policies, should be guided by the academic progress of students and their instructional needs, rather than by rigid adherence to age.

RECOMMENDATION D: TEACHING

This recommendation *consists of seven parts. Each is intended to improve the preparation of teachers or to make teaching a more rewarding and respected profession. Each of the seven stands on its own and should not be considered solely as an implementing recommendation.*

1. Persons preparing to teach should be required to meet high educational standards, to demonstrate an aptitude for teaching, and to demonstrate competence in an academic discipline. Colleges and universities offering teacher preparation programs should be judged by how well their graduates meet these criteria.
2. Salaries for the teaching profession should be increased and should be professionally competitive, market-sensitive, and performance-based. Salary, promotion, tenure, and retention decisions should be tied to an effective evaluation system that includes peer review so that superior teachers can be rewarded, average ones encouraged, and poor ones either improved or terminated.
3. School boards should adopt an 11-month contract for teachers. This would ensure time for curriculum and professional development, programs for students with special needs, and a more adequate level of teacher compensation.

4. School boards, administrators, and teachers should cooperate to develop career ladders for teachers that distinguish among the beginning instructor, the experienced teacher, and the master teacher.

5. Substantial nonschool personnel resources should be employed to help solve the immediate problem of the shortage of mathematics and science teachers. Qualified individuals, including recent graduates with mathematics and science degrees, graduate students, and industrial and retired scientists could, with appropriate preparation, immediately begin teaching in these fields. A number of our leading science centers have the capacity to begin educating and retraining teachers immediately. Other areas of critical teacher need, such as English, must also be addressed.

6. Incentives, such as grants and loans, should be made available to attract outstanding students to the teaching profession, particularly in those areas of critical shortage.

7. Master teachers should be involved in designing teacher preparation programs and in supervising teachers during their probationary years.

RECOMMENDATION E: LEADERSHIP AND FISCAL SUPPORT

We recommend *that citizens across the Nation hold educators and elected officials responsible for providing the leadership necessary to achieve these reforms, and that citizens provide the fiscal support and stability required to bring about the reforms we propose.*

Implementing Recommendations

1. Principals and superintendents must play a crucial leadership role in developing school and community support for the reforms we propose, and school boards must provide them with the professional development and other support required to carry out their leadership role effectively. The Commission stresses the distinction between leadership skills involving persuasion, setting goals and developing community consensus behind them, and managerial and supervisory skills. Although the latter are necessary, we believe that school boards must consciously develop leadership skills at the school and district levels if the reforms we propose are to be achieved.

2. State and local officials, including school board members, governors, and legislators, have *the primary responsibility* for financing and governing the schools, and should incorporate the reforms we propose in their educational policies and fiscal planning.

3. The Federal Government, in cooperation with States and localities, should help meet the needs of key groups of students such as the

gifted and talented, the socioeconomically disadvantaged, minority and language minority students, and the handicapped. In combination these groups include both national resources and the Nation's youth who are most at risk.

4. In addition, we believe the Federal Government's role includes several functions of national consequence that States and localities alone are unlikely to be able to meet: protecting constitutional and civil rights for students and school personnel; collecting data, statistics, and information about education generally; supporting curriculum improvement and research on teaching, learning, and the management of schools; supporting teacher training in areas of critical shortage or key national needs; and providing student financial assistance and research and graduate training. We believe the assistance of the Federal Government should be provided with a minimum of administrative burden and intrusiveness.

5. The Federal Government has *the primary responsibility* to identify the national interest in education. It should also help fund and support efforts to protect and promote that interest. It must provide the national leadership to ensure that the Nation's public and private resources are marshaled to address the issues discussed in this report.

6. This Commission calls upon educators, parents, and public officials at all levels to assist in bringing about the educational reform proposed in this report. We also call upon citizens to provide the financial support necessary to accomplish these purposes. Excellence costs. But in the long run mediocrity costs far more.

A FINAL WORD

This is not the first or only commission on education, and some of our findings are surely not new, but old business that now at last must be done. For no one can doubt that the United States is under challenge from many quarters.

Children born today can expect to graduate from high school in the year 2000. We dedicate our report not only to these children, but also to those now in school and others to come. We firmly believe that a movement of America's schools in the direction called for by our recommendations will prepare these children for far more effective lives in a far stronger America.

APPENDIX D

EXCERPT FROM *GOALS 2000: EDUCATE AMERICA ACT,* JANUARY 25, 1994

The following is section 102 from National Education Goals of H.R. 1804.

The Congress declares that the National Education Goals are the following:

(1) SCHOOL READINESS. —
  (A) By the year 2000, all children in America will start school ready to learn.
  (B) The objectives for this goal are that —
    (i) all children will have access to high-quality and developmentally appropriate preschool programs that help prepare children for school;
    (ii) every parent in the United States will be a child's first teacher and devote time each day to helping such parent's preschool child learn, and parents will have access to the training and support parents need; and
    (iii) children will receive the nutrition, physical activity experiences, and health care needed to arrive at school with healthy minds and bodies, and to maintain the mental alertness necessary to be prepared to learn, and the number of low-birthweight babies will be significantly reduced through enhanced prenatal health systems.

(2) SCHOOL COMPLETION. —
  (A) By the year 2000, the high school graduation rate will increase to at least 90 percent.
  (B) The objectives for this goal are that —

(i) the Nation must dramatically reduce its school dropout rate, and 75 percent of the students who do drop out will successfully complete a high school degree or its equivalent; and

(ii) the gap in high school graduation rates between American students from minority backgrounds and their non-minority counterparts will be eliminated.

(3) STUDENT ACHIEVEMENT AND CITIZENSHIP. —

(A) By the year 2000, all students will leave grades 4, 8, and 12 having demonstrated competency over challenging subject matter including English, mathematics, science, foreign languages, civics and government, economics, arts, history, and geography, and every school in America will ensure that all students learn to use their minds well, so they may be prepared for responsible citizenship, further learning, and productive employment in our Nation's modern economy.

(B) The objectives for this goal are that —

(i) the academic performance of all students at the elementary and secondary level will increase significantly in every quartile, and the distribution of minority students in each quartile will more closely reflect the student population as a whole;

(ii) the percentage of all students who demonstrate the ability to reason, solve problems, apply knowledge, and write and communicate effectively will increase substantially;

(iii) all students will be involved in activities that promote and demonstrate good citizenship, good health, community service, and personal responsibility;

(iv) all students will have access to physical education and health education to ensure they are healthy and fit;

(v) the percentage of all students who are competent in more than one language will substantially increase; and

(vi) all students will be knowledgeable about the diverse cultural heritage of this Nation and about the world community.

(4) TEACHER EDUCATION AND PROFESSIONAL DEVELOPMENT. —

(A) By the year 2000, the Nation's teaching force will have access to programs for the continued improvement of their professional skills and the opportunity to acquire the knowledge and skills needed to instruct and prepare all American students for the next century.

(B) The objectives for this goal are that —

(i) all teachers will have access to preservice teacher education and continuing professional development activities that will provide such teachers with the knowledge and skills needed to teach to an increasingly diverse student population with a variety of educational, social, and health needs;

(ii) all teachers will have continuing opportunities to acquire additional knowledge and skills needed to teach challenging subject matter and to use emerging new methods, forms of assessment, and technologies;

(iii) States and school districts will create integrated strategies to attract, recruit, prepare, retrain, and support the continued professional development of teachers, administrators, and other educators, so that there is a highly talented work force of professional educators to teach challenging subject matter; and

(iv) partnerships will be established, whenever possible, among local educational agencies, institutions of higher education, parents, and local labor, business, and professional associations to provide and support programs for the professional development of educators.

(5) MATHEMATICS AND SCIENCE. —

(A) By the year 2000, United States students will be first in the world in mathematics and science achievement.

(B) The objectives for this goal are that —

(i) mathematics and science education, including the metric system of measurement, will be strengthened throughout the system, especially in the early grades;

(ii) the number of teachers with a substantive background in mathematics and science, including the metric system of measurement, will increase by 50 percent; and

(iii) the number of United States undergraduate and graduate students, especially women and minorities, who complete degrees in mathematics, science, and engineering will increase significantly.

(6) ADULT LITERACY AND LIFELONG LEARNING. —

(A) By the year 2000, every adult American will be literate and will possess the knowledge and skills necessary to compete in a global economy and exercise the rights and responsibilities of citizenship.

(B) The objectives for this goal are that —

(i) every major American business will be involved in strengthening the connection between education and work;

(ii) all workers will have the opportunity to acquire the knowledge and skills, from basic to highly technical, needed to adapt to emerging new technologies, work methods, and markets through public and private educational, vocational, technical, workplace, or other programs;

   (iii) the number of quality programs, including those at libraries, that are designed to serve more effectively the needs of the growing number of part-time and midcareer students will increase substantially;

   (iv) the proportion of the qualified students, especially minorities,who enter college, who complete at least two years, and who complete their degree programs will increase substantially;

   (v) the proportion of college graduates who demonstrate an advanced ability to think critically, communicate effectively, and solve problems will increase substantially; and

   (vi) schools, in implementing comprehensive parent involvement programs, will offer more adult literacy, parent training and life-long learning opportunities to improve the ties between home and school, and enhance parents' work and home lives.

(7) SAFE, DISCIPLINED, AND ALCOHOL- AND DRUG-FREE SCHOOLS. —

  (A) By the year 2000, every school in the United States will be free of drugs, violence, and the unauthorized presence of firearms and alcohol and will offer a disciplined environment conducive to learning.

  (B) The objectives for this goal are that —

   (i) every school will implement a firm and fair policy on use, possession, and distribution of drugs and alcohol;

   (ii) parents, businesses, governmental and community organizations will work together to ensure the rights of students to study in a safe and secure environment that is free of drugs and crime, and that schools provide a healthy environment and are a safe haven for all children;

   (iii) every local educational agency will develop and implement a policy to ensure that all schools are free of violence and the unauthorized presence of weapons;

   (iv) every local educational agency will develop a sequential, comprehensive kindergarten through twelfth grade drug and alcohol prevention education program;

   (v) drug and alcohol curriculum should be taught as an integral part of sequential, comprehensive health education;

   (vi) community-based teams should be organized to provide students and teachers with needed support; and

   (vii) every school should work to eliminate sexual harassment.

(8) PARENTAL PARTICIPATION —
  (A) By the year 2000, every school will promote partnerships that will increase parental involvement and participation in promoting the social, emotional, and academic growth of children.
  (B) The objectives for this Goal are that —
    (i) every State will develop policies to assist local schools and local educational agencies to establish programs for increasing partnerships that respond to the varying needs of parents and the home, including parents of children who are disadvantaged or bilingual, or parents of children with disabilities;
    (ii) every school will actively engage parents and families in a partnership which supports the academic work of children at home and shared educational decisionmaking at school; and
    (iii) parents and families will help to ensure that schools are adequately supported and will hold schools and teachers to high standards of accountability.

APPENDIX E

STATE CHARTER SCHOOL LEGISLATION, ENROLLMENT, AND OPERATION, 2002

The dynamic and continuing growth of the charter school movement is evident in the following chart, which notes the year state charter laws were passed in each of the 39 states (and the District of Columbia) that permit them, the number of charter schools in operation and their total enrollment in 2001, charter schools in operation in 2002, and the approved increase of charter schools in 2003.

State	Year Charter Law Passed	Schools Operating, Fall 2001	Enrollment, Fall 2001	Schools Operating, Fall 2002	Approved to Open, Fall 2003
Alaska	1995	15	1,965	15	0
Arizona	1994	419	69,884	465	11
Arkansas	1995	6	1,806	8	0
California	1992	358	134,425	427	7
Colorado	1993	89	24,352	93	0
Connecticut	1996	16	2,445	16	0
Delaware	1995	11	4,335	11	0
District of Columbia	1996	41	10,356	39	0
Florida	1996	180	38,313	227	4
Georgia	1993	46	24,999	36	3
Hawaii	1994	22	3,087	25	0
Idaho	1998	11	1,350	13	1
Illinois	1996	28	5,110	29	0
Indiana	2001	...	...	10	3
Iowa	2002	...	...	0	0
Kansas	1994	28	2,389	30	0
Louisiana	1995	26	5,925	20	0
Massachusetts	1993	43	13,911	46	6
Michigan	1993	196	61,148	196	12
Minnesota	1991	75	9,600	87	0
Mississippi	1997	1	334	1	0
Missouri	1998	22	4,838	26	2
Nevada	1997	9	1,636	13	0
New Hampshire	1995	0	0	0	0
New Jersey	1996	55	13,652	56	0
New Mexico	1993	21	3,287	28	4
New York	1998	32	7,008	38	10
North Carolina	1996	96	20,259	93	2
Ohio	1997	68	15,278	97	0
Oklahoma	1999	10	1,559	10	0
Oregon	1999	17	998	25	1
Pennsylvania	1997	77	26,749	91	2
Rhode Island	1995	6	823	8	0
South Carolina	1996	8	595	14	0
Tennessee	2002	...	...	0	0
Texas	1995	214	53,263	228	0
Utah	1998	9	587	12	1
Virginia	1998	6	768	8	0
Wisconsin	1993	96	12,846	115	0
Wyoming	1995	0	0	1	0
Nationwide Total	...	2,357	579,880	2,699	69

Note: States that do not have a charter school law: Alabama, Kentucky, Maine, Maryland, Montana, Nebraska, North Dakota, South Dakota, Vermont, Washington, West Virginia. Ellipsis points indicate that no law existed in that state.

Source: Center for Education Reform, information compiled through state departments of education and charter school resource centers.

APPENDIX F

EXCERPTS FROM *SUSAN TAVE ZELMAN, SUPERINTENDENT OF PUBLIC INSTRUCTION OF OHIO, ET AL. V. DORIS SIMMONS-HARRIS ET AL.*, JUNE 27, 2002

(Note: footnotes and references have been omitted)

CHIEF JUSTICE [William] REHNQUIST delivered the opinion of the Court.

The State of Ohio has established a pilot program designed to provide educational choices to families with children who reside in the Cleveland City School District. The question presented is whether this program offends the Establishment Clause of the United States Constitution. We hold that it does not.

There are more than 75,000 children enrolled in the Cleveland City School District. The majority of these children are from low-income and minority families. Few of these families enjoy the means to send their children to any school other than an inner-city public school. For more than a generation, however, Cleveland's public schools have been among the worst performing public schools in the Nation. In 1995, a Federal District Court declared a "crisis of magnitude" and placed the entire Cleveland school district under state control. Shortly thereafter, the state auditor found that Cleveland's public schools were in the midst of a "crisis that is perhaps unprecedented in the history of American education." The district had failed to meet any of the 18 state standards for minimal acceptable performance. Only 1 in 10 ninth graders could pass a basic proficiency examination, and students at all levels performed at a dismal rate compared with students in other Ohio public schools. More than two-thirds of high school students either dropped or failed out before graduation. Of those students who managed to reach their senior year, one of every four still failed to graduate. Of those students who did graduate, few could read, write, or compute at levels comparable to their counterparts in other cities.

It is against this backdrop that Ohio enacted, among other initiatives, its Pilot Project Scholarship Program. The program provides financial assistance to families in any Ohio school district that is or has been "under federal court order requiring supervision and operational management of the district by the state superintendent." Cleveland is the only Ohio school district to fall within that category.

The program provides two basic kinds of assistance to parents of children in a covered district. First, the program provides tuition aid for students in kindergarten through third grade, expanding each year through eighth grade, to attend a participating public or private school of their parent's choosing. Second, the program provides tutorial aid for students who choose to remain enrolled in public school.

The tuition aid portion of the program is designed to provide educational choices to parents who reside in a covered district. Any private school, whether religious or nonreligious, may participate in the program and accept program students so long as the school is located within the boundaries of a covered district and meets statewide educational standards. Participating private schools must agree not to discriminate on the basis of race, religion, or ethnic background, or to "advocate or foster unlawful behavior or teach hatred of any person or group on the basis of race, ethnicity, national origin, or religion." Any public school located in a school district adjacent to the covered district may also participate in the program. Adjacent public schools are eligible to receive a $2,250 tuition grant for each program student accepted in addition to the full amount of per-pupil state funding attributable to each additional student. All participating schools, whether public or private, are required to accept students in accordance with rules and procedures established by the state superintendent.

Tuition aid is distributed to parents according to financial need. Families with incomes below 200% of the poverty line are given priority and are eligible to receive 90% of private school tuition up to $2,250. For these lowest-income families, participating private schools may not charge a parental co-payment greater than $250. For all other families, the program pays 75% of tuition costs, up to $1,875, with no co-payment cap. These families receive tuition aid only if the number of available scholarships exceeds the number of low-income children who choose to participate. Where tuition aid is spent depends solely upon where parents who receive tuition aid choose to enroll their child. If parents choose a private school, checks are made payable to the parents who then endorse the checks over to the chosen school.

The tutorial aid portion of the program provides tutorial assistance through grants to any student in a covered district who chooses to remain in public school. Parents arrange for registered tutors to provide assistance to their children and then submit bills for those services to the State for payment. Students from low-income families receive 90% of the amount charged for such assistance up to $360. All other students receive 75% of that amount. The number of tutorial assistance grants offered to students in a covered district must equal the number of tuition aid scholarships provided to students enrolled at participating private or adjacent public schools.

The program has been in operation within the Cleveland City School District since the 1996–1997 school year. In the 1999–2000 school year, 56 private schools participated in the program, 46 (or 82%) of which had a religious affiliation. None of the public schools in districts adjacent to Cleveland have elected to participate. More than 3,700 students participated in the scholarship program, most of whom (96%) enrolled in religiously affiliated schools. Sixty percent of these students were from families at or below the poverty line. In the 1998–1999 school year, approximately 1,400 Cleveland public school students received tutorial aid. This number was expected to double during the 1999–2000 school year.

The program is part of a broader undertaking by the State to enhance the educational options of Cleveland's schoolchildren in response to the 1995 takeover. That undertaking includes programs governing community and magnet schools. Community schools are funded under state law but are run by their own school boards, not by local school districts. These schools enjoy academic independence to hire their own teachers and to determine their own curriculum. They can have no religious affiliation and are required to accept students by lottery. During the 1999–2000 school year, there were 10 start-up community schools in the Cleveland City School District with more than 1,900 students enrolled. For each child enrolled in a community school, the school receives state funding of $4,518, twice the funding a participating program school may receive.

Magnet schools are public schools operated by a local school board that emphasize a particular subject area, teaching method, or service to students. For each student enrolled in a magnet school, the school district receives $7,746, including state funding of $4,167, the same amount received per student enrolled at a traditional public school. As of 1999, parents in Cleveland were able to choose from among 23 magnet schools, which together enrolled more than 13,000 students in kindergarten through eighth grade. These schools provide specialized teaching methods, such as Montessori, or a particularized curriculum focus, such as foreign language, computers, or the arts.

In 1996, respondents, a group of Ohio taxpayers, challenged the Ohio program in state court on state and federal grounds. The Ohio Supreme Court rejected respondents' federal claims, but held that the enactment of the program violated certain procedural requirements of the Ohio Constitution. The state legislature immediately cured this defect, leaving the basic provisions discussed above intact.

In July 1999, respondents filed this action in United States District Court, seeking to enjoin the reenacted program on the ground that it violated the Establishment Clause of the United States Constitution. In August 1999, the District Court issued a preliminary injunction barring further implementation of the program, which we stayed pending review by the Court of Appeals. In December 1999, the District Court granted summary judgment for respondents. In December 2000, a divided panel of the Court of Appeals affirmed the judgment of the District Court, finding that the program had the "primary effect" of advancing religion in violation of the Establishment Clause. The Court of Appeals stayed its mandate pending disposition in this Court. We granted certiorari, and now reverse the Court of Appeals.

The Establishment Clause of the First Amendment, applied to the States through the Fourteenth Amendment, prevents a State from enacting laws that have the "purpose" or "effect" of advancing or inhibiting religion. There is no dispute that the program challenged here was enacted for the valid secular purpose of providing educational assistance to poor children in a demonstrably failing public school system. Thus, the question presented is whether the Ohio program nonetheless has the forbidden "effect" of advancing or inhibiting religion.

To answer that question, our decisions have drawn a consistent distinction between government programs that provide aid directly to religious schools, *Mitchell* v. *Helms, Agostini, supra; Rosenberger* v. *Rector and Visitors of Univ. of Va.*, and programs of true private choice, in which government aid reaches religious schools only as a result of the genuine and independent choices of private individuals, *Mueller* v. *Allen, Witters* v. *Washington Dept. of Servs. for Blind, Zobrest* v. *Catalina Foothills School Dist.* While our jurisprudence with respect to the constitutionality of direct aid programs has "changed significantly" over the past two decades, *Agostini, supra*, our jurisprudence with respect to true private choice programs has remained consistent and unbroken. Three times we have confronted Establishment Clause challenges to neutral government programs that provide aid directly to a broad class of individuals, who, in turn, direct the aid to religious schools or institutions of their own choosing. Three times we have rejected such challenges.

In *Mueller*, we rejected an Establishment Clause challenge to a Minnesota program authorizing tax deductions for various educational expenses, including private school tuition costs, even though the great majority of the program's beneficiaries (96%) were parents of children in religious schools. We began by focusing on the class of beneficiaries, finding that because the class included "*all* parents," including parents with "children [who] attend nonsectarian private schools or sectarian private schools," the program was "not readily subject to challenge under the Establishment Clause. Then, viewing the program as a whole, we emphasized the principle of private choice, noting that public funds were made available to religious schools "only as a result of numerous, private choices of individual parents of school-age children." This, we said, ensured that "'no imprimatur of state approval' can be deemed to have been conferred on any particular religion, or on religion generally." We thus found it irrelevant to the constitutional inquiry that the vast majority of beneficiaries were parents of children in religious schools, saying:

> *We would be loath to adopt a rule grounding the constitutionality of a facially neutral law on annual reports reciting the extent to which various classes of private citizens claimed benefits under the law.*

That the program was one of true private choice, with no evidence that the State deliberately skewed incentives toward religious schools, was sufficient for the program to survive scrutiny under the Establishment Clause. In *Witters*, we used identical reasoning to reject an Establishment Clause challenge to a vocational scholarship program that provided tuition aid to a student studying at a religious institution to become a pastor. Looking at the program as a whole, we observed that "[a]ny aid . . . that ultimately flows to religious institutions does so only as a result of the genuinely independent and private choices of aid recipients." We further remarked that, as in *Mueller*, "[the] program is made available generally without regard to the sectarian-nonsectarian, or public-nonpublic nature of the institution benefited." In light of these factors, we held that the program was not inconsistent with the Establishment Clause.

Five Members of the Court, in separate opinions, emphasized the general rule from *Mueller* that the amount of government aid channeled to religious institutions by individual aid recipients was not relevant to the constitutional inquiry. Our holding thus rested not on whether few or many recipients chose to expend government aid at a religious school but, rather, on whether recipients generally were empowered to direct the aid to schools or institutions of their own choosing.

Finally, in *Zobrest*, we applied *Mueller* and *Witters* to reject an Establishment Clause challenge to a federal program that permitted sign-language interpreters to assist deaf children enrolled in religious schools. Reviewing our earlier decisions, we stated that "government programs that neutrally provide benefits to a broad class of citizens defined without reference to religion are not readily subject to an Establishment Clause challenge." Looking once again to the challenged program as a whole, we observed that the program "distributes benefits neutrally to any child qualifying as 'disabled.'" Its "primary beneficiaries," we said, were "disabled children, not sectarian schools."

We further observed that "[b]y according parents freedom to select a school of their choice, the statute ensures that a government-paid interpreter will be present in a sectarian school only as a result of the private decision of individual parents." Our focus again was on neutrality and the principle of private choice, not on the number of program beneficiaries attending religious schools. Because the program ensured that parents were the ones to select a religious school as the best learning environment for their handicapped child, the circuit between government and religion was broken, and the Establishment Clause was not implicated.

Mueller, Witters, and *Zobrest* thus make clear that where a government aid program is neutral with respect to religion, and provides assistance directly to a broad class of citizens who, in turn, direct government aid to religious schools wholly as a result of their own genuine and independent private choice, the program is not readily subject to challenge under the Establishment Clause. A program that shares these features permits government aid to reach religious institutions only by way of the deliberate choices of numerous individual recipients. The incidental advancement of a religious mission, or the perceived endorsement of a religious message, is reasonably attributable to the individual recipient, not to the government, whose role ends with the disbursement of benefits. As a plurality of this Court recently observed:

> *[I]f numerous private choices, rather than the single choice of a government, determine the distribution of aid, pursuant to neutral eligibility criteria, then a government cannot, or at least cannot easily, grant special favors that might lead to a religious establishment.*

It is precisely for these reasons that we have never found a program of true private choice to offend the Establishment Clause.

We believe that the program challenged here is a program of true private choice, consistent with *Mueller, Witters,* and *Zobrest,* and thus constitutional. As was true in those cases, the Ohio program is neutral in all respects toward religion. It is part of a general and multifaceted undertaking by the State of Ohio to provide educational opportunities to the children of a failed school district. It confers educational assistance directly to a broad class of individuals defined without reference to religion, *i.e.*, any parent of a school-age child who resides in the Cleveland City School District. The program permits the participation of *all* schools within the district, religious or nonreligious. Adjacent public schools also may participate and have a financial incentive to do so. Program benefits are available to participating families on neutral terms, with no reference to religion. The only preference stated anywhere in the program is a preference for low-income families, who receive greater assistance and are given priority for admission at participating schools.

There are no "financial incentive[s]" that "ske[w]" the program toward religious schools. Such incentives "[are] not present . . . where the aid is allocated on the basis of neutral, secular criteria that neither favor nor disfavor religion, and is made available to both religious and secular beneficiaries on a nondiscriminatory basis." The program here in fact creates financial *dis*incentives for religious schools, with private schools receiving only half the government assistance given to community schools and one-third the assistance given to magnet schools. Adjacent public schools, should any choose to accept program students, are also eligible to receive two to three times the state funding of a private religious school. Families too have a financial disincentive to choose a private religious school over other schools. Parents that choose to participate in the scholarship program and then to enroll their children in a private school (religious or nonreligious) must copay a portion of the school's tuition. Families that choose a community school, magnet school, or traditional public school pay nothing. Although such features of the program are not necessary to its constitutionality, they clearly dispel the claim that the program "creates . . . financial incentive[s] for parents to choose a sectarian school."

Respondents suggest that even without a financial incentive for parents to choose a religious school, the program creates a "public perception that the State is endorsing religious practices and beliefs." But we have repeatedly recognized that no reasonable observer would think a neutral program of private choice, where state aid reaches religious schools solely as a result of the numerous independent decisions of private individuals, carries with it the *imprimatur* of government endorsement. The argument is particularly misplaced here since "the reasonable observer in the endorsement inquiry must be deemed aware" of the "history and context" underlying a challenged program. Any objective observer familiar with the full history and context of the Ohio program would reasonably view it as one aspect of a broader undertaking to assist poor children in failed schools, not as an endorsement of religious schooling in general.

There also is no evidence that the program fails to provide genuine opportunities for Cleveland parents to select secular educational options for their school-age children. Cleveland schoolchildren enjoy a range of educational choices: They may remain in public school as before, remain in public school with publicly funded tutoring aid, obtain a scholarship and choose a religious school, obtain a scholarship and choose a nonreligious private school, enroll in a community school, or enroll in a magnet school. That 46 of the 56 private schools now participating in the program are religious schools does not condemn it as a violation of the Establishment Clause. The Establishment Clause question is whether Ohio is coercing parents into sending their children to religious schools, and that question must be answered by evaluating *all* options Ohio provides Cleveland schoolchildren, only one of which is to obtain a program scholarship and then choose a religious school.

Justice Souter speculates that because more private religious schools currently participate in the program, the program itself must somehow discourage the participation of private nonreligious schools. But Cleveland's preponderance of religiously affiliated private schools certainly did not arise as a result of the program; it is a phenomenon common to many American cities. Indeed, by all accounts the program has captured a remarkable cross-section of private schools, religious and nonreligious. It is true that 82% of Cleveland's participating private schools are religious schools, but it is also true that 81% of private schools in Ohio are religious schools. To attribute constitutional significance to this figure, moreover, would lead to the absurd result that a neutral school-choice program might be permissible in some parts of Ohio, such as Columbus, where a lower percentage of private schools are religious schools, but not in inner-city Cleveland, where Ohio has deemed such programs most sorely needed, but where the preponderance of religious schools happens to be greater. Likewise, an identical private choice program might be constitutional in some States, such as Maine or Utah, where less than 45% of private schools are religious schools, but not in other States, such as Nebraska or Kansas, where over 90% of private schools are religious schools.

Respondents and Justice Souter claim that even if we do not focus on the number of participating schools that are religious schools, we should attach constitutional significance to the fact that 96% of scholarship recipients have enrolled in religious schools. They claim that this alone proves parents lack genuine choice, even if no parent has ever said so. We need not consider this argument in detail, since it was flatly rejected in *Mueller*, where we found it irrelevant that 96% of parents taking deductions for tuition expenses paid tuition at religious schools. Indeed, we have recently found it irrelevant even to the constitutionality of a direct aid program that a vast majority of program benefits went to religious schools. The constitutionality of a neutral educational aid program simply does not turn on whether and why, in a particular area, at a particular time, most private schools are run by religious organizations, or most recipients choose to use the aid at a religious school. As we said in *Mueller,* "[s]uch an approach would scarcely provide the certainty that this field stands in need of, nor can we perceive principled standards by which such statistical evidence might be evaluated."

This point is aptly illustrated here. The 96% figure upon which respondents and Justice Souter rely discounts entirely (1) the more than 1,900 Cleveland children enrolled in alternative community schools, (2) the more than 13,000 children enrolled in alternative magnet schools, and (3) the more than 1,400 children enrolled in traditional public schools with tutorial assistance. Including some or all of these children in the denominator of children enrolled in nontraditional schools during the 1999–2000 school year drops the percentage enrolled in religious schools from 96% to under 20%. The 96% figure also represents but a snapshot of one particular school year. In the 1997–1998 school year, by contrast, only 78% of scholarship recipients attended religious schools. The difference was attributable to two private nonreligious schools that had accepted 15% of all scholarship students electing instead to register as community schools, in light of larger per-pupil funding for community schools and the uncertain future of the scholarship program generated by this litigation. Many of the students enrolled in these schools as scholarship students remained enrolled as community school students, thus demonstrating the arbitrariness of counting one type of school but not the other to assess primary effect. In spite of repeated questioning from the Court at oral argument, respondents offered no convincing justification for their approach, which relies entirely on such arbitrary classifications.

Respondents finally claim that we should look to *Committee for Public Ed. & Religious Liberty v. Nyquist,* to decide these cases. We disagree for two reasons. First, the program in *Nyquist* was quite different from the program challenged here. *Nyquist* involved a New York program that gave a package of benefits exclusively to private schools and the parents of private school enrollees. Although the program was enacted for ostensibly secular purposes, we found that its "function" was "*unmistakably* to provide desired financial support for nonpublic, sectarian institutions," (emphasis added). Its genesis, we said, was that private religious schools faced "increasingly grave fiscal problems." The program thus provided direct money grants to religious schools. It provided tax benefits "unrelated to the amount of money actually expended by any parent on tuition," ensuring a windfall to parents of children in religious schools. It similarly provided tuition reimbursements designed explicitly to "offe[r] . . . an incentive to parents to send their children to sectarian schools."

Indeed, the program flatly prohibited the participation of any public school, or parent of any public school enrollee. Ohio's program shares none of these features. Second, were there any doubt that the program challenged in *Nyquist* is far removed from the program challenged here, we expressly reserved judgment with respect to "a case involving some form of public assistance (*e.g.*, scholarships) made available generally without regard to the sectarian-nonsectarian, or public-nonpublic nature of the institution benefited." That, of course, is the very question now before us, and it has since been answered, first in *Mueller*, "[A] program . . . that neutrally provides state assistance to a broad spectrum of citizens is not readily subject to challenge under the Establishment Clause," then in *Witters*, "Washington's program is 'made available generally without regard to the sectarian-nonsectarian, or public-nonpublic nature of the institution benefited'" (quoting *Nyquist, supra,*), and again in *Zobrest*, "[T]he function of the [program] is hardly 'to provide desired financial support for nonpublic, sectarian institutions'" (quoting *Nyquist, supra,*). To the extent the scope of *Nyquist* has remained an open question in light of these later decisions, we now hold that *Nyquist* does not govern neutral educational assistance programs that, like the program here, offer aid directly to a broad class of individual recipients defined without regard to religion.

In sum, the Ohio program is entirely neutral with respect to religion. It provides benefits directly to a wide spectrum of individuals, defined only by financial need and residence in a particular school district. It permits such individuals to exercise genuine choice among options public and private, secular and religious. The program is therefore a program of true private choice. In keeping with an unbroken line of decisions rejecting challenges to similar programs, we hold that the program does not offend the Establishment Clause.

The judgment of the Court of Appeals is reversed.

It is so ordered.

INDEX

Page numbers in **boldface** indicate biographical entries. Page numbers followed by *g* indicate glossary entries.

Index

Index

Index

Index

Index